the complete guide to

investing
in property

the complete guide to

investing
in property

BARNET LIBRARIES	
Bertrams	14.04.06
333.338	£11.99

liz hodgkinson

**KOGAN
PAGE**

London and Philadelphia

First published in Great Britain and the United States in 2006 by Kogan Page Limited

120 Pentonville Road   525 South 4th Street, #241
London N1 9JN   Philadelphia PA 19147
United Kingdom   USA
www.kogan-page.co.uk

© Liz Hodgkinson, 2006

ISBN 0 7494 4493 2

British Library Cataloguing-in-Publication Data

A CIP record for this book is available from the British Library.

Library of Congress Cataloging-in-Publication Data

Hodgkinson, Liz.
   The complete guide to investing in property / Liz Hodgkinson.
      p. cm.
   Includes indexes.
   ISBN 0-7494-4493-2
   1. Real estate investment. 1. Title.
HD1382.5.H63 2006
332.63'24—dc22

                                    2005030878

Typeset by Saxon Graphics Ltd, Derby
Printed and bound in Great Britain by Cambridge University Press

Contents

bluepropertygroup

Rent-2-Buy for a Landlord

The Benefits

- You benefit from no void periods, no maintenance costs no re-let inventory fees.

- A regular rental stream – if the tenant does not pay they lose the right to buy.

- Even after allowing for the tenant's share in any increased value of the property, it still provides a similar return to a Buy-to-Let investment.

- Your property is let on an assured shorthold tenancy for six years, providing you with protection under the 1988 Housing Act.

- If your tenant does not exercise their option to buy, you can still enjoy the benefits during the term of the tenancy, without giving up a share of the increased value.

For more information please contact Andrew Brassey on:
E-mail: Andrew@blue-properties.com
Website: www.blue-properties.com
Tel: 0151 236 3366

The logical approach...

Launched in November 2003, Urban Logic has developed exclusive relationships with a number of the UK's leading NHBC registered housebuilders, enabling it to offer its clients discounts of up to 20% on a range of residential properties at prime sites across the north of England and Scotland.

With a client database, which includes first time, experienced and high net worth investors and celebrity and sporting personalities, Urban Logic has established itself as the leading off plan property specialist offering a selection of well-researched investment opportunities to its clients.

A unique consultancy, Urban Logic operates with a team of property professionals who are trained to address all aspects of the off plan property investment process. The company has the resource and experience to deliver a full service package including in depth market research, maximum discount, bespoke mortgages, conveyancing, property management, interior design and letting & selling support.

Urban Logic's team offers simple and straightforward advice, discussing every single step of the off plan process with its clients so that a clear understanding of the offering is achieved before any commitment is made. Full market research is undertaken to identify capital appreciation and buy-to-let potential so that only the best investment opportunities are presented to the clients.

To stand out in the property investment market as an expert and trusted team, Urban Logic is currently forging a path through the industry which will ensure that it is renowned for the quality of its service and regarded as a standard-bearer for its competitors.

The aim of its directors is to raise the bar for off plan property investment providers and to become the leader in this field, forming exclusive relationships with quality housebuilders.

Partnerships have also been formed with leading financial advisors, conveyancing specialists, estate agents and interior design specialists to ensure that Urban Logic offers hassle-free investment opportunities resulting in turn-key operations for those who wish to rent out their properties and support for those who want to sell on.

Although there is talk of the property market stabilizing, the amount of investors continuing to consider off plan property investment is on the rise. Urban Logic operates in this climate to help its clients make considered choices, take the best advice and work with parties that they can trust.

We are expert at sourcing property hotspots, carrying out the most complete due diligence, negotiating the best discounts and working with the most highly sought after professionals associated with off plan property investment.

There are still many pockets of opportunity in the North which continue to open up thanks to the Government's plans for further regeneration and housebuilders best efforts to utilise the land available and we will continue to seek out these 'hotspots' for the benefit of our clients.

The proof of the pudding is in the eating and at the end of 2005 Urban Logic finalised its 500th sale, sailing past its forecast mid-year target of 300. We have recently announced flotation plans for 2006 and the company is on track to treble profitability to £740,000 during its current financial year. Last year, the directors sold 15 per cent of Urban Logic to AIM-listed property expert Nadlan plc, valuing the company at £3.5m. We have also been short listed for a number of prestigious awards.

FPIBC

Paying too much tax? Wasting time on administration?

We deliver services that maximise your profits, privacy, asset protection and reduce operating costs and bureaucracy. Including Offshore Companies, Nominee Directors, Nominee Shareholders, Trusts and International Structures.

FPIBC Worldwide establishes and administers secure and efficient corporate and trust structures for expatriates, businesses, entrepreneurs, private individuals.

This means that we set up and manage offshore companies and offshore trusts and other types of international structures, to meet the specific personal or business objectives of our clients.

Broadly,these objectives include wealth protection and tax reduction, international business and market entry, but there are many different reasons and benefits attached to utilising international corporate or fiduciary trust structures to arrange one's affairs advantageously.

Our focus is to understand, assess, design and implement a solution that best fits our clients' specific needs and goals while maximising the available benefits.

Briefly, our focus includes the areas of:
- Company formation and company management.
- Banking facilities
- Offshore and onshore companies
- Trusteeship
- Corporate structuring
- Corporate Management
- International tax planning
- Nominee Directors
- Nominee Shareholders
- Accounting
- Property Investments
- Business Finance

Contact us for a confidential consultation on:
0033 468 81 62 17 or 0033 614 202 106
E-mail: **advice@wwmdirectory.com**
website: **www.wwmdirectory.com**

Introduction

Why invest in property?

This book is written in the belief that for the person who wants to attain financial security, and have some fun, excitement and flexibility in the process, property makes the best kind of modern investment.

But what does it actually mean to 'invest' in property? What is the real difference between 'owning' property, which the vast majority of people do anyway nowadays, and 'investing' in it?

Don't we automatically 'invest' when we buy property, given that property generally goes up in value? Yes, in a sense, but the main difference is that when you consciously invest in property, as with any other type of investment, you are buying with the express and overriding intention of making a profit.

When you specifically invest in property, you are doing more than just depending on a rising market. Instead, you are hoping to make a gain whatever the market, as you are using moneywise skills rather than just wishful thinking.

At its most basic level, when you invest in something, you put a certain amount of money into that commodity in the hope that you will get vastly more money out, and that during your ownership, that commodity will have increased enormously in value.

This is the theory behind all kinds of investments. Investing is seen as a way of making money over and above what could be made either by earning, or by simply saving up.

Investing is a different matter from just saving, where you put your money into a totally safe, if unexciting and low-yielding bank or building society account. There is no risk but there is precious little gain, either.

Just hoarding money up will never make you rich; you have to make your money work harder than that. And in fact, whenever you put money into ultra-safe deposit accounts, you will in effect be losing, as not only will interest rates be below the rate of inflation, you will have to pay tax on the interest, and the capital sum will never increase.

In real terms, its value will diminish over time.

And if you act like a French or Spanish peasant and put all your money under the mattress, you may never have to pay tax on it, but you will never make on it, either.

BUT – when you invest, as opposed to just saving, this means you are taking an element of risk with your money. Unless there is some risk, it is not investing. And while you may make a lot of money from your investments, you will stand to lose as well. Investments are never guaranteed, but wise investors balance the risk so that the scales are heavily weighted in their favour.

When you invest, whether in property or any other commodity, you are basically backing a hunch, but you cannot know for an absolute certainty that you will gain.

But of course, the more you know what you are doing, the smaller the risk becomes. Although this may sound an obvious thing to say, all day and every day people are investing in products about which they know nothing at all. Nowhere is this more true than on the money markets, where amateur investors are losing fortunes all the time because they haven't a clue what they are doing, and have not bothered to understand the nature of their investment.

Some people dismiss the whole concept of investing, believing it is a euphemism for gambling and that there is in effect little difference between the two. But although the unexpected, whether local or global, can always happen, investing is not exactly the same as putting money into fruit machines or onto a roulette wheel in the wild hope of winning the jackpot. Investing has elements of gambling, true, in that the eventual outcome can never be guaranteed, but it is not, or should not be, a matter of random chance.

There are many products to invest in, from equities to fine art, antiques, wine and classic cars, and many investment 'opportunities' are being advertised all the time.

This book explains what is meant by investing in property, as opposed to merely buying property, and why the author believes that property is probably the best and safest choice for the amateur or part-time investor, so long as you know what you are doing, and why you are making certain choices.

Over the past few years, property has generally increased in value so much that there is a general belief that you just can't lose. This impression is underlined by the growth of property clubs, where you pay to invest in newbuild and off-plan properties bought at a discount. Such clubs tend to be heavily advertised and appeal to people's greed and laziness by suggesting that you can become a property millionaire in no time, for little or no money down, and whether the market is rising or not.

The truth is that you can lose, but even so, property does historically come good most of the time – eventually. And thanks to major changes in government policy, residential property can, under certain conditions, now be 'wrapped up' in a Self-Invested Personal Pension (SIPP), free from the grasping claws of the HM Revenue and Customs.

Also, investors in property can now, quite literally, have the whole wide world in their hands – or in their portfolios. It is now possible to invest in property in most countries in the world, so that your property portfolio can look as international as you like. Nowadays, anybody can be an international investor and financier! Anybody can swagger around brandishing an impressive-looking international property portfolio!

So why do I believe that property, in general, makes a good type of investment?

In the first place, everybody understands property, simply because everybody has to have a roof over their heads. Everybody also understands that home occupiers have to pay rent or a mortgage in order to continue living there. It is also self-evident that even when fully owned and mortgage-free, there are continuing costs attached to living in a home.

This is knowledge that we all have. By contrast, you have to be quite financially sophisticated to understand how equities and other aspects of the money markets work. You also have to be numerate and actually enjoy number-crunching. Successful city people are doing sums in their heads the whole time; it is second nature to them. But few ordinary people really understand how and why stock markets crash, or how the stock market performance in, say, Japan, can intimately affect other stock exchanges around the world.

Few people, too, readily understand futures, hedge funds or derivatives. You have to be quite deeply interested in money and all its ramifications to be able to play money markets. It is a mindset which not all of us have. Yet everybody knows what estate agents and letting agents do.

Then, historically, at least, property is solid and substantial and far less liable than equities to stock market fluctuations, to crashes and recoveries. Obviously house prices fluctuate, but there has rarely, if ever, been a complete crash. One reason for this is that all real estate is built on land which will never go away. A further reason for the dependability of property is that everybody needs a home, whereas we can manage without a car, foreign travel, the latest electronic gadgetry, if we have to.

Then, there is almost always a shortage of housing.

And while house prices can go up and down, there is always going to be some value in land. By contrast, the entire value of an equity can be wiped out, in a severe downturn of the market, when major contracts are lost, when there is a takeover, or poor performance in the High Street. And there is little the individual shareholder can do about this, except to buy and sell at the right time.

When you invest in stocks and shares, you may have very little control over whether their value rises or falls. To take a famous example, when former jewellery retailer Gerald Ratner made his notorious remark at a City dinner that his sherry decanters were 'crap', £500 million was immediately wiped off the value of Ratner shares, with the result that many shareholders lost very large sums indeed, through no fault of their own.

But even if somebody calls your house 'crap' – as 'specialists' on TV home design programmes often come perilously close to doing – it is still unlikely to lose all its value.

Property is also a very versatile type of investment. Not only can you see it, feel it, touch it, there are many things you can do with it. You can buy it and go and live in it yourself, you can buy a wreck to do up and sell on, you can rent your property out or you can buy land and build your own home. In other words, you can enjoy property in a hands-on way which would be difficult to do with purely financial investments.

You can stamp your personality on a piece of real estate, which you cannot do with equities. You can make your home look lovely, you can renovate, decorate or extend it.

You can use a property as your main residence, or for holidays. You can enjoy your home for part of the year and rent it out for the rest of the year. Or you can have lodgers or paying guests, run holiday cottages or use part of your home as an office. You can create a separate flat in the basement or in the garden. As opposed to equities, you can use and enjoy your property as a full- or part-time home all the while it is (with any luck) making you money.

Then for many people, property has an emotional pull which merely playing the money markets does not possess. There is only one kind of beauty in a share – when it goes up in value. But you can take an aesthetic interest in a beautiful home which you cannot do with a beautiful share. A home can be an architectural gem or 'full of charm and character' in estate-agent speak. You can fall in love with a property in a way that would be difficult when just moving money around.

It is this aspect, I think, which gives property its special appeal. You are not merely hoarding for the future, you are getting pleasure and excitement from it in the present.

In my adult life, I have owned or lived in more than 20 different homes and each one has been exciting, challenging or highly profitable. Not all the homes have provided every ingredient on the wish list, but each has been important in its way, and each has had something special about it, at least to me. And while I lived in or owned them, I put something of myself in them. Then, when they were sold or I moved away, the next owner changed their personality again.

These are the considerable upsides of investing in property. What are the downsides?

Here are the main ones:

1. Property is much less easy to liquidize than stocks and shares. Although you can sell a share at any time, or instruct your broker to sell, you may have to wait a year or more to sell a house or a flat. Because any property represents a considerable sum of money, you have to wait for a buyer to come along. With a share, you can sell at any time, even though you may not make a profit.

2. It is more difficult and expensive to sell a property than other types of investment. This is mainly because property is subject to the laws of tenure, some of which go back to Roman times. In selling, title has to be established, plus any costs or debts attaching to the property, and searches have to be carried out. All these not only take time but cost money. Then mortgages have to be arranged, stamp duty paid, utilities sorted out. Buying and selling property is a complex and time-consuming business, even when you have a ready and willing buyer.

3. Property is not always 'owned' in the way other commodities are owned. Although most houses are sold on a freehold basis, the majority of apartments, at least in the UK, are leasehold. This means you have bought the right to occupy the property for a certain length of time, and not the property itself. When the lease ends, the property reverts to the freeholder for nothing. Not everybody realizes that the shorter the lease, the more value the property loses. The fact of 'leasehold' is peculiar to property ownership, and is yet another complication. Short leases are the main reason why some properties go down in value.

4. Property is expensive to purchase. You can buy a share for just a few pounds, but any piece of real estate is going to cost five figures minimum, and usually six figures, these days. And the purchase price is not the only cost involved. There will be stamp duty to pay, lawyers and agents to pay, surveyors to pay, removal costs, insurance costs and, possibly, renovation costs.

5. Although most people buy property through mortgages, in most cases you still need to have a considerable deposit available. This is particularly the case when buying property purely for investment. You will also have to have spare cash for incidental costs. Then when you sell, there will be Capital Gains Tax to pay, unless the property is your principal private residence.

6. Property is a high-maintenance investment. You can't just buy it and forget it, as you can with stocks and shares or when putting money into a bank account. All property needs constant updating and modernizing.

7. There are also ongoing costs when owning property, such as council tax, utilities, mortgage payments, service charges and repair bills. All these can add up, so you have to be sure that your property constitutes an asset and not a liability.

So – do the upsides outweigh the downsides?

In my view yes, very much so. The main upside is that property is much less liable to intense market fluctuations than other types of investment.

If you invest in, say, fine art or antiques, the artist or furniture-maker you have confidently backed may well go out of fashion. Property is vastly less subject to the vagaries of fashion and style than most other commodities.

A further point is that it is relatively cheap to borrow money to buy property. Mortgages on your own home constitute very low-interest loans, and even mortgages on buy-to-let or investment properties, while higher, are still lower than loans for other types of goods. This is because property is generally seen as good security for the lender, and mortgage providers will not usually advance more money on any property than they believe it to be worth – and what they could get for it on repossession, come to that.

So, lending money for property purchases has come to be seen as safe for the lenders. This is in itself an indication of the relatively low level of risk in property investment; lenders are actually falling over themselves to lend you money to buy ever more property. You might find it hard to raise such a cheap loan to buy a cellar full of vintage wines, or Lord Montagu's collection of antique cars or, indeed, any product where it is not easy to determine resale value.

These are the main advantages of investing in property but overwhelmingly, the greatest appeal is that with property, you remain in control. You do not abdicate the care of your valuable investment to fund managers who may not have your best interests at heart. It is up to you to buy, sell, rent, upgrade or whatever.

If you put your property into a SIPP, you lose some of this control – all will be explained in Chapter 9.

But in general and historically, you the owner are responsible for your property. Yes, you have to look after it and yes, owning property can certainly cause anxious moments and sleepless nights. And you cannot control every aspect of your property investments, such as freak weather conditions or neighbours from hell. But while you are the owner, a property remains your concern and yours only.

It is fun, creative, challenging and exciting to invest in property. I have been doing it for many years and still get a thrill from it.

My personal story

I am not clever with money or figures and indeed, I am almost innumerate. My number-blindness has been a severe handicap throughout my adult life and is rather like dyslexia in the world of words. But even so, I have made a lot of money and am heading towards an extremely financially comfortable old age by investing over many years in property.

By contrast, not one of the purely financial investments I have entered into over the years has been even remotely worth while, from the Savings Certificates given to me at birth, to the Save and Prosper scheme, where I Saved but never Prospered, to pension funds (Robert Maxwell took mine) or any kind of bank account.

Mind, for a long time I didn't even realize I was 'investing' in property. So far as I knew, I was just doing my best to buy nice homes in attractive locations that I would enjoy inhabiting. The fact that in the main they turned out to be highly profitable investments was an added bonus.

Also, I have enjoyed the buying, selling, renovating, developing and buy-to-let processes that I have got into over the years. Dabbling in property has been an exciting addition and sideline to my life as it has never been my 'day' job.

But don't just listen to me. Marion Mathews and Renske Mann have amassed three very nice homes, two in London and one in Devon, simply through property trading over the years. Renske says: 'In reality, most people cannot save from their salary. Most of us never earn enough to save for a decent pension and in any case, it is virtually impossible to discipline yourself to save out of your net salary.

'Marion and myself could never have saved enough or contributed enough to any kind of pension scheme to give a decent retirement. But through investing in property we not only have more than enough assets to see us out, we have choices about where to live as well as being able to earn income on our properties. Even our main home is producing income, as it is partly commercial premises.'

What does Renske believe is the secret of successful property dealing? 'You have to be prepared to hang onto it until the market is right for selling. I would say you cannot be in it for the quick buck but have to wait 10 years for it to come good. Also, any property you buy, whatever its condition, has to be a little bit special. The bog-standard properties will never really gain that much in value. The old adage, location, works best every time.

'If the property is not very special in itself, it has to be in an exceptionally attractive location to increase significantly in value.'

Writer Val Hennessy decided to sell her big house in Totnes, Devon and move to a two-up, two-down cottage in Whitstable, Kent, which cost less than half the selling price of the Totnes house. Val says: 'Thanks to selling my main house, which had no mortgage on it anyway, I now have enough money in the bank to see me out and if ever I can't earn any money by writing, I will never have to worry financially.'

Totnes, near Torquay, is in any case a highly desirable part of Devon, and Val's beautiful house, with its stupendous views, sold for the full asking price in only two days. The secret is always to buy highly desirable properties.

Because property can have so many wild cards, you need to know that the places you buy always have the edge over the competition.

At Christmas, I went on a very expensive Swan Hellenic cruise; the passengers were mainly ordinary-looking people who, nevertheless, had mostly been on many, many such cruises. I asked one passenger how they could all afford it and he replied that they had all made a lot of money from property. In the evening of their lives, they were able to afford to keep cruising round the globe, enjoying a luxurious life on the ocean waves without a financial care in the world.

So far as I am concerned, at this stage of my life I have several hundred thousand pounds in the bank, four fully-owned properties, no debts, no dependants and no absolute need to work for a living.

And that is without being remotely clever, or dishonest, with money. I am so naïve about money that I would not even know how to be dishonest. And most of my moneywise friends inform me that I have a peasant mentality when it comes to money. This is in common with many writers and artists who like to live 'like a poor person with money', as Picasso once put it. We have other things on our mind, so that if we do end up with money in the bank, we have been extremely fortunate.

Many writers and artists earn large sums in their lifetime, only to end up with nothing in the bank. Examples include Scott Fitzgerald, Simon Raven and Roy Boulting. Why? It never occurred to them to invest in property during their high-earning years; instead, they just spent.

Because I currently have four properties in my portfolio, I can mix and match according to circumstances. At the moment, one property is my main home, another, in the same building, serves as a self-contained guest suite and study. The third is my London home and the fourth is rented out. This gives me a town home, a seaside home, a buy-to-let investment and a place for my guests to stay where they can be on their own, as with a hotel suite. It is all luxurious living at the moment, but if I fell on hard times, I could just live in one property and rent out the other three, thus giving myself a liveable income.

My London flat was rented out successfully for many years, as was the studio flat currently used as a guest suite. The whole point, I believe, of successful property investment is to give yourself lifestyle options as well as money in the bank.

My present happy financial state of affairs is purely the culmination of buying and investing in property since my early twenties. And I have, like many people these days, had a divorce along the way, thus halving my monetary assets at a stroke.

This is how it all began. After renting a series of extremely grotty flats, I bought my first house in 1967 with a small legacy of £1,000 from an aunt. The six-bedroom house in Newcastle on Tyne, where I was then working, cost just under £3,000. Even in those days, it was cheap for such a large house and it was cheap because at the time Victorian properties were not highly desirable. Most people wanted to live on modern estates, plus, you could not get a full mortgage for an old property. Because I was able to put down a one-third deposit, it was easy to secure a mortgage for the rest.

The top floor had already been converted into a flat, which my then husband and myself rented out to university students. Later, another student rented our spare bedroom, and the rent from these three students more than paid our mortgage.

Thus we lived rent-free. When we sold the house three years later to come to work in London, we hardly made any money on resale, just a few hundred pounds. But because the rental income had more than covered the mortgage, it was still a good buy.

We found we could hardly afford anything in London, and eventually struggled to buy a tiny two-up, two-down cottage in Richmond, Surrey, for £7,800. We had two small children by now and were ridiculously overcrowded. We were also poverty-stricken and had no spare rooms to rent out. It was altogether hellish and we stuck it for just one year before putting the immaculate cottage on the market for £11,500. It sold for the full asking price, thus making us a terrific gain in that time. This tiny house, therefore, proved to be a good investment although it was far from being an ideal place to live.

We bought the tiny cottage because we could not get a mortgage on a rundown property, which we would have preferred. However, our next house was more like it: a four-bedroom terrace house on the slopes of Richmond Hill, which we bought for £14,000. Because of the great gain made on the tiny cottage, we could secure a mortgage on this very dilapidated house. We stayed there for seven years, in that time renovating it completely. Then the lack of a garden meant we had to move again to accommodate our growing family.

We sold this house easily and quickly for £34,000 – a good gain in that time, although it was back on the market in 2004 for £1 million!

The next purchase was a large, five-bedroom Edwardian house with a huge garden, again in Richmond, which we bought for £33,000. This too was in dreadful condition and we set about extensive renovation. Seven years after this, my then husband and myself were out on an evening walk by the river when we saw a For Sale sign up at a beautiful but totally dilapidated Queen Anne house on the river.

We had to have it! The house contained squatters, had trees growing through the living room floor and there was no parking. It was a pig in a poke and a ridiculous buy, really, but anyway we went ahead and bought it for just under £200,000; selling the Queen's Road house for £170,000. A legacy of £24,000 from an aunt of my husband's came in useful here as well.

We then set about trying to get planning permission to turn the space in front of the house into two parking spaces. This resulted in an almighty, two-year-long fight with the local council, but eventually the decision went in our favour, meaning that the value of the Grade Two listed property doubled overnight.

Not long after we won our epic fight with the council, somebody rang up out of the blue and offered us £550,000 for the house, about a hundred grand more than it was really worth at the time.

We took the money and ran – in opposite directions. This bonanza enabled us to afford to get divorced, and we moved into separate establishments, this time in Prime Central London, as it is now called. I went to live in Notting Hill and my now ex-husband bought a place in South Kensington, after taking a 50 per cent share each of the proceeds of the Richmond sale.

My large maisonette in W11 was again very rundown. I bought it for £300,000 and sold it in perfect condition six years later for £415,000 – not such a great gain in that time, but it was a wonderfully trendy and vibrant place to live in those years.

With the family now grown up and gone, it was time to downsize and I bought a three-bedroom terrace house in Hammersmith, London W14, outright for £200,000, thus not only zapping the mortgage but giving myself some useful capital as well. I now started investing in buy-to-let properties, buying and selling as markets changed. I also began buying properties on the south coast with my new partner, who died in 2004, leaving me our joint purchases.

The Hammersmith house was sold in 2004 for the full asking price of £650,000, within a day of going on the market. This time I did not even have to pay removal costs, as I walked out leaving my buyer everything, even down to cutlery and crockery. He was extremely grateful, as he had been thrown out of his house by his ex-wife, and had nothing to call his own.

Meanwhile, the remaining properties on the south coast had increased in value, which meant I still had a fully-owned property portfolio worth in excess of £600,000.

I tell this story, not to boast about how clever I have been, because I am not that clever. Also, when I was buying and selling, there were no property investment seminars, no investor shows, no makeover programmes on television and certainly no books about the best ways to invest in property; in fact, there was no expert advice available at all. I had to learn as I went along and I made plenty of mistakes along the way.

Looking back, what has been the main secret of my property success, modest enough by Donald Trump standards, but quite impressive for a financial klutz? Firstly, I would say that I am good at location and secondly, that I am good at adding value. Again, initially I did not realize I was good at choosing locations, and I hope that having said this I don't now become like the centipede who didn't know how to walk when asked the secret of putting one leg in front of the 999 others.

I just tried to imagine myself living in the place, before it was bought, and also always asked myself how I could improve it. Looking back, I have never been afraid to buy something in bad condition and do it up – gradually. I think that if you are serious about investing in property, you have to be prepared to live with one cold tap, sleep on a mattress on the floor and suffer endless privations, such as doing without a kitchen or bathroom, and having builders constantly in the house. Some people are not prepared to live like this, and maybe property investment is not for them.

When investing in property, you have to be prepared to suffer short-term discomfort for long-term gain and also, keep updating as tastes and ideas change. I have spent Christmas Day up a ladder painting a ceiling, gone to DIY warehouses on Bank Holidays, and got up at five in the morning to do painting and decorating. Why? I have to say that in some masochistic way, I enjoy it.

If you seriously want to invest in property, it is also important to have at least some competence with DIY as otherwise you are constantly getting stuck because of having to rely on a workman being available. It is not always practical, and it is always expensive, to call workmen out for tiny jobs.

Nor do you, I think, have to be the kind of person who swans around like a lord or lady of the manor. You really do have to be prepared to get your hands dirty and do a lot of stuff yourself. I don't much like humping heavy sacks but I have gouged out bricked-up fireplaces and taken the sacks of bricks to the dump. Also, I am always asking myself whether this or that piece of furniture, picture, mirror or object would look good in another property, and this means humping household goods up and down the country. I also take stuff to auctions when I no longer need it myself, and this has often given me a bit of spare cash to buy something new for another property.

I am an avid repainter and recycler of old or dated furniture. Much stuff can be given a new lease of life with a paint job, with new handles or a new cover. If you can paint stuff yourself and coordinate colours, you can save thousands of pounds on equipping interiors. Charity shops often yield good finds, as well, when trying to match up.

The secret, I think, lies in knowing where to spend and where to save, but unless you are prepared to put in quite a lot of work yourself, the cost of property renovation and development will probably be prohibitive. My friend Ivan Twigden, who became a multi-millionaire through building and construction, is always prepared to mend a drain or get up onto a roof himself. If it's cheaper to do it himself, he will always have a go, rather than pay over the odds for an emergency call-out service. Even as a rich man – particularly as a rich man – he doesn't like to waste money.

Most people who have been successful property developers and investors have been prepared to get their hands dirty and pile in themselves.

But it is not a good idea to try to do highly technical or skilled jobs yourself, such as electrics or plumbing. These must be done by a qualified professional.

Then, nothing beats doing your own research, slogging round streets and looking at properties, whether or not you intend to buy. I am always poking my nose into new developments, show homes and houses for sale. That way, I keep getting ideas of both what to do and what not to do. Otherwise, your tastes can get stuck and you can become old-fashioned in your thinking.

Everything in property is a learning experience, whether you always make or not. As Robert Kiyosaki, author of the best-selling book *Rich Dad, Poor Dad*, puts it: 'Sometimes I make money – and sometimes I learn.'

But by putting in the right kind of effort, you can greatly minimize the chance of losing, and maximize the possibility of gaining.

Nowadays, there are many more opportunities to invest in property than when I first set out, and the whole game has been made much easier by the availability of buy-to-let mortgages, property clubs, self-build magazines and advice from every quarter. Buy-to-let has become a mature industry and there are many ways to invest in property that were not easy or possible in the past. Overseas mortgages are becoming ever easier to obtain and self-build mortgages are also available.

Also, when I bought my early properties, most people did not regard their homes as 'investments'. You bought in order to have somewhere decent to live, as there was very little acceptable rental property available. In those days, property development was only for the rich and the few. Now, at least in theory, everybody has the opportunity to invest in property. The whole business has become democratized, much as the business of buying stocks and shares was democratized in the 1980s.

But even without the advantages that today's property investors possess, buying property has eventually provided me with the type of pension and retirement income that no other product could possibly have done. In most cases, you have to have earned a lot of money to stack up a decent pension; as a writer I have had good years and bad years, good decades and bad decades. But property has been much more reliable.

There are, I believe, two overriding aspects to successful property investment: always be prepared to sell, and never sell out of desperation.

Always be prepared to sell

That is, provided the right buyer at the right price comes along. This has happened to me twice in my lifetime and I have not passed up the opportunities which may not have come my way again.

Such luck cannot, of course, be guaranteed, but sometimes you have to make your luck by agreeing to sell when and if the right buyer shows up. That is what investment means – there is no room for lingering sentiment, even with your own home.

Never be desperate to sell

I always remember the words of a millionaire art dealer who said the secret of his success was that he held on to his artworks until the market was right to sell. Never be so desperate that you have to sell at any price – as this way you will never get a good price.

House markets fluctuate all the time, but eventually the right buyer will come along. If you sell for a knockdown price, though, you will never be able to recover that money and may curse yourself for years to come when, if you had waited another few months, your ideal buyer would have happened along.

Of course, the property must be correctly priced. Estate agents are fond of saying that if you put your house on the market at a price that is too high, you will end up selling it for a price that is too low.

An example: in 2004 I sold my London house for £650,000 as soon as it went on the market. My neighbours, with a virtually identical house, believed it sold so quickly because it was under-priced, and put their house on the market for £680,000. A year later, they were forced to accept an offer of £560,000. Yet if they had put it on at £640,000, say, it would have sold instantly for the asking price. Moral: never be too greedy!

Finally, if you want to invest in property, I do believe you have to have a definite 'feel' for the product, which is a mixture of interest, knowledge and insight. Robert Kiyosaki believes that unless you love real estate, you shouldn't invest in it because 'if you don't love it, you won't take care of it', and, as we have seen, property takes a lot of care. There also has to be some chemistry between you and the property. However much the deal works on paper, if you feel unhappy with the property, or uncomfortable with it, you should always walk away. I always work out the figures very carefully before buying, but I definitely go on instinct and gut feeling as well.

So, if you are a beginner to property investment, or are keen to expand your portfolio, where do you start? There are so many options to choose from that it can seem difficult to hit on the 'best buy'.

We will now take a look at the extent of today's ever-expanding property investment opportunities.

supermodels and houses.

the only things to just stand there and make money.

A supermodel was once quoted saying she wouldn't 'get out of bed for less than 10,000 dollars'. This time next year you could be thinking the same.

Year on year, property has proved to be one of the safest, yet, most profitable investment ventures. And with professional guidance from Inside Track, in twelve months, you could have built yourself a substantial property portfolio.

We are the UK's largest and most respected providers of specialist property education, helping people generate wealth through property. And now is the time to invest.

Our seminars have helped thousands on their way to becoming property millionaires. On them you'll discover how to:

- Obtain properties with minimum investment.
- Buy property at up to 30% less than market price.
- Maximise your income, capital growth and profit.
- Minimise risk (make money in the good times and the bad, buy the right properties at the right price, avoid bad tenants and vacancies).

Book your place on our free first step workshop. Free tax software worth £95* for all who attend.

INSIDE TRACK
Profit • Growth • Stability

For a full list of upcoming workshops text: **WEALTH** to 84222

Or Call Now on: 0870 042 5544

Or visit: **www.insidetrack.co.uk**

*Limited period only.   Quote reference: KOGAN1

Property has long been a major investment sector in the UK and people have always appreciated the benefits of owning property over the long term, particularly in terms of capital appreciation. This is hardly surprising when you consider that the property market has consistently generated good returns for UK investors over the past 40 years and residential property has on average doubled in value every seven years.

Despite its historically positive performance, property continues to be the victim of an onslaught of negative press which promises an imminent crash just around the corner. There are a number of very good reasons to doubt these predictions.

Firstly, interest rates remain low by historic standards and mortgages are at their cheapest for more than 25 years. The predicted property crash is also more unlikely to materialise when you consider the fact that the UK has high GDP growth and employment levels and a shortage of housing supply. In fact, the quantity of newly developed units is more than 100,000 behind current demand levels and the gap is expected to widen, with house building in the UK at its lowest since the Second World War.

Property as an investment vehicle (apart from owning your own home) has for long been overshadowed by the various investment opportunities provided by banks, building societies, pensions, investment and unit trusts, and stocks and shares.

Investment markets of all kinds are cyclical in nature - they rise and fall over time - but investment in property and in particular residential property, was hampered for many years through legislation which was clearly biased against the investor.

More recently the UK investment scene has changed quite a bit, so much so that property has once again come into favour as an investment medium, particularly for the individual investor, but this time on a scale as never seen before.

Having said all of this, investing in property is not without its risks. For anyone looking to take the first step on the ladder, education of the risks and how to minimise their effects is essential, from learning the essentials of carrying out successful due diligence to grasping the legal considerations of property investment. A comprehensive education is the first step on the road to financial independence.

Inside Track Seminars was launched in 2001 to finally unlock the substantial benefits of successful property investment for the individual investor. Too long the exclusive domain of a relatively small number of very wealthy and financially sophisticated investors, the company provides the education and end-to-end support services required to enable a much wider audience to benefit.

Start with a free two-hour workshop. This will introduce you to the basics to see if property investment might be right for you. If it is, come to one of Inside Track's two-day seminars at which you will have all those vital questions answered. You will hear from a range of independent experts who will talk you through all you need to know.

In the last 12 months, Inside Track has produced more than £100 million of 'instant equity' for its network of UK investors through sales of UK and overseas property valued at more than £600 million.

Join the thousands of individuals who have taken the Inside Track route to become successful property investors. Two days of learning could make all the difference to the rest of your life.

For more information on Inside Track or to book a place on one of their free two-hour introductory workshops, visit their website at **www.insidetrack.co.uk** or telephone **0870 042 5544**.

1 Determining the market

There is so much choice when it comes to investing in property that it can be hard to know where to start, or what to do for the best, as there are many more options than most people imagine. Of course, none of these is mutually exclusive! Many investors have a go at several types of property investment, in order to have a varied portfolio.

At one time, house prices may rise, and your own home becomes ridiculously valuable. At other times, prices may stick or plummet, and buy-to-let becomes a more attractive option. Buying overseas may sometimes make more sense than investing in the home country, and so on. Commercial property can also be a good bet for some people. It is as well to note that the smart money always moves to where the best investments are at any one time, and when one type of investment has outlived its usefulness, moves on without sentiment or regret to the next up and coming opportunity. Smart money, for instance, would not have continued to invest in horses and carts once the motor car had been invented, but put money instead into the new horseless carriages.

Although that may sound obvious with the beauty of hindsight, it has to be remembered that, at the time, many 'experts' were predicting that the motor car would never catch on. As with all investments, the smart operator has to know when it is time to forget about one type of product and move on to the next.

In this chapter, we shall take a look at the main modern types of property investment, and briefly mention the pros and cons of each one.

Here they are:

1. Investing in your own home
2. Investing in buy-to-let
3. Buying a second home or holiday cottage
4. Buying overseas
5. Buying off-plan, either home or abroad
6. Buying a wreck and doing it up (developing)
7. Buying commercial property
8. Buying a business such as a hotel or B&B
9. Buying property to put into a SIPP
10 Selling your main home and pocketing the proceeds
11. Buying ground rents and leaseholds
12. Buying at auction.

1. Investing in your own home

What it is: You buy somewhere to live in yourself and it will be your main home, or principal private residence. However, you fully intend to use it as an investment or financial asset in that you will sit tight there until the market is at its peak, at which time you will sell and move on somewhere else. In other words, the primary consideration is always the investment potential, rather than a cosy home.

Here, you obviously have to be fairly sure that the place you have chosen to live is a present or future 'hotspot' and that it is likely to increase greatly in value during your residence there.

Pros: Because you are choosing a place as your main home, you are likely to take more care over it than when buying purely for investment, as with a buy-to-let or off-plan purchase, where you may be beguiled by sales talk and smart show homes. Also, because the place is your own home, you will not be liable for capital gains tax when you sell.

If you are building a new home from scratch, you will also be able to claim VAT relief on the new build. But beware: this can be a high-risk strategy as you must not be seen by the taxman to be buying or self-building purely for profit.

Cons: You may be in danger of entering into a nomadic lifestyle, where you are constantly buying with an eye to future profit rather than looking for a nice place for you and your family to live. This attitude can set in motion a rootless, temporary type of existence.

Also, although you are avoiding capital gains tax, it is expensive to keep moving. Every time you move, you will encounter legal fees, estate agents' fees, stamp duty, removal costs and renovation costs, for instance. The furniture and fittings which suited your last place may not fit into the new home. A further point is that you will not be able to claim any tax relief on renovations or improvements, which you can do with investment properties and second homes.

There is also the temptation to renovate your own home to a far higher standard than you could hope to recoup on the open market. The trick is renovate to just the right standard, and this is not always easy to determine.

2. Investing in buy-to-let

What it is: You buy a place that is not your main home in order to make money by renting it out or, alternatively, you bank on the property making a huge capital gain in a few years and rent it out to make it pay for itself in the meantime. These days, most investors look at the total yield, that is, rental return plus potential capital gain, when deciding whether to buy.

Pros: Buy-to-let, in all its various guises, has become by far the most popular method of investing in property in recent years, and is the main way used of making money – or turning you into a 'property millionaire' – at property clubs and investment seminars. The idea is that you get regular income through rental yield which offsets the many costs involved in buying and maintaining a property, and in the process you become a landlord.

Although you incur capital gains tax on resale, there are very many costs you can set against this tax, such as refurbishment and improvement, utility bills, council tax, service charges, accountancy fees, purchase costs and legal fees. Plus, the process of indexation on capital gains tax means that the longer you own the property, the less of this tax you pay on resale.

A further benefit is that buy-to-let mortgages are easily available and constitute cheap borrowing. The idea is that you make a killing by selling at a profit when you have bought with cheaply borrowed money. Mortgages are still the cheapest kind of long-term loan available, and a prime reason for so many people investing in buy-to-let.

Cons: There can never be any guarantee that your place will successfully rent out. Although many property developers are now offering a 'guaranteed rental' for a period of time, you as the owner do not know whether this is a genuine rent, or whether the property will rent out at that amount when the guarantee period ends. Or, indeed, that it will rent out at all.

In many areas, landlords struggle to find tenants as the buy-to-let phenomenon has caused serious oversupply of properties, with many developers now building apartment blocks specifically aimed at this sector, and canny tenants negotiating rents ever downwards. Rents also do not always cover mortgages, as Tony and Cherie Blair found to their cost when they had to keep lowering the rent on their West London house.

Being a landlord is hard work and requires input from you. Renting out a property is emphatically not the same as hiring out a car, for instance, as the complicated rules of tenure always apply. Tenants are human beings, and being a landlord involves very human transactions – it is emphatically not simply a matter of moving money around.

There are very many regulations governing renting out properties and also many ongoing costs associated with buy-to-let. Figures have to be worked out very carefully indeed, to make sure the expected rental will adequately cover your costs – and not merely the mortgage.

Tenants nowadays expect smart, modern, clean properties, and this means constant work maintaining and renovating your property to a high standard. The unexpected – such as no tenants, the boiler breaking down, the roof coming off in a high wind – can always happen.

The other major factor here is that if buying mainly for capital gain, you are taking a big gamble as you can never know for sure that the capital gain on resale will be worth it. You are looking into the future, a place where nobody has a reliable crystal ball.

Although many property professionals are in the business of prediction, as with all financial predictions, they can actually only go on past performance. Anybody who could genuinely and accurately predict future trends would indeed soon be a billionaire, but that person has never yet come forward.

3. Buying a second home or holiday cottage

What it is: You buy a second home that is not your main home, either because you believe the area or the property will rise in value, or because you want to make the place pay for itself by renting it out as a holiday cottage when you are not there yourself.

Pros: you enjoy a second home which, if you rent it out, helps to pay for itself, and with any luck, you will be both getting rental income and enjoying capital growth. Also, the rents from holiday cottages and short lets are higher than with the assured shorthold tenancies you will be entering into with buy-to-let.

Another plus is that renting out a holiday cottage is considered a business, which means there are many more things you can offset against tax than with buy-to-let, which continues to be assessed as unearned income.

Cons: it is almost always the case that the times of highest rental interest will be the times you will want to use the property yourself. Also, you will have to keep the place meticulously tidy to satisfy the rental agency, and have plenty of changes of linen, towels and so on. Holiday cottages and flats have to come completely equipped with everything.

As occupants usually stay only a week or so – and stays are becoming ever shorter, with many holiday homes being rented only for weekends – the quick turnover means a lot of cleaning,

If you're moving...look for the BAR Badge!

The British Association of Removers (BAR) is the largest and most recognised trade association representing the professional remover in the UK for over 100 years. So whether you are moving house or office in the UK or abroad, make sure your moving company is a member of BAR and here's the reason why...

All BAR member companies must meet the strict criteria necessary for membership. We inspect their premises, vehicles, warehousing facilities, financial records, equipment and expertise on a regular basis to ensure they meet and maintain these high standards. In fact, fewer than 700 removal companies in the UK can claim to be members of BAR.

In addition, BAR provides industry recognised training services to our members; we lobby at European level to improve laws and legislation affecting the removals industry and all our members operate and uphold the principles of the BAR's Code of Practice for the benefit of the general public.

All moves are stressful enough without having to worry about who is handling your worldly possessions. By choosing a professional mover and planning your move well in advance you can often avoid many of the stressful factors associated with moving. Ask your mover what services they can provide – packing, for instance, can be the most time consuming part of any move. Many people leave it until the last minute and often enough, don't have the correct packing materials. That's why BAR always recommends that you leave the packing to a professional. They have the knowledge and experience to pack your goods safely and efficiently leaving you to relax and concentrate on other parts of the move.

BAR is dedicated to promoting professional excellence and service in the removal industry for the mutual benefit of removers and their customers.

Choose a remover you can trust...look for the badge. For further information, please contact BAR on **01923 699 480** or visit their website **www.bar.co.uk**

Paul Swindon
Membership Services Manager
The British Association of Removers

Moving home? If you're choosing a removals company...

...choose a professional.

Moving home is stressful enough without worrying about who's doing what and when on the big day. There's the safety of your personal and cherished belongings to consider as they're being packed, loaded, transported and delivered. And then there's storage!

So who should you go to when choosing the right removals company?

The British Association of Removers (BAR) is the largest established and recognised Trade Association for removals companies.

All member companies must meet strict standards and agree to inspection on a regular basis to ensure that their facilities, equipment and expertise remain at the highest level. In fact, fewer than 700 removals companies in the whole of the UK can claim to be members.

Many of our members are also accredited with the European Quality Standard for Removals: BS EN 12522.

● All member companies must use trained staff and appropriate vehicles.

● They must provide written quotations before any work is undertaken and offer service schedules and plain English contracts to ensure any confusion is avoided.

● BAR is dedicated to promoting professional excellence and service in the removal industry for the mutual benefit of removers and their customers.

If you're planning on using a removals company, be sure to approach one you can trust.

If you're moving, look for the badge.

British Association of Removers
Tangent House
62 Exchange Rd
Watford
Herts
WD18 0TG

T 01923 699 480
F 01923 699 481
E info@bar.co.uk

For more information go to www.bar.co.uk

clearing and preparing – and wear and tear. As one holiday cottage owner said: 'It's three times the money and six times the work of ordinary rentals.'

The other thing is that the holiday home must be in an area of high rental potential, where you may well be competing with other holiday cottages. As with buy-to-let, holiday lets have become a competitive business, both fuelled by the easy availability of mortgages.

4. Buying abroad

What it is: You buy a place abroad in the belief that by doing so you will make more money than by investing in the home country. You may also, into the bargain, hope to get some enjoyment from the place yourself, although increasingly investors are buying abroad purely for investment and do not ever expect to visit their foreign properties.

Pros: Buying abroad is exciting, challenging and exotic. It is often much cheaper to buy abroad than in the UK and there are dramatic opportunities for capital growth, as many foreign markets are emerging, are nowhere near their peak, and have plenty of growth potential. It is possible to make a far greater capital gain by buying abroad than in the home country.

It is now also possible to buy on a mortgage in most currencies, and is becoming easier all the time. The other huge advantage of much of 'abroad' is the vastly better weather. There is also the aspect that you are buying a dream, and that people will pay a lot of money to realize a dream. Your investment could rise hugely in value, if you have bought into a highly desirable area or country.

Cons: There are many unknowns about buying abroad, so while it can be an extremely profitable exercise, it can also be very risky. Changes of government, currency differences, developers going bust, labyrinthine legal procedures, poor infrastructure, language problems, high-pressure sales talk, fragile economies, can all mean you have been sold a pup in the belief you were buying a reliable investment.

Also, the actual process of buying abroad can be more expensive than buying in the UK. Then there is the cost of flights, getting to and from your investment, as well as paying ongoing costs such as local taxes, service charges and land taxes. Each country has its own financial and legal rules, and you may well find that you are bound by the rules of the country when it comes to inheritance, buying and selling, renting and advertising.

5. Buying off-plan, either home or abroad

What it is: You buy a property long before it is finished in the belief that by so doing, you will make a significant profit on resale, maybe renting it out for a time before you come to sell. Here, you are buying a place you will never inhabit yourself as you are purchasing purely for investment purposes.

Pros: You buy at an early stage in the development, at a discount, because you have to use your imagination to visualize what the property or development will look like on completion. Because the property is unfinished, you pay in stages, often over several years, so do not tie up all your money at once. You buy cheaply because you are buying something which does not yet exist. The idea is that you gain a cash incentive by helping the developer to defray some of his costs, and enable the project to continue and be completed.

Cons: Buying off-plan is the most heavily marketed of all property investments. You are taking a risk that (a) the finished property will be as attractive in reality as on the computer-generated pictures and (b) that the completed development will rise in value as much as the hype. Marketing people point to previous growth figures but with future developments, nobody really knows. Not all off-plan properties are sold at a discount, either. The more the developer reckons he can obtain full price, the less likely he is to offer discounts to early buyers. When buying discounted properties through a property club, the club will also extract its fee. You have to be sure that the purchase price plus the property club's fee plus the buying and running costs plus interest on the loan add up to a genuine cut-price deal.

In any case, your money will be tied up for a long time, maybe several years, before the development is even ready. Very many developments go seriously over time. There may be service charges, council tax and other ongoing costs to pay as well as the stage payments.

Property clubs – those which promise to make you an instant millionaire – are heavily into off-plan buying, and there are many unscrupulous operators in this game.

Other risks are that developers can go bust, the apartments may not be finished to the high standard expected, and the hoped-for capital growth may not happen, especially if there is a serious downturn in the market. These are all potential risks that the off-plan investor has to take on board.

There are two main ways to make money from off-plan developments: one is to rent the completed property out until such time as its value has increased enough to secure a substantial profit, and the other is to 'flip' – sell on at completion without either yourself or anybody else ever having lived in it.

At times of quickly rising house prices, flipping can be a sensible option. When house prices are levelling off or plummeting, you stand to lose a lot of money, bearing in mind that you have to pay interest on borrowed money all the time, whether or not you make a profit yourself.

6. Buying a wreck and doing it up (developing)

What it is: You buy something in bad condition, renovate it and immediately sell it on for a high profit. This type of amateur property developing is beloved of countless of property shows on television, where we are almost always shown the things that can go horribly wrong.

Pros: Developing property is exciting and challenging, not least because you are turning something horrible into something wonderful. Property developing appeals to some deep instinct in us, which is to make something beautiful and usable out of unpromising material. In fact, all kinds of makeovers have this appeal, which is why they make such popular television, from *House Doctor* to *What Not to Wear* to *Extreme Makeover* and *Look 10 Years Younger*. We all love this kind of transformation, of turning the ugly duckling into a swan.

Cons: It can be difficult to make money unless you are extremely strict with yourself and work to the tightest budget and the shortest timescale. You have to know where to spend and where to save, where to cut corners and where to be lavish; also, you must be very exact with the market you are aiming at, and what that particular market requires. This is again where research comes in.

In order to make this kind of developing work, you have to be able to coordinate builders and building trades; work out your realistic expenses at every stage, not forgetting interest charges, council tax, stamp duty, VAT, capital gains tax, estate agents' fees, for instance. There are very many costs involved in developing, including 'dead' costs such as stamp duty. These all have to be recovered on resale, otherwise you have not made a profit. You cannot just look at the purchase price and the selling price, and assume you have thereby made a killing.

When developing an existing property, as opposed to building from scratch, you cannot reclaim VAT. This means you have to add on 17.5 per cent (in the UK – VAT levels may differ in other countries) to all your building and renovation costs, including kitchen and bathroom appliances.

It is also difficult to make a good profit from a quick turnaround on property. Usually, a house or flat takes several years to reach its peak value and recoup buying and selling costs.

7. Buying commercial property

What it is: You are buying property for commercial or business purposes rather than for residential use. As with residential buy-to-let, you can buy this type of property to rent out, except that this time you are renting to a business, rather than a person. Commercial property can include offices, shops, sheds, warehouses and factories, and as with buy-to-let you have two bites of the profit cherry: rental yield and capital growth when you come to sell.

Historically, it has also been possible to put commercial property only into a SIPP (Self-Invested Personal Pension), although new rules allow residential property to be invested in this way.

Pros: In the recent past, yields from commercial property have vastly outstripped not only shares and bonds but also residential property.

Commercial tenants tend to be far less hassle than residential tenants as they are usually responsible for all the repairs and renovation to the property. They also tend to stay longer – 15 years is not uncommon – and as well as being responsible for all maintenance and repairs, they agree to regular, upward-only rent reviews. Residential tenants, by contrast, can negotiate rents down for agreeing to stay.

Commercial tenants must also hand the property back in perfect condition, agree to insure the place, handle any planning permission and pay for any improvements.

Cons: There is more to go wrong when investing in commercial property, and much more to understand than with residential property. Many investors go for residential property simply because they understand it, and are frightened off by commercial property. You would definitely need a qualified expert to guide you through the maze and this, of course, will cost you. Every commercial lease is different and each has to be separately analysed. Then there is such a bewildering choice of commercial property that it can be hard for the beginner to know which might be best to choose.

Some swanky new office blocks, for instance, fail to attract the expected tenants and lose thousands daily. It can also be difficult and expensive for the individual investor to break into commercial property as the entry level is high.

Petermans
Residential Sales • Lettings • Management Agents

Family-owned and run estate agency, Petermans is the first estate agency to offer a complimentary 'House Doctor' service. 'House Doctor' helps home-owners prepare and transform their properties to ensure they attain their optimum market appeal and therefore achieve their maximum value for sale.

Petermans is including the 'House Doctor' service as part of its package to vendors for sole agent instructions on properties for sale over £300,000. The estate agency is offering the consultation and make-over in conjunction with London-based Milc Property Stylists.

Selling a property can be a time consuming and stressful process. Taking a step back and considering the property from prospective buyers' points of view to make it more saleable, attract the right buyer and prompt a successful sale is an invaluable process. For example, by adding finishing touches and applying useful tricks of the trade to present the property as an appealing product will prove most helpful in this process.

Wendy Peterman, Director at Petermans, commented, "Milc Property Stylists are a leader in their field and Petermans is delighted to be working with the company to help our clients enhance their properties ahead of a sale and achieve the best price possible for them. Additionally, knowledge of how to present a property for the rental market is critical in attaining its maximum revenue."

Polly Maxwell, co-founder of Milc Property Stylists, commented, "Too many house doctors offer the same standardised recommendations for every property. However, Milc Property Stylists rethink the way vendors present their home, recognising it as a commodity that requires an individual strategy, and focusing on the features that are key to selling it at its maximum value."

The 'House Doctor' process begins with a member of Milc Property Stylists viewing the property through the eyes of a potential buyer, looking at every interior and exterior aspect of the property, and identifying any problems which may hinder its sale.

Recently Petermans worked with Milc Property Stylists to improve the exterior presentation of a property, advised on de-cluttering and storage solutions and space planning and arranging furniture.

Following the phenomenal success of 'House Doctor', Petermans has teamed up with Richard Lush and is launching a 'Garden Doctor' service. This too will be offered as a complimentary service on sole agent instructions on properties for sale over £300,000. Richard has been a garden designer for over ten years, working with clients of society and television fame. Through the provision of these services, Petermans will be helping its clients with all aspects of preparing their properties ahead of its sale.

Wendy Peterman commented, "It is so easy to concentrate and become fixated on the interior of a property that sometimes the outside space can become an afterthought, which is often neglected, and its importance overlooked. To really maximise the potential of any home, there needs to be a good balance and flow both inside and out with thought given to the target audience. It is on the basis of the exterior that prospective buyers form their first impressions. The 'Garden Doctor' consultation will assess and advise on some methods to help create favourable impressions. These need not necessarily be time consuming or expensive, for example, easy to maintain window pots."

Photography is critical in creating that first impression and capturing the attention of a potential buyer. It is vital that the marketing of a property is with stylish and professional shots that highlight the property's best features.

Petermans was founded in 1962 and offers residential sales and lettings and property management services across South East London from its head office located at Herne Hill. The North West of London is covered from its Edgware branch. Additionally, its team has expertise in buying and selling property in Spain and can advise on this from either branch.

Contact Petermans at:

63-65 Herne Hill
London
SE24 9NE
020 7733 5454

8, The Promenade
Edgwarebury Lane
Edgware, HA8 7JZ
020 8958 5040

8. Buying a business such as a hotel or B&B

What it is: You are buying a property which gives you both a home and an income.

Pros: Going for this option may well mean that you are living in a much nicer, bigger and grander place than you could otherwise afford. And whatever the hotel or guest house may produce in income, the chances are that the real estate will keep increasing in value.

Cons: It is difficult to make a living from a small hotel or bed and breakfast, and very hard work. Also, you constantly have strangers in your house. You have to enjoy the actual process of running a hotel and also be the kind of person who can cope easily with strangers. Definitely not for everybody!

It is also essential that the hotel is situated in a location which will attract a high number of visitors, but where there is not already oversupply. Many, many hotels in seaside towns in the UK, for instance, have had to close as there are simply not enough summer visitors to enable the business to keep going.

You will also have to keep meticulous records of incomings and outgoings. Also, you will have to conform to current health and safety regulations, and may need licences for running a restaurant or selling liquor, for instance.

9. Buying property to put into a SIPP

What it is: You buy property which is then transferred to a trust and 'wrapped up' in a pension scheme which will yield you, with any luck, an excellent return when you retire.

Pros: Such investments are protected from the taxman and thus, as tax-free vehicles, yield far more money than they would if you had to pay tax on them. Investments put into SIPPs can be bought and sold in the same way as other properties, and rents can be received from buy-to-let investments – all tax free. Some overseas investments are also suitable for putting into SIPPs. You can bequeath these investments to your heirs, thus creating the famous, or notorious, 'trustafarians'. You can also avoid paying inheritance tax, or your executors can, when you die.

Cons: By 'wrapping up' your investments, you are not only protecting them from the taxman, but also from yourself and your heirs! The point about putting property – or indeed, any other type of investment – into a SIPP is that you can never yourself get at the bulk of the capital.

The reason for this is that the investment does not belong to you any more, but to a trust you have created. You can administer the trust, but you remain a trustee, not the owner. As such, you only benefit from the interest or yield received.

Also, these vehicles need professional management and you will have to pay a fee to fund managers. Another aspect is that, really, you need to be quite rich to invest in a SIPP. There are also upper limits to the amount and type of property you can put into a SIPP. Because there are many rules, it is imperative to take professional advice, and you need to know that your adviser is completely trustworthy.

10. Selling your main home and pocketing the proceeds

What it is: This is the famous 'downsizing' that older people are increasingly choosing to do when the family has grown up and gone, and the big house and garden are no longer needed.

Pros: By downsizing, you get your hands on a large lump sum you can use how you like. By choosing this option, you avoid all costs, fees and complications. There is also nobody to take your money off you, such as fund managers or other financial advisers, and nobody is making any money out of you either. You become a totally free, financially independent individual, living like the camel, off your hump. The huge hike in property values in recent years has enabled ever more people to take advantage of this simple option.

Cons: Can there possibly be any cons to this option? Yes, just a few. In the first place, the fabulous lump sum you have in the bank is extremely vulnerable to the taxman. You will not only pay tax on the interest received, but in effect, your capital will lose value just sitting in the bank.

Then, with 'unwrapped' money, you will also have to pay your full whack of inheritance tax on your estate – or your executors will – when you die. As you never know how long you have to live, or what care you may require in later years, it is hard to budget for having just enough to last you out – a financial planning difficulty that has not escaped the taxman.

11. Buying ground rents and freeholds

What it is: Now that there are many more flats and apartments being built than houses, leaseholds, once rare, are becoming ever more common. All apartments in blocks are sold leasehold as to have a freehold property means that you own the land on which the property is built; clearly this cannot happen with a third-floor apartment, for instance.

All leasehold properties are owned by a freeholder; that is, somebody who owns the whole building, and who leases out the separate apartments to the leaseholders. But freeholds frequently change hands, for a variety of reasons. The initial freeholder or developer may have gone bust, they may have died, or they may have tired of the business of collecting ground rents, service charges and so on. It is possible to buy the ground rents off the freeholder and so own the building. This business is only going to grow as ever more apartment blocks are created.

Pros: Ground rents and freeholds are often sold extremely cheaply. You see ground rent investments being advertised for as little as £4,500. But the collectable ground rents may only come to £300 a year. People who buy ground rents and freeholds usually view them as a very long-term investment, and as their business. It's no use just buying one; you have to own a lot to make it work.

Cons: You have now got yourself a huge responsibility! One reason freeholders offload their freeholds is because collecting charges from leaseholders can be a thankless task. In some cases, people may not have paid service charges for years. In addition, the property may be in very bad condition and need six figures spending on it. That money has to be raised from the leaseholders, a group of people who notoriously hate paying out, especially when they believe they are putting money into the hated free-holder's pocket. In general, the business of buying ground rents and freeholds is a specialist business not really suitable for the amateur investor. Another aspect is that leaseholders are now allowed to enfranchise, which means they can buy the freehold for themselves and so wrest control from an outside freeholder. As against this, investors can make a lot of money from selling the freehold to the residents.

When buying abroad, it can be difficult to establish title, which can make buying the freehold extremely risky, as you think you own the building, then discover that you do not.

12. Buying at auction

What it is: Instead of going through an estate agent, you buy property at a property auction. These are becoming increasingly frequent and many investors nowadays only buy at auction.

Pros: You can get bargains at auction in a way that might be difficult otherwise. In general terms, properties sell at auction for 10–15 per cent less than through ordinary estate agents.

Cons: If there are many people bidding for the same property, it may end up being the opposite of a bargain. At one recent property auction, a garage valued at around £7,000 went for £14,500. You must have all the finance, surveys, mortgage and so on in place before going to the auction, as when the hammer comes down, the property will be yours. Buying at auction has become sophisticated and most auctions are now full of profes-sional auction-buyers. You are competing with these.

There is usually a very good reason why something is sold at auction, which is that it cannot, for some reason, be sold in the ordinary way. Properties sold at auction may have a sitting tenant paying £6 a week rent; they may be in truly terrible, uninhabitable, condition; they may be in out of the way places; not have a high value; or there may be legal problems attaching. You would need to find out exactly why a particular property is being sold at auction.

You would also need to act fast as there is usually a gap of only a few weeks before the catalogue is sent out and the auction itself. The kind of places that often go at auction are unmodernized houses which need total renovation and houses with sitting tenants, which often come at about 30 per cent cheaper than those sold with vacant possession. Then when the tenant leaves, the property gains its full value. But if the tenancy is regulated, and the tenant is paying hardly any rent, you may have a very long wait indeed, as they can never be evicted.

Brief guide to buying at auction

Catalogues are published around two weeks before the sale, and guide prices are included, usually on a separate sheet. Note: the guide price is expected to be exceeded at the sale. Lots are identified by description, such as Vacant House, Ground Rent Investment, Commercial Property and so on.

Dates and times of viewings are also published on a separate sheet in the catalogue. These are almost always block viewings and there is no need to book in advance. The property will be open for about 15 minutes only. Tenanted properties are not usually viewed in advance.

If you are interested in a particular property, you can obtain a legal pack from the agents, and this should be sent to your solicitor. You can also contact the vendor's solicitor; the agent can put you in touch.

Finance must be arranged before the auction sale. There are financial companies which specialize in auction sales, and your agent should have a list. They will also usually advertise in auction catalogues.

Pre-auction offers can be made by phone, fax, e-mail or in writing. If you make an offer you must be in a position to exchange contracts immediately. A lot will not be withdrawn from the auction until a legally binding contract is exchanged.

It is possible to bid by proxy, via the internet or telephone if you are unable to attend the sale personally. We have all seen footage of such bidding on television.

If you plan to attend the sale, you should first check as to whether there have been any last-minute alterations, as lots are sold subject to these alterations. The auctioneer will announce the lot by number and invite bids at a suggested level. You bid in the usual manner, by raising either your hand or the catalogue. If you are the highest bidder, the auctioneer will strike the gavel and the property is yours – there and then. A legal and binding contract happens at the time of the sale.

Then you will be asked to complete a purchase slip and attend the contract desk where the legal formalities will be concluded. You then have to pay the 10 per cent deposit plus a purchaser's administration fee of, typically, £150 including VAT for each lot purchased.

The balance of the purchase money must be paid within 28 days of the auction. If you are interested in seeing the progress of a property auction before taking the plunge, you can obtain a Result Sheet the day after the auction.

(Information courtesy of Andrews and Robertson: 020 7703 2662; auctions@a-r.co.uk)

There is a lot to take on board in the complicated business of buying property for profit!

The important questions to ask yourself

When considering investing in property, you have to ask yourself why you are investing and what you hope to get out of the investment, whether in the short, medium or long term. Property investment is currently extremely fashionable and 'everybody' seems to be doing it, but that doesn't mean everybody is automatically on their way to vast wealth.

All forms of property investment are highly complex, and every aspect of the transaction needs to be completely understood before you proceed. This is what is known in the trade as 'due diligence' and you would be extremely unwise to proceed without it, as there are very many sharks out there, waiting to take your money off you.

Never forget that there are very many ways of making money out of you, the investor. There are mortgage lenders, who make vast sums from borrowers, there are surveyors, project managers, builders, insurers, developers, property seminar providers, furnishers, decorators, paint manufacturers, financial advisers, letting and estate agents, pension providers, managing agents, freeholders, solicitors, investment advisers – just to name a few. And let us also not forget that the government too makes huge sums out of you, the investor, as well, through income tax, stamp duty, capital gains tax, VAT, inheritance tax, council tax. Every time a property changes hands, the government takes its whack, one way or another. VAT is just as much a tax as income tax, stamp duty and capital gains tax.

Because there are so many ways, both legitimate and fraudulent, that money can be taken off you, you have to make sure that you come out on top, even when taking all these people and their fees and commissions into account. It is true to say that the more possibilities there are of making money from property, the more ways there are of taking at least some of that money off you. The only reason buying and selling your main home is such a good idea is that the government have not yet found a way of taxing the profits. But one day, they will, and there is already talk of taxing homeowners who make more than a certain percentage of profit from their house sales.

As such you have to be sure that you know exactly what you are doing, and that you are very clear about WHY you are investing in property – and what you hope to get out of it in the long run.

If you need usable income now, you would probably consider some form of renting or letting. If you have a spare room or rooms, you can rent those out to lodgers or paying guests. This is the time-honoured way of making money from your property, and still the most popular.

There is, of course, a big difference between making a usable, useful extra bit of cash and earning an income you can live on. You would need to have a very big property portfolio indeed in order for it to yield a full-time income, and the bigger the property portfolio, the more work and effort it takes. There will always be repair jobs, difficulties with tenants, plus ongoing administration.

If you are looking for financial independence in the future, then you will be thinking about pensions, or pension alternatives, or maybe buying bigger and better homes to live in with a view to eventually downsizing and living off the capital.

You may also consider buying off-plan in order to sell in 10 or 15 years' time at a sizeable profit.

It may be that you are looking to afford the otherwise unaffordable, such as a second home overseas or in the country. In which case, you will buy a place that can be rented out when you are not using it yourself.

Whatever your eventual aim, you have to ask yourself some searching questions about property investment, such as:

■ Am I prepared to put in the necessary work of maintenance, repairs and renovation? Building costs can easily run away with you and make no mistake – all property will need maintenance and regular updating. The property that looks after itself has not yet been invented.

■ Am I prepared to put in the kind of research that sensible property purchases demand? This means never buying anything on impulse, but only after careful consideration and evaluation of the costs involved in buying and owning the property.

■ What kind of risk am I prepared to take which will allow me to sleep at night? Everybody has their own 'risk profile' and this needs to be carefully assessed before making any investment purchase. The more risk-averse you are by nature, the more you need to proceed with caution. The kinds of risks you are taking on include: interest rates rising, house prices plummeting, no tenants appearing for your lovely property, tenants trashing your apartment, an unexpected huge repair bill such as for a new roof or new boiler, and your investment turning out to be worth much less than you were led to believe.

■ Am I good at working to a very tight budget? When investing in property, every last penny has to count and costs can include petrol or air fares to get to your investment, phone calls (more than you would ever believe possible), accountants' fees, legal fees and continuous overheads. However big your budget, you can always expect fees to run away with you and there will always, always be unforeseen costs.

■ Over how long a period do I want to invest? Obviously, for anybody who invests, there comes a time when they want to see a return on their investments. With buy-to-let or holiday lets, there can be an instant return in the form of rents, but when developing property, you will only realize a return when you successfully sell. In general, the advice is to regard property as a medium- or long-term investment, as it can take time to realize its full potential.

As well as all these, there is another important consideration – what kind of property interests me most? Am I more interested in smart newbuild properties which (with any luck) are absolutely perfect at the time of completion, or romantic hideaway cottages? Am I an urbanite or a country person? Can I stand living cheek by jowl with other people, as in an apartment building, or must I have a big house standing in its own grounds? Everybody has strong preferences when it comes to property, and with which they feel most comfortable. I always feel most at ease with property where I can add my own touches and add some value, rather than somewhere highly designed by somebody else.

I never felt really at home in the tiny Richmond house, not just because of its dolls' house size, but also because it was absolutely immaculate and needed no work or improvement at all. Totally immaculate new homes frighten me with their 'soullessness'. Although I like to buy brand-new cars that nobody else has driven, I much prefer homes that have already been lived in to an all-new abode.

But others prefer to buy places that need no work and no immediate maintenance; such people are highly targeted by the off-plan developers.

Then, different places appeal as your lifestyle changes. When I was bringing up a family, I would not have wanted to live in a flat; now, flats make more sense as they offer more security and, in general, take less maintenance than a house. Your work may require you to live in a big town or city; then, when you retire, you may prefer to move to the country, to another country, or to the seaside. All these considerations will affect your attitude towards the kind of property investment that will most suit you.

Investing in Property

NCB Associates Ltd are pleased to be title sponsors of *The Complete Guide To Investing In Property* and we hope that our knowledge will help some of you invest in property in the future.

NCB has been helping its existing clients invest in property for over 5 years. Property investment is a great way to make a living or earn extra money, but it isn't easy and it isn't straight forward. To go it alone there are long hours required and much commitment. Working with a company such as NCB enables you the investor to earn money from your very first project, rather than treating it as a learning curve and hoping to come out the other side with some profit. There are many areas of developing property that people don't think of, overlook or just get wrong which is where we can help.

You are obviously interested in investing in property or you would not have purchased this book. Don't get it wrong now, let the experts help you. What can NCB do for you? As experts in our field, we have a client driven customisable service that tailors around the individual client's needs, from property sourcing, to fully managed packages. This is just some of the services we can help you with.

Whichever individual or combination of services our clients choose an experienced Project Manager will be allocated to ensure that our high levels of service standards are maintained. This enables all our clients to tailor our services to their specific requirements.

Property Sourcing

This is one of the most important areas of property developing. To be successful in developing you must buy the right property. NCB have a specialist property team who have the sole responsibility of sourcing properties for development from our extensive contacts.

Project Management

Found the site, know what you want to do, but just don't know what to do when? Get a Project Manager. You will spend more than the cost of a Project Manager on overspends on time, labour and materials. How do we know this? Because we have been told this by clients time and time again.

Refurbishment Management

Our Refurbishment Management service is one of our most comprehensive available. This service has proved extremely successful with existing clients, with little knowledge of the building or property industries or where they don't have the time to dedicate their working week to a building project. If you choose to proceed with a fully managed refurbishment, NCB will source, refurbish, market and sell your property for you. Leaving you to carry on with your normal day-to-day life. Your involvement can be increased if you wish, but your assigned project manager will take care of your project for you from start to finish. At first we will establish the project budget with you to ascertain how much funding is available and how it is to be raised. Then we select a suitable, and more importantly, a profitable refurbishment project that fits within your budget requirements. On approval from you the property will be purchased and specifications will be issued to both client and builder for the works to be carried out. Your builder will be selected by your project manager depending on the location and project type. All builders used by NCB are insured to appropriate levels and have many years experience. Once the project is under way, your project manager will provide you with weekly progress reports and if required emails with digital images of your project. If you wish to visit the site at any time this can also be arranged. On completion of the works your property will be marketed with a local estate agent, again chosen by your project manager based on his local knowledge and expertise.

Land Acquisition

NCB can help you find land either with or without planning permission. Purchasing land can often be the hardest type of purchase in property investment due to its popularity with not only developers of all sizes but also self builders. If you would like to build your own dream home or you want a new build project then finding the right land is imperative. Land prices vary greatly dependant on whether they have any planning permission at all or even between outline and detailed planning permission. Many plots that become available are "back land" or "infill" sites that are usually someone's back or side garden that they have managed to get planning permission to build on. These sites may carry an option from the vendor also. This can and should be negotiated on any purchase.

Buy To Let Investments

Buy to Let can be an attractive long term investment, but of course this too has its pitfalls if not managed correctly. NCB can offer you help and support in searching for the perfect investment property. A good investment property should not only generate enough money to cover the mortgage but it should also be selected in an area where property prices are on the rise. You should never rely entirely on a rise in the normal housing market.

Project Finance

Get this right. If you enter into the wrong finance deal then you will pay penalties throughout your development, either in interest payments or redemption penalties for ending your mortgage early. As experts in the investment field and with our own independent financial advisors we can secure you the best possible finance on your project. When investing in property your other mortgage commitments will need to be taken into consideration. NCB are happy to offer finance advice for one of their developments or a development you may be completing independently. Whatever your circumstances you can be assured that you will be given independent advice that is tailored to meet your individual circumstances.

Home Search

Some would regard finding their home as a normal routine task and not an investment, NCB would disagree. Even the purchase of a home, usually the single most expensive thing you buy, should be considered an investment. After all, you are going to want to sell it at a profit when you move on, the profit may take the form of equity rather than cash, but it is all important to help you take the next step up the ladder. Because of the specialist nature of the search and relocation business, NCB have launched a sister company, Mayfield's, to help you with your potential home search. The services offered by Mayfield's are extensive and can be viewed at **www.mayfieldshomefinders.co.uk**

As you will see NCB can offer you many solutions to your property needs, so please give us a call, **0845 230 9797**, *send us an email* **enquiry@ncbassociates.co.uk** *or visit our website at* **www.ncbassociates.co.uk**

Property Search & Relocation

Are you looking to move house?
Not finding the right property for you?
Relocating to an unfamiliar area?
Too busy to view all the properties sent to you?
Agents sending you details you just don't want?

If you can answer YES to any of these questions then Mayfields Search & Relocation could well be your answer.

Mayfields are a leading property search and relocation company offering families, individuals and organisations a professional and friendly service.

At Mayfields we aim to ensure that our clients have the easiest and smoothest relocation possible. We understand that for an individual, family or organisation searching for a home or relocating is a stressful time, and Mayfields aim to make this as stress-free and seamless as possible.

In addition to finding your property Mayfields can also arrange orientation tours of the location. We assist our clients with everything from arranging schooling for their children to finding the nearest supermarket. Mayfields will also be happy to help you with all aspects of your move from organising removal firms to dealing with the utility companies at your new home.

We are not Estate Agents and therefore can offer a wider variety of property from many different sources. Estate Agents are hired by the vendor of the property and are paid a percentage of the sale price. Because of this Estate Agents will always want to secure the best possible price for a property to ensure that they earn the best possible commission. As Mayfields are working for you, we ensure that we secure the best possible deal for you and our fees are structured around the discount we negotiate on your behalf.

At Mayfields we recognise that our clients have many different requirements and as a result have created a unique 4 tier pricing structure. Whether we assist you under our basic Bronze service, our Gold service or our latest "DEVELOPER" service you can be assured that you will receive the same commitment and professionalism from your appointed relocation agent at Mayfields.

t: 0845 230 9897
e: enquiry@mayfieldshomefinders.co.uk
w: www.mayfieldshomefinders.co.uk

2 Using your own home

There are a number of ways you can use your own home as a property investment, thus killing two birds with one stone – enjoying your property as it makes you money, the ideal scenario! You cannot do this with a bond or a share.

For the purposes of this chapter, 'your own home' is defined as your principal private residence as opposed to a second home, a buy-to-let, holiday cottage, home abroad or any other type of property other than what is designated your main abode.

There are many tax advantages to using your own home as an investment, but the government only allows each person ONE principal private residence (PPR). If you are an unmarried couple, you are each allowed a PPR but if you are married, then it's one between you. The new Civil Partnership Bill, which came into force in December 2005, allows same-sex couples in genuine relationships to leave property to each other free of inheritance tax. This right does not extend to cohabiting heterosexual couples, on the grounds that they could marry if they wished.

Buying a house together – advice for couples

If you are a married couple buying a house together, you will usually be joint tenants. This means that you both own the whole of the property and if one dies the survivor automatically inherits. But if you are a cohabiting couple, you would be wise to choose the tenants in common option, whereby you each own half the property. Where this happens, it is vital for each partner to make a will stating that, on death, the deceased's half of the property goes to the remaining partner. Otherwise, it just goes into the estate.

A HOME TO FIT
YOUR SITE – YOUR BUDGET – YOUR LIFE

Fleming Homes specialise in the design, manufacture and supply of **"one-off"** timber framed homes. We provide a professional, friendly and flexible service where quality always comes first.

We supply throughout the UK. We have our own in-house design team who are familiar with the regional variations of house style in England, Scotland, Ireland and Wales. Every project is overseen by key personnel who have over 30 years experience in the timber frame industry. Where the Client has his or her own Architect we work closely with him to maintain our rigorous high standard.

An unsurpassed knowledge of the timber industry ensures that the materials used are the very finest. Only slow grown timber from sustainable Scandinavian and Canadian Forests, kiln dried and treated, is used for the main structural timbers. The Scandinavian levels of insulation bring low running costs, excellent acoustic properties and a home which is comfortable, cosy and environmentally friendly.

When it comes to internal and external finishes the range and choice is very large and we can help guide you to the finishes which best suit you.

When design flexibility, speed, budget and performance are the critical factors – you will find a timber frame solution from Fleming Homes.

Why not ask us to quote for the timber frame components for your new home.

If you do not already have a design why not give us a chance at designing a home for you based on you own design brief? **We do offer this service free of charge.** This can lead to significant savings in the overall cost of your new home.

We will also carry out the necessary drawings and submissions for Planning and Building Regulations.

The very personal service the Fleming Homes Team offers ensures that your ideas and requirements become a reality in the building and completion of your new home.

Fleming Homes bring the same standard of design, care, finish and manufacture to commercial projects.

Check out our website at www.fleminghomes.co.uk

Inheritance tax does apply, however, as the only exemption is for married couples leaving property to each other, or same-sex couples who have declared a civil partnership.

I bought three properties jointly with my partner, who died suddenly in 2004. Because we had each drawn up a will specifically stating that the survivor would own the properties, I automatically inherited them on his death. Otherwise I would have had to sell them to administer the estate. The question of joint or common ownership is very important indeed when investing in property and cannot be left to chance.

There are other vital considerations when you are investing in property with another person, such as: Does one person have ownership and if so, what rights does the other person possess? Who pays the mortgage and how will this affect the equity on resale? What happens when one party wishes to sell and the other does not? What happens in the event of death? How are outgoings to be apportioned? What about life insurance? What if there is negative equity? Who pays for repairs?

Before you ever start investing with another person, whether this is your spouse, partner or friend, it is essential to draw up a legally binding document. If you are a close friend or intimate partner, it can seem harsh and calculating to do this, but it is essential.

If my late partner and myself had not drawn up a Deed of Covenant and each amended our wills, there would have been a fearful muddle on his death. It is also important to draw up these documents in case of splitting up, or the friendship coming to an end.

If you have decided that the best and safest way to invest in property is to use your own home, you must be very careful that you are not seen to be running any kind of property development business for profit, as the HM Revenue and Customs will take a very dim view if you are, and tax you accordingly.

The main methods of using your own home as an investment are:

■ buying a place in an up-and-coming area, living in it for a few years, then selling it on at, you hope, a vast profit;

■ buying a wreck, doing it up and then selling it on, while living in the place in the meantime;

■ building your own home from scratch, living in it and then selling it on when finished;

■ having lodgers or paying guests;

■ renting out your home to overseas visitors as a holiday let when you are not there yourself;

■ buying a place that has a self-contained flat in the basement or in the loft, or converting part of your home into a self-contained flat;

■ letting out your home to TV and film crews;

■ running a small hotel or B&B at the same time as living in the place yourself.

Finance

The first, and most important, aspect to any investment is getting the finance right. First of all, you must do all you can to save costs on the actual buying process, as these are 'dead' costs which cannot always be recouped on resale. And when you are using your own home for investment, you cannot claim anything back on tax, as you can with properties acquired purely for investment. So far as the government is concerned, your own home is supposed to be a tax-free zone, apart from paying stamp duty on purchase and VAT on just about everything else, of course.

So far as estate agents and lawyers are concerned, it is important to remember that, contrary to what most people believe, it is always possible to negotiate on costs and fees – these are not as fixed as you might imagine. Most professionals charge what they believe they can get away with, and it is up to you to obtain the best price possible.

When choosing a conveyancing solicitor, get three quotes, as with builders. You can simply call them and ask what they charge for conveyancing, or for their scale of charges. Firms of solicitors like to believe they are above 'quoting' but they are only people touting for business, after all. As all firms of solicitors are pretty much the same when it comes to conveyancing, it makes sense to go for the cheapest. The most expensive solicitors are by no means always the best.

Last time I sold a property I was quoted fees ranging from £600 to £1,000 – for an identical service. The same goes for surveyors, estate agents and removals firms. If you can be bothered, always get three quotes.

When making an offer on a property, always ask what will be included in the sale, as this can make a huge difference to the eventual costs of purchase. Most agents' particulars quote 'space' for washing machine, fridge and so on. I always ask vendors to throw in the white goods as there is little resale value, they are a lot of effort to move, and always look dingy and second-hand in the new property, apart from which it saves me from having to buy appliances right away. Carpets and curtains should always be included in the sale as well; again, they have little or no resale value. And even if they are not to your taste, they will serve for a while.

In the olden days, I used to try to charge for curtains and buyers never wanted to pay anything for them. So I ended up taking them down, storing them for a few years then throwing them away as they never fitted my next windows. Now I can't be bothered, and I just leave the curtains and blinds without ever entering into negotiations. Curtains and blinds also go out of fashion after a few years, as with other furnishings.

Whatever deal you are able to secure from your lawyer or agent, remember that there are always many costs involved in moving house. These have to be calculated and set against any profit you may make when selling one place and buying another.

As well as the price of the house, these costs also have to be taken into account: land registry fee; stamp duty; local searches; Mortgage Indemnity Guarantee; valuation fee; homebuyer or full survey fee; fees for specialist tests where applicable, such as damp or drains; lender's arrangement fee; mortgage broker's fee; insurance premiums; removal firm; storage costs; van hire; disconnection and reconnection of services and utilities; carpet laying or other flooring; animal care; mail redirection; change of address notices; purchase of appliances; immediate redecoration or renovation.

Although some of these costs, such as redirection of mail, may be small, they all add up and eat into your wonderful profit.

Getting a mortgage

(Note – this section applies only to mortgages or loans taken out on your principal private residence. Mortgages for the specific purpose of buying investment properties are discussed in Chapters 6 and 8.)

There are very many different types of mortgages and also fierce competition for custom from mortgage providers. Even so, whatever the incentives from particular companies, a mortgage amounts to borrowed money on which you pay interest.

Many people imagine the word 'mortgage' refers to the loan itself. In fact, the term denotes the document which puts up the property as security for the loan. This ensures that the property cannot be sold without the loan being paid off. In the UK, this is unlikely to happen, but when buying property abroad, care has to be taken that there is not a loan outstanding on the property, which frequently happens.

A mortgage has two main elements – the capital plus the interest. All mortgages are repaid with the interest calculated at variable, fixed or discounted rates. The usual length of time for a mortgage to be paid off is 25 years, although some mortgages can stretch to 40 years. The longer the period, the lower the monthly repayments, but the overall cost of the loan will be greater as you are paying interest for longer.

There are usually penalties for paying off your mortgage early, as the mortgage provider considers that by so doing you have reneged on the deal by doing them out of their full whack of interest.

The mortgage business, regulated in the UK by the Financial Services Authority, is complicated and becoming ever more so.

Find the right location for your buy-to-let mortgage

If you're looking for an investment that could provide you with a regular income and long term capital growth, you might not expect to find it in an estate agent's window. Yet buying a property to rent out has become increasingly popular in recent years with money-minded homeowners looking to capitalise on the continuing rise in house prices and the accompanying demand for rental homes.

The income from a buy-to-let property can be very attractive compared with the returns from other investments. Even more so, now that relatively low interest rates have made mortgages more affordable.

The foundations of a great investment

A report from the Council of Mortgage Lenders (CML) claims that the number of first time buyers has fallen, partly because of high house prices but also because renting provides the flexible lifestyle a lot of people are looking for. Not only that, many tenants say that renting enables them to live in a better property in a better area than they would be able to buy.*

The Association of Residential Letting Agents (ARLA) backs this up. ARLA reports that demand exceeds supply in most areas of the country, and their chief executive Adrian Turner believes that 'It may not be long before there is a shortage of property in the private rented sector.'**

This could be great news for anyone interested in the buy-to-let market.

Finding the right property

As always, location is everything. A house or flat in an area with excellent amenities will be easier to let and is more likely to appreciate in value. Do your research. Talk to estate agents and local people, too, if you can.

Bear in mind that rental markets vary from area to area. And when you're doing your sums, you'll need to work out a balance between a rental value that will attract tenants and one that will cover your borrowings, maintenance costs, service charges and allow for the possibility of periods without a tenant.

Buying-to-let in an area you know well is often the best policy. But you don't have to stay close to home. A number of parents buy a property for their children to live in while they're at university – over a three or four year period, the rise in equity in the house or flat can often cover the cost of student living. Even if you don't have children yourself, college towns are well worth looking into. With rooms on campus often being very limited, you could have a regular supply of tenants right on your doorstep.

Choosing the right mortgage

Buying a property to let should be seen as a medium to long term investment. It's a big commitment. That's why your choice of mortgage is just as important as the one you would choose for your own home. Going to an experienced buy-to-let mortgage provider can take an enormous amount of pressure off your shoulders, and leave you free to concentrate on finding the right property.

Opening doors

Choose a name you know and trust. For example, Lloyds TSB Scotland has the expertise to make the whole process as straightforward as possible.

As a buy-to-let customer you'll have the opportunity to choose from the full range of mortgages – including, Fixed Rate and Tracker. And you'll benefit from competitive rates designed to help you maximise your returns.

There's no lender's valuation fee, no higher lending charge and you can borrow up to 85% of the property's value or purchase price whichever is lower. The advantage of a wide choice of options gives you the chance to build a mortgage with the flexibility you could be looking for.

Your next move

With the right property and a mortgage designed to help you make the most of your income potential, buying-to-let could be a great investment move.

Whether you're new to the market or want to add to your rental properties, Lloyds TSB Scotland could be the ideal home for your buy-to-let mortgage.

For more information, visit your nearest Lloyds TSB branch or call **0845 3000 000.**

YOUR HOME MAY BE REPOSSESSED IF YOU DO NOT KEEP UP REPAYMENTS ON YOUR MORTGAGE.

You must be at least 18 years old to take out a loan. Before agreeing a loan we will want to satisfy ourselves about the suitability of your application. This will include assessing your ability to afford the payments and normally valuing the property. Buy-to-let mortgages are not regulated by the Financial Services Authority. An administration fee may be payable. Telephone calls may be monitored or recorded. Call costs may vary depending upon your Service Provider. Lloyds TSB Scotland plc, Henry Duncan House, 120 George Street, Edinburgh EH2 4LH. Registered in Scotland, number 95237. Telephone No: 0131 225 4555

* Source: Guardian Unlimited www.money.guardian.co.uk/news
  Press Association, Tuesday July 5, 2005

** Source: www.thisismoney.co.uk/mortgages
  Michael Clarke,14 September 2005

You first Lloyds TSB Scotland

Safe
hands

By moving day our Lloyds TSB Scotland
mortgage had taken care of all the big
problems, leaving us plenty of time to
take care of all the small ones.

Call **0800 056 0156*** for more information
or log on to **www.lloydstsb.com/scotland**

**YOUR HOME MAY BE REPOSSESSED IF
YOU DO NOT KEEP UP REPAYMENTS ON
YOUR MORTGAGE.**

Here is a handy guide through the maze to enable you to decide which sort of mortgage would most suit your needs.

Although there are hundreds of different mortgages on offer, they fall broadly into half a dozen types.

Variable

The basic mortgage rate which most lenders offer is a standard 'variable' rate (SVR). Here, the interest paid varies according to Bank of England base rate charges. Where there is a special rate, this reverts to the SVR at the end of the deal period.

Fixed

This type of mortgage sets the interest rate payable for a given period of time – not the entire length of the mortgage. This type of mortgage enables you to budget for a certain length of time as you know for certain what the outgoings will be. But when the fixed period expires, the mortgage reverts to the SVR.

Fixed-rates mortgages can be both good and bad news. If interest rates rise above the level you are paying during the deal period you will save money, but if they go down, you will lose out.

Fixed-rate mortgages usually last for between one and five years, although some lenders offer fixed-rate mortgages for up to 10 years. In a few cases, you can get a fixed rate for the entire mortgage term, although these rates will be higher than usual. Fixed-rate mortgages have been extremely popular, but they are not such a good idea when interest rates keep falling. At the moment, the government (in fact all governments) are doing their utmost to keep inflation low, so fixed-rate mortgages may not be such a good deal in future as they have been in the past.

Capped

These mortgages guarantee that your monthly payments will never go above a certain figure. Below that set figure, the rate can move up and down in line with the SVR. The advantage of a capped-rate mortgage is that you can be certain of the maximum amount you will have to pay and may benefit from lower rates if interest rates fluctuate downwards.

Discount

This type of mortgage gives a discount on the lender's standard rate for a specified period of time.

Tracker

These mortgages track the Bank of England base rate so that every time this changes, your payments will change as well. Tracker mortgages are good news when rates are going down, but if interest rates go up, your monthly payment rise accordingly and you could be paying above the odds.

Flexible

These mortgages calculate interest rates daily and also allow over-payments, so that your mortgage can be paid off early. Most flexible mortgages allow you to make underpayments and go on mortgage 'holidays' as well.

Although the mortgage business is hugely competitive, never forget that mortgage providers are only in it to make money out of you – lots of it! So the sensible advice is never to be tempted by wonderful-sounding offers but work out the full cost of the deal, including the lending fee, valuation fee, legal fees and any redemption penalties. The mortgage does not start and end with the repayments.

Every time you move home, you will have to go through all the mortgage business all over again, with another set of unavoidable fees.

Warning: many mortgages which purport to discount interest rates come with extra charges for arranging the loan. Application fees for discounted and fixed-rate mortgages come in at around £400. Only a small proportion of mortgages do not charge this application fee.

Then there is often an exit fee, of typically £300, when you change mortgage providers. The advice here is to shop around, as many apparent deals come with high entry and exit costs.

Also, many of the mortgage options are, in reality, so much window-dressing and their differences are more apparent than real.

Jesus saves, Moses invests – but what about Mohammed?

Many Muslims are interested in investing in property, yet the Koran emphatically states that they must not lend or borrow at interest.

The idea, in Sharia law, is that there should be no interest on money for no effort. Yet few Muslims, in common with others, probably have the entire cash sum sitting in their accounts ready to buy property. The solution has been to set up special 'Muslim mortgages' which operate differently from the usual ones.

Lloyds TSB, for instance, have both a current account and mortgage on offer which comply with Sharia law. The current account pays no interest and charges no interest because there is no overdraft facility. With the mortgage, the bank buys the home for the customer who pays for it with a fixed monthly sum plus rent.

Bristol and West have a Muslim-type mortgage on offer, and the Islamic Bank of London also offers a current and savings account which makes an arrangement charge rather than interest charges.

Before you ever buy a property for investment purposes, take careful note of:

Freehold or leasehold?

When buying property with a view to its future investment potential, you need to know, not just whether the property is being sold leasehold or freehold, but the length of the lease, and whether the property is being sold with a share of the freehold. Also, what the service charges are and whether there is a sinking fund, as all intimately affect the future value of the property.

In the old days, leasehold properties were relatively rare, but now that more flats are being built than houses, leaseholds are increasingly becoming the more common type of tenure. And anybody buying with investment potential in mind needs to look very carefully at all aspects of the lease before making an offer.

The main difference between leasehold and freehold is that with the latter, you own not just the home, but the land on which it is built; the 'real estate'. With a leasehold property, by contrast, you don't own anything at all! All you have bought is a length of time. You have bought, in effect, an extremely long rental, whether this is 99 years or 999 years. You can sell this lease on, but you are not buying or selling the actual property, which continues to belong to the freeholder, or landlord.

All types of property where there is more than one self-contained dwelling sharing common parts, a roof and foundation, are likely to be sold leasehold. Examples include: newbuild apartments, mansion blocks, conversions from large houses, conversions from former commercial buildings, such as 'The Old Fire Station', 'The Old Vicarage', 'The Old Post Office', and residential premises over shops or offices.

Many buyers, when looking at the length of lease, imagine that the longer it is, the safer they are. But this is an illusion. Whenever there is an outside freeholder, you, the leaseholder, can be charged thousands of pounds for repairs and renovation. When this happens, the value of your investment goes out of the (new) windows that have been forced on you by the freeholder, as subsequent buyers look at service charges very carefully before deciding to buy. Any leasehold property that has high service charges attached will put off potential purchasers and reduce the value of your unit.

Nowadays, very many people are buying newbuild flats – always leasehold – as investments, whether or not they intend to inhabit these properties themselves. But unless the property comes with a share of the freehold, your investment could actually lose value in time. And certainly, by the time the lease ends, your property will be worth nothing, and you will have nothing to sell.

Because newbuild apartments are heavily marketed, they can seem extremely attractive. In addition, service charges – always an aspect of living in an apartment building – tend to be very low, at first. This is because the building is unlikely to need repairs and maintenance for many years – although this is by no means always the case.

It is common for the service and maintenance charges to rise heavily after a few years of being kept artificially low. Also, the freeholder can sell the freehold on at any time he or she likes, above the heads of the residents, although residents must by law be offered the 'right of first refusal'. This very often happens, as selling freeholds is yet another way property investors can make serious money.

Is there any way round this? Yes – whenever contemplating buying leasehold properties, always ask whether they come with a share of the freehold. If they do, this means that you, and the other residents, are in charge and there is no outside freeholder. But beware if the property does not come with a share of the freehold, as you are then buying into something over which you have no control. Whenever there is an outside freeholder, you can find yourself, as a leaseholder, paying very high sums for renovation, painting, new windows or a new roof. In some cases, these bills can come to £90,000 or more per leaseholder.

There is especial danger here in buying a flat in a local authority block, where leases can be very short, mortgages difficult to obtain and leaseholders mugged with huge bills for repairs. The council tenants in the block, meanwhile, pay nothing except their own very low rent.

Ever since Mrs Thatcher announced the Right to Buy scheme in 1980, buyers have snapped up local authority flats as they are cheaper to buy than others. In addition, the flats are often in extremely desirable locations, and come with very low annual service charges. Again, the annual service charges on a local authority block are about half of what is charged by a private freeholder.

But if the council decided to update the building, you as the leaseholder would have to pay your share of this updating. And with a short lease and unknown service charges, you could discover that your apparent bargain buy is extremely difficult to sell.

Mortgage providers also are not keen to lend money on high-rise blocks; in any case, it is difficult to get a mortgage for a property with a lease of 80 years or less.

In general terms, the longer the lease the more valuable the property, but you are still extremely vulnerable if your flat is not sold with a share of the freehold. Apart from unknown bills and levies in the future, your lease can be forfeited if you do not comply with its terms, or fail to pay service charges. Many people buying leasehold properties do not realize that they are never the owners of their property, but in effect, long-term tenants. Mortgage providers often do not understand leaseholds, either, as they grant mortgages on the length of the lease, not whether the property comes with a share of the freehold.

So, always ask whether it comes with a share of the freehold. If it does, this means that you, and the other residents, are in charge and no outsider can impose heavy repair and maintenance bills. Having a share of the freehold means, in effect, that the lunatics are running the asylum.

If the property you own or are considering buying does not come with a share of the freehold, you should seriously consider enfranchising, which means clubbing together to buy the freehold from the existing freeholder. Current laws mean that leaseholders in a block are allowed to enfranchise if enough of them want to do it – but there has to be a majority decision.

Enfranchising can be expensive, as the freeholder naturally will want to get as much money as possible from relinquishing control of the building, and also lawyers specializing in enfranchisement law are extremely expensive. The legal fees alone for enfranchising can come to around £4,000 per leaseholder. There may also be people living in the building who complain that they cannot afford to enfranchise; alternatively, that the lease will 'see me out'.

It can sometimes be very hard work persuading the majority of residents that enfranchisement is worth it.

The real problem with apartment blocks is that, although everybody wants them to be smart, clean and in good repair, nobody wants to spend any money on them. And although property generally goes up in value, an apartment block in bad repair will lose value, and you will be left with a liability rather than an asset.

It can be the same story with property overseas; much of it is bought on a leasehold which means that you are never the real owner.

Now we will take a look at the various ways of making money from your own home.

Buying a wreck in an up and coming area, doing it up and then selling on at a massive profit

I have taken advantage of this option on many occasions, and it has worked wonderfully. Here, you need to be very sure that an area *is* up and coming – and that it will not take forever to come up. Also, you have to be very sure that you can add value.

Be very careful when watching television property shows, as they never include all the many costs of renovation, development and time taken. They virtually never factor in costs such as stamp duty, interest paid on mortgages or other loans, loss of income if you have given up your job to renovate the property, estate agents' fees, or moving costs. Nor do they give the true cost of renovation, which is much, much more than the one or two grand stated on the shows.

The impression given on many television shows is that you can buy cheap and sell dear, while spending hardly anything on reno-vation in the process. For instance, it is common for TV programme producers to 'allow' gardeners around £300 for total landscaping and paving of a neglected garden. (Not all viewers realize that the owner of the property, and not the television

OVERLAY MAY BECOME A TV STAR

A problem cropped up during a major refurbishment project on a detached house in Crosspool on the outskirts of Sheffield City Centre. Central heating was required in the concrete-floored kitchen and in the new 'wet room' extension outside it. The rest of the house was radiator heated but brand new kitchen units had already been installed leaving little wall space in the kitchen and, with a shower area and patio doors, the same applied to the 'wet room'. Underfloor heating was clearly the preferred choice but time was short and, with concrete floors and especially a newly-fitted kitchen, the disruption caused by installing a conventional screeded system would have been enormous and time consuming.

Polyplumb's Overlay system offered the perfect solution. The Overlay preformed floor panels are only 18mm deep, are easily cut or sawn to shape and can be laid directly on any reasonably flat surface be it

concrete or floor boards. Once the floor panels are laid it is simple to 'walk' the ultra-flexible 12mm polybutylene pipe into the panel grooves from a large roll. In the case of the Sheffield house a single Zonal Regulation Unit was used to connect the new installation

to the boiler feeding the existing radiator heating system. Installation was completed in just over half a day with minimal disruption and the owner, David Wilson Wolfe was able to lay a new tiled floor over the Overlay that evening.

The refurbishment of David's home is to be featured by ITV Network in a series entitled *Don't Move, Improve* later this year so Polypipe's Overlay system may have star billing.

For further information, please contact:
Martin Dootson,
Polypipe Building Products
Broomhouse Lane, Edlington
Doncaster DN12 1ES
Tel: **01709 770000**   Fax: **01709 770001**
Email: **info@ppbp.co.uk**   Website: **www.polypipe.com/b**

CONFUSED ABOUT HOME TECHNOLOGY? – IT'S SIMPLE WITH CRESTRON

Home automation technology should simplify your life, not complicate it. Technology should protect you, entertain you, keep you comfortable and give you more free time for the things that really matter. But faced with the bewildering array of options, where should you go to simplify the process? Help is at hand through home technology specialists, Crestron. The company specialises in delivering a *'total home technology'* package to manage, integrate, and control all the systems and technologies that keep you comfortable, entertained and secure at home.

In fact the options are endless. The only limitations are your imagination and budget. Talking to experts in the field, such as Crestron, you will discover the exciting possibilities available – and then working with their extensive network of dealers, develop an installation for your home which suits you and your lifestyle.

The ultimate in control
Imagine tapping the "Start Movie" button on a touch panel in your lounge to automatically dim the lights, draw the curtains, then lower the screen and projector from the ceiling, while the movie you've selected from the DVD jukebox starts to play! Or select the music you want to listen to in different rooms. And you can use the same touchpanel to adjust the room temperature – and see and hear your children via the Babysitting camera for your peace of mind.

Essential to any home, Crestron's family of lighting products allow you to control the lighting throughout your home. You can create different lighting effects at the touch of a button thanks to their award-winning systems which can give you effortless lighting throughout your home.

It's amazing what's on offer. Talk to your local Crestron dealer for their advice on what options are available and what would work best for you and your family – not to mention your budget.

Today's dream homes require sophisticated new technology, along with the power to control it. You can rely on Crestron to provide you with the technology to realise your dreams, now and for the future.

Visit **www.crestron.co.uk** or call **0208 439 7272**
to find your local Crestron dealer.

company, pays for all improvements.) Very few people would be able to find a garden firm that would do a total landscaping and replanting job for £300; £3,000 would be nearer the mark.

In general terms, you must allow at least £4,000 for a new bathroom, £5,000 for a new kitchen; £1,000 for redecoration of one room; £30,000 for a side extension or loft conversion and around £2,000 for garden landscaping. And these are minimum, not maximum amounts.

Then, all the time it stays on the market, the property will be costing you – in mortgage fees, parking fees, utilities, council tax, and service charges for a leasehold property. All these costs have to be added up before you can safely say you have made a profit.

But apart from the cost of renovation and selling, there has to be something special about your property which will make it stand out from the rest, and give it a certain cachet.

This is where cutting corners can cost you dear. In 2003, I had an expensive conservatory extension built onto my Victorian terrace house. I designed the extension so that the living room flowed into the dining room extension – great for parties and entertaining. By contrast, a neighbour who had an identical extension, undertaken by the same firm of builders, kept the original back wall and window, to save money.

When she put her house on the market, the feedback she got from disappointed viewers was that there was no 'flow through' from the living room to the extension. I sold my house for £650,000 and my neighbour's best offer was £595,000 – and that was only after it had been on the market for a year.

Also, beware of the 'my house' syndrome! Estate agents all complain that people selling their own homes frequently fall into this mindset, which means that however terrible it may appear to viewers, the 'my house' syndrome means that the owners refuse to see its faults and tend to overvalue it as a consequence. This psychological stumbling block means that people's own homes very often stay on the market for a very long time, because their owners remain emotionally attached to them. You can see this syndrome very clearly on television shows, where it reigns supreme.

The prevailing attitude is: if it's mine, it must be wonderful.

The other tendency is to overvalue your own home, ignoring the market.

A friend put her immaculate, beautifully designed studio flat on the market for £120,000. At the time, such flats were selling for a maximum of £90,000. After lingering on the market for a year, my friend had to accept an offer of £75,000. Here, the 'my house' syndrome prevailed to such an extent that my friend tried to bypass estate agents' fees by selling it privately, expecting that people would fall over themselves to pay over the odds for the flat.

In the end, not only did my friend have to accept a low offer – incurring service charges and council tax all that time – but had to pay estate agents' fees of 1.5 per cent plus VAT – another £1,321.87 to add to the selling costs.

Many people, when selling their homes, pin their hopes on cash buyers. But you can never do this. Most people buy on a mortgage, which means the property will be valued according to what the mortgage provider is prepared to lend.

In my time, I have made wonderful profits on my main home, and the secret has always, always been that old cliché of location, location, location. That, plus always buying character properties.

Some research carried out by London agents Ludlow Thompson showed that most buyers prefer older, character homes over newbuild. I have never in my life bought a new property, and would say, looking back, that many homes built from the 1950s onwards never do acquire a 'period' feel. Property developer Ivan Twigden, who started building houses in the 1960s, said that although some of his homes were now more than 40 years old, they still looked modern.

Wherever there is character, or period features, your home will attract a premium. So never destroy all the original character by ferocious updating.

Also, never forget that buyers are emotional people, too, and buy homes for many strange reasons. One buyer fell in love with a house of mine simply because it had a lovely expensive green curtain right across the back wall of the living room. 'I just had to buy it because of that curtain!' she enthused.

WISE BUYERS SET SIGHTS ON NEW HOMES

NHBC statistics show that new homes are more popular than ever and with their spangley bathrooms, swish fitted kitchens and savvy décor, who can blame home buyers for snapping them up? NHBC, the UK's leading warranty provider for new homes was established almost 70 years ago, since then its purpose has been to help raise the standards of new homes and provide protection for new home buyers through the ten year Buildmark insurance and warranty. Here are just a few reasons why buying new is so attractive to today's homebuyers:

- Many builders offer new homes buyers a range of attractive financial options, from offers to buy your old property at market value, to paying your deposit.

- There is no chain when buying a new home which allows you to sell your home in your own time and, often, move in when you're ready to.

- You're covered – if the builder is registered with NHBC, the property will receive NHBC's full ten year Buildmark Cover once it is completed. NHBC's Buildmark currently protects 1.8 million homes throughout the UK. Here are the different stages.

  - Before Completion – This part applies even before your home is finished, protecting your deposit if the builder goes bust before the work is complete.

  - The first two years – During the first two years the builder is responsible for sorting out any problems which do not comply with NHBC's Technical Standards. If the homeowner and the builder do not agree on what repair work is required, NHBC can offer its free, independent Resolution Service. They can also instruct the builder to carry out repair works where necessary.

  - Years three to ten – If a homeowner finds a problem more than two years after they have moved in, they should contact NHBC. At this point the Buildmark covers a range of structural aspects as well as double-glazing and staircases.

- New homes are built to higher insulation standards and have more efficient heating systems than ever before which means lower heating bills.

- Most house builders provide quality design, use energy efficient materials and the latest gadgets to finish their homes. They may also offer a choice of kitchens, bathrooms, fixtures, fittings and internal colour scheme.

- Long live the DIY free Sunday! New homes require less maintenance and repair than older homes and areas that would commonly require attention, like window frames and skirting boards, are just beginning their life span.

For more information on the Buildmark Cover contact NHBC on **01494 735363** or visit their website at **www.nhbc.co.uk**

From inspection to protection

no-one's more constructive

Successful and profitable selling of your own home – which contains, of course, much of your character, aspirations and lifestyle – depends not just on working out figures as exactly as possible, but on appealing to people's emotions. Even the right book on a coffee table can help to sell your house to the perfect purchaser. Never dismiss the amount of sheer emotion tied up in buying and selling homes.

I am always inclined to put in an offer on a home containing the latest hardback novels, and tempted to walk away from a property containing much hi-tech recording equipment, even though the properties may be, in effect, identical.

Yet a potential buyer of one of my homes admitted that seeing all my books on bookshelves made her feel sick and claustrophobic. She had never willingly read a book in her life.

Building your own home and selling it on

It is estimated that you can make 35 per cent more profit by building your own home than by buying a wreck and then renovating it. You also are allowed to do this work free of VAT. When you renovate an old house, you pay 17.5 per cent VAT, but no VAT on building your own house. The current situation, therefore, encourages people to knock down existing buildings and start again rather than renovate a wreck.

But you have to be very careful indeed, when doing this, that you are not seen to be property developing, or building purely for profit. If you want to avoid capital gains tax on selling, your property must not have been purchased for the sole purpose of making a profit, and you may have to prove this to the HM Revenue and Customs; in addition, the property must be your only or main residence throughout the period of ownership. This means that you cannot build one house while living in another – at least, you can, but only one can count as your PPR, even if it is not yet built.

If you keep moving, the HM Revenue and Customs may start asking awkward questions, as they are looking very carefully at the 'serial self-builders' who eventually may be taxed or deemed to be professional developers. In order to avoid capital gains tax, the property or land must emphatically NOT have been purchased for the sole purpose of making money, but rather, to provide a home for yourself and your family.

Obviously the Revenue have to accept that you must live somewhere before your self-build home becomes habitable. This is how it works at present: if the building work is completed within 12 months of purchase, the self-builder is not liable to CGT while inhabiting two homes. In order to avoid this, most self-builders live in a caravan on the site while building is in progress. You can hire caravans for the specific purpose of temporary accommodation during the build.

You must show a degree of permanence, so the best advice is to try to live in your completed self-build house for more than just a few months before putting it on the market. As the Revenue are very likely to swoop down, it is imperative that you keep all council tax bills, and all bills must be sent to the self-build address. If the self-build is seen to be driven by commercial considerations, then the exemption from VAT does not apply.

The biggest advantage of starting from scratch, as opposed to improving an existing building, is that you are exempt from VAT. But – what is starting from scratch, and if you live in a caravan on a site while your house is being built, does the caravan count as your main home? What about if you continue to live in your existing home while the new one is being built?

One way round this, of course, might be to rent, but even a rented home can count as your principal private residence. It is the occupation rather than the tenure that counts.

Self-build is becoming ever more popular, as by this means homeowners get exactly what they want. There is a big and growing business nowadays in selling plots for self-builders, who all have to be very careful that they are not seen to be commercial developers.

Mortgages

The problem with getting a self-build mortgage is that the lender has no collateral – that is, the house itself – to act as security for the loan. So with self-build, a different type of mortgage is required.

Here, you borrow in the short term to pay for materials and labour, then once the house is completed, you borrow in the long term just as with any other type of mortgage.

During the build, the funding is provided in four or five stages, each being linked to a phase in completion. Funds are released retrospectively after each stage is completed and approved by a Building Control inspector. There are a number of companies now offering self-build mortgages, and this is likely to increase as self-build becomes ever more popular.

Most self-builders believe you can save up to 30 per cent on building your own home as opposed to renovating a wreck or buying at the top of the market, and at the end of the build you have something unique to put on the market. (But not suspiciously soon after completion.)

Renting out a room (or rooms)

This option will not exactly make you rich, but is a time-honoured way of helping to pay the costs. Although I have been a buy-to-let landlord for many years, I have also rented out rooms in my own home over the years, and this has often enabled me to live in a better or more expensive home than I could afford otherwise, plus the rental income has enabled me to carry out renovations and improvements, thus greatly adding to the value of the property.

Under the government's rent-a-room scheme, you are allowed to charge up to £4,250 a year for rent without paying tax. Above this sum, you will be liable for income tax. But even without tax, the rental money will not be all profit. There will be greater wear and tear, your utility bills will increase with each new tenant, and you will have to pay more council tax if you are on the single person's 75 per cent rate. For this reason, many ad-hoc landlords prefer bona fide students, as they are exempt from paying council tax.

The usual thing with renting out rooms in your own home, as opposed to letting self-contained properties, is that the rent is an all-in amount. With an Assured Shorthold Tenancy, the utilities are paid by the tenant on top of the rent.

The practicalities you have to consider are these: Do your tenants eat with you or get their own meals? If the latter, do they have use of the kitchen at certain times? What about baths and washing? Internet connections and telephone lines, including broadband? What if they want, or expect, satellite television?

Here are the experiences of Mike, somebody who has been renting out rooms for many years to mature students – mainly people aged 25 to 30 doing MBAs or other higher qualifications and who are simply there to work.

Mike says: 'It does not make me a fortune but is enabling me to stay in a home I would otherwise have to sell, as I am no longer employed. This means I can stay in the house until it reaches its maximum value on the market; otherwise I would have had to sell simply because I could not afford to continue to live here.'

BUT – be careful here, as the HM Revenue and Customs are looking hard at people who rent out their homes for big events, such as Wimbledon tennis. At the moment, such people are banking a large amount of tax-free money, but the Revenue are considering ways to tax this form of income.

In the 2001 novel *Fingersmith*, set in Victorian times, one house owner makes a lot of money renting out her upstairs rooms to people wanting to watch public hangings, which took place opposite. The taxman now has his beady eye on modern versions of this wheeze.

Renting out your home to holidaymakers and overseas visitors

Ever more people are now doing this and, as a result, many companies have sprung up which do all the arrangements for you. In most cases, your overseas visitors will be staying for a couple of weeks, and they are people who prefer to be in a real house rather than staying in a hotel. All the money is taken upfront, and it is advisable to rent out your house through a reputable agency. They will advise what you have to do to prepare your house for visitors and how much money you are likely to make. Again, you have to be careful that you are not seen to be using your house for profit, thus incurring the dreaded CGT when you sell.

You do not have to clear your house out but just make sure that the visitors have somewhere to hang their clothes and live free of your personal clutter. But those who take on other people's houses for holidays and visits are people who vastly prefer a family home to a hotel.

In general terms, you are not liable for tax if your home is just let out for a few weeks a year. In order to count as a holiday letting on a commercial basis, the home must be available for letting for at least 140 days a year, and actually let for 70 of those days. Also, the property must not be occupied by the same person or family for more than 31 days at a stretch. But as we have just seen, this could soon change.

Using part of your home as a hotel or B&B

If your home is used partly for business purposes, or for income, you could lose the capital gains tax exemption which applies on your principal private residence. It is obviously wise here to take advice from a tax expert on whether some of all of your home will become liable for CGT when you sell.

Renting out a self-contained flat within your home

Here again you have to be careful, as the self-contained flat no longer counts as part of your home and will be liable for CGT when you sell, as you have been using your home partly for profit. If the house is divided into two, or more than two parts, each with its own separate utility supply, council tax bands will be affected.

You will also have to decide, if going for this option, whether you would sell the entire property as a going concern, or market the self-contained flat as a separate entity. If the latter, you would have to draw up a lease, as the property then becomes leasehold, and for this you would need the services of an expert property lawyer. In order to sell as separate entities, the flats have to be genuinely self-contained, in that you do not have to go through one flat to get to another.

Problems can arise if you have outbuildings on your property which you would like to turn into self-contained apartments. Here, before going ahead, it is essential to contact the council and ask how this will affect council tax. You would have to get planning permission, as well.

Some councils discourage homeowners from turning their houses into separate flats, while other councils actively encourage the provision of smaller units.

Three of my homes have had separate self-contained flats, and in every case, the flat was sold as an integral part of the main house, meaning that no capital gains tax was incurred, or necessity for drawing up leases.

Inheritance tax

This is one of the biggest concerns of everybody who invests in property; indeed, anybody who invests at all, in any assets, liquid or illiquid, above the current (2006) threshold of £275,000 is liable for inheritance tax of 40 per cent, and there is no quarter given, no relief, no way out.

Briefly, the situation is that for married couples or those in recognized civil partnerships, the joint home can pass free of tax to the surviving spouse. But that is all. Properties passed to your children are liable for this tax, as are properties owned by cohabiting partners. The only exemption is for the legally married

TRUSS LOFT CONVERSIONS

With today's variable housing market, cost of relocation and changing social considerations there are more reasons than ever for people to invest in a loft conversion rather than relocate. Many homeowners have changed the bathroom, kitchen etc., and are settled into the area. However find themselves looking for additional space. Social and working practices have altered the way people spend time in their home – the advent of cheap internet and working from home has made it difficult to switch off from the office – "I simply want to close the door and forget work for the weekend" or "The children are older and we need the spare room back" are quotes heard many times from people wishing an out of the way office. Families today generally need more space to live in – children with a computer each, quiet space to do the homework, younger children wanting play rooms. Home entertainment systems have made home cinema rooms a desirable investment. For all, many or any of these applications homeowners are more and more looking to the loft space to achieve that lifestyle change and increase the value of their home.

From inception in 1985 Truss Loft Conversions was founded on the basis of providing a high quality product that exceeds our customers expectations in terms of their lifestyle requirements, product quality and delivery. As a national specialist we have undertaken loft conversions of diverse sizes and requirements including second homes on the south coast, residential/office conversions in Scotland and family homes in Oxfordshire, Hertfordshire, Lancashire, Norfolk, North Yorkshire, Middlesbrough… Truss Loft Conversions has converted hundreds of properties throughout the UK, each to it's own specification, and each to comply with full building regulations. Our designers work alongside clients to deliver the best possible conversion from design through planning to completion.

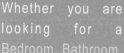

spouse – and when that person dies, the family home goes back into the estate to be assessed for IHT.

Make no mistake, IHT is a terrible business and you may have to sell your investment properties to pay it. Also, all assets belonging to the deceased are frozen until probate is granted. Then you have to have all properties independently assessed by an estate agent (valuing properties for probate has become a lucrative sideline for selling agents); also, if the HM Revenue and Customs are not satisfied, they may poke their noses in as well, quite legally.

Of course, there are ways round inheritance tax, and these will be discussed in Chapter 9 on SIPPs. But tax-avoidance schemes are in themselves very expensive to set up and you may be sure that the government has worked very diligently to plug as many loopholes as possible.

Also, the government is now cracking down on those who have put their properties into trust to avoid or minimize inheritance tax.

Letting out your home to film and TV crews

If you have an interesting or unusual home, you may consider making money from it by letting it out for films and TV shows. There is a huge demand for all kinds of homes, with the following provisos: they must have rooms which are big enough to take film equipment and crews, and there must be easy parking. In particular, there must be enough room somewhere nearby to park the canteen van – most important!

In the old days, finding suitable locations was a hit and miss affair, with freelance location managers having to source suitable venues for filming. But now, all is made easy with the Envenio website, whereby any property owner can post their home on the site and add to the database which is constantly being scoured by film and television companies. Advertising agencies are also always looking for unusual homes as backgrounds or foregrounds for ads. Even the naff and the kitsch can have their uses!

In order to be suitable, your home must have some special quality, but this doesn't mean it has to be grand. An intact 1950s kitchen, even an unusual cupboard, can fit the bill, and there is constant demand for suburban semis of all ages, from Georgian and Victorian, to thirties, fifties and modern.

You can post your property on the website for nothing, and should somebody want to film there, you will be paid anything from £400 to £2,500 a day. Filming lasts between one day and several weeks, and in order to allow filming to proceed uninterrupted, obviously all occupants have to make themselves scarce during proceedings.

The film company hiring your home may want to paint your walls a different colour or move in different furniture, but they will undertake to return your home in the condition they found it, even if this means complete redecoration.

Obviously it is very disruptive to have a film crew hanging around your house for days, maybe weeks, on end but if your home suits the purpose, then it is good money for nothing, really, and an excellent way of turning your home into yet another money spinner.

David Rudland, founder of the leading website for this work, says: 'We get numerous requests from people wanting to have their homes used for locations, and have found some spectacular properties in this way. We have council houses, grand mansions, old and new. We even have apartments used solely for film and TV work on our database. We take 15 per cent commission and try to get all the money upfront for our clients.

'Modern apartments are very popular for ads, but they must be very minimal, and large enough to fit in a film crew of, typically, 10 people.

'It can be a good way of making money from your property, so long as you have the right kind of property.'

Tax matters

If you hire out your home to film companies on a regular basis, or otherwise rent it out for a short time, say for Wimbledon fortnight, you may be liable to tax on the rental income.

Homeowners who receive income from short-term lettings, from letting their home while they are away on holiday, or hire out their house for profit, must make sure they declare this income on their tax return forms. Any undeclared income could come back to haunt homeowners and may result in substantial penalties.

All profit received on your own home is fully taxable, although you may be able to set some expenses against tax, such as the cost of advertising your home, repairs, letting agent's fees, painting and decorating, gardening and window cleaning. Make sure you keep all bills.

If you are considering hiring or renting out your home for short periods, first take advice from your accountant as to whether generating income from your own main home will incur any capital gains tax liability. In general terms, the HM Revenue and Customs will take a view on this, as tax and capital gains tax liability will depend on how much your home is used for purposes other than simply living.

The Bedroom

The bedroom – More than just a place to sleep!

Our lives are moving at a faster pace than ever before and the bedroom can be the perfect haven to escape. The bedroom should be a place to relax, to unwind, to dream and to invent - it should be your personal sanctuary. Yet, it is also a room that says much more about your personality than it has ever done before.

Once upon a time, people's bedrooms where out of sight and people invested very little in styling them to reflect their personality. Yet today, It is well know that on average we spend around one third of our lives in our bedrooms and with more people living in smaller 'open-plan' homes and apartments, the bedroom is becoming increasingly a functional room in the house - a room to enjoy and be proud of.

Be-Yourself!

The bedroom furniture market has never being so energetic. With an increasing choice of styles, materials and designs to choose from, there has been no better time to revamp your bedroom and create your own perfect living sanctuary.

What will it cost? Well, gone are the days when you needed to buy an entire bedroom suite of matching bed, wardrobe and dressing table. Today, eclectic style is in! Feel free to mix and match individual pieces of furniture to create your own exclusive look and spend as little or as much as you like. Simply, painting the walls or adding a new designer bed will completely revitalise a bedroom.

The focal item in a bedroom – the bed!

It goes without saying that the most important item of furniture in a bedroom is the bed. Therefore, it is essential to compare the different benefits of each bed pick the right one for you. Good Beds can range from as little as £149 to over £5000 and come in a variety of styles from traditional Victorian to contemporary metal to stylish upholstered storage beds. Most people keep their bed for approximately 17 years and yet, often compromise on price and quality. Consider that a typical bed retailing at £699 will only cost you about 11pence per night over 17 years.

Also, look for a brand. Brands such as Jay-Be have manufactured beds for many years and offer substantial guarantees, which is your assurance of quality.

Sleep better – in a clean and organised environment.

Research shows that people are living in smaller homes but have more possessions. Consequently, storage is becoming more important. Jay-Be has developed a new genre of storage beds offering as much as 4 times more storage than the old 4 drawer storage beds whilst still offering great design. A clean, uncluttered, comfortable and organised bedroom is likely to contribute to a better night's sleep and consequently improve the quality of your decisions and actions the next day.

What's Comfortable?

Comfort is a matter of personal preference so what feels comfortable to one person may feel uncomfortable to another so it is essential that whoever is going to sleep in the bed should try several different models before deciding which one they should buy.

Choose the support and comfort that suits your weight and build – every 'BODY' suits different firmnesses. Also, don't forget that the comfort of your bed relies on the mattress and the base working in harmony together.

The ideal base for any bed is one with sprung slats. Sprung slats provide long lasting evenly distributed support optimising the effectiveness of the mattress properties. They also allow good Air circulation through the mattress, which is a key factor for healthy sleep! During the night it is estimated that a human body can perspire as much as 1 pint of water. By allowing the mattress to 'air' it helps reduce the build up of moisture making a fresher sleeping environment.

Award winning bed designer and UK manufacturer, Jay-Be offers an extensive range of beds, all with sprung slatted bases and a variety of complimentary mattresses. With an excellent choice of styles from contemporary metal beds in a choice of colours to, stylish upholstered beds in over 50 fabric options, you are sure to find a bed that suits you!

Visit **www.jaybe.co.uk** or call on **01924 517820**

Ballard and Bailey

If you are looking for a quality chimney piece Ballard and Bailey has over 30 authentic designs spanning the Georgian , Victorian and Art Nouveau/Edwardian era. What sets our fireplaces apart from others is the extremely fine casting detail. Visitors to your home will assume that you are fortunate enough to have the originals still in situ.

The Ballard and Bailey range has been selected by drawing upon 25 years of experience gained from the restoration and installation of period fireplaces. These fireplaces have been developed with the aim of combining traditional elegance and the necessity for modern practicality.

We believe a Ballard and Bailey fireplace is unrivalled in terms of quality of casting , attention to detail and after service. Our family run business takes pride in hand assembling every item which is then given a thorough inspection. Finally each fireplace is then hand polished to either a highlighted or traditional graphite finish depending on the customers choice.

Any of our fireplaces will make a welcome addition to your home and a focal point which your family and friends will enjoy for many years to come.

Ballard and Bailey fireplaces are available through our specialist retailers who supply and install throughout the United Kingdom and the Republic of Ireland. For a copy of our latest brochure and details of your nearest stockist visit **www.ballardandbailey.com** or alternatively please contact us on this number **02392 241111**

Ballard and Bailey

BOSHAM CAST IRON SURROUND
WITH
DROXFORD CAST IRON INSERT

DETAIL SHOWING DROXFORD INSERT

Give your home kerbside appeal

Windows and Doors – what you need to know

Windows are the first thing people see when they visit your house, so it's no surprise to learn that badly fitted windows can affect the value of your home. Your best bet is to choose a member of the Glass and Glazing Federation (GGF).

Especially as all replacement glazing now comes under Building Regulations Control.

This means that if you want to replace your windows, those new windows will have to be energy efficient. The reason for this is the Government's drive to ensure we, like the rest of the world, pollute the atmosphere as little as possible.

If in the future you then decide to sell your property, the purchaser's solicitors, when undertaking the necessary search, will ask for evidence that any replacement windows installed after April 2002 comply with the new Regulations.

You can prove that your windows comply in two ways:-
1. a certificate showing that the work has been done by an installer who is registered under the FENSA Registration Scheme
   or
2. a certificate from the local authority saying that the installation has approval under the Building Regulations

If you want to ensure that you comply with these Regulations and that the company undertaking the work will do a good job, you should make sure that you use a Glass and Glazing Federation (GGF) member who is FENSA Registered.

Conservatories – let the light in!

Sunshine is a vital element in our lives. This is reflected in the popularity of holidays abroad in countries where temperatures are in the 90s and the sun is guaranteed. It is also apparent when people buy a new home. Recent surveys have indicated that home owners say the more light there is in their homes, the happier they feel.

The British craving for light is also indicated by the popularity of conservatories. During the Victorian and Edwardian periods, the conservatory was most often used as a winter garden, allowing plants to flourish all year round. These days, it tends to be used as extra living space, making the design specifications ever more important.

The majority of all conservatories built today are double glazed and allow the household to make year round use of their additional space and to appreciate the aesthetics and benefits provided by its glass walls.

As The Conservatory Association – a specialist division of the Glass and Glazing Federation – points out, conservatories can come in all shapes and sizes in both modern and traditional styles, but the one thing that unites them is glass. Glass enables us to sit in a conservatory even on a cold and blustery day, and bask in the sun.

What design?
Among the most popular designs are:

The Victorian
Characterised by a ridge with ornate cresting and multi faceted bay end – usually either 3 or 5 facets.

The Edwardian
Typically this has a square end which makes good use of space, and a pitched roof.

Lean-to
Great for both big and small awkward spaces like corners.

When you choose a GGF Member, you can be assured that they:

1. Will comply with the new Building Regulations (relating to windows) and ensure you get the appropriate certificate via the Fenestration Self Assessment Scheme (FENSA).

2. Will have been in business for at least three years.

3. Have all been vetted to ensure they provide a quality service, the vetting procedure includes taking up references, looking at their accounts and site visits.

4. Work to the Federation's Code of Good Practice and technical guidelines.

In addition the GGF will provide you with:

1. A free conciliation service – should you and a Member company not see eye to eye over work carried out.
2. Protection for your deposit – the GGF Deposit Indemnity Scheme is backed by Norwich Union and safeguards deposits up to £3,000 or 25% of the contract price, whichever is lower.
3. A Customer Charter.

Contact us on: **0870 042 4255** for a list of members in your area or see **www.ggf.org.uk**

Safe as....

Choosing a new conservatory or replacement windows but don't know who to trust?

Every GGF member must work within our Code of Good Practice. Everyone that installs conservatories, windows and doors is also registered with FENSA to simplify working within the new Building Regulations. We offer a scheme to secure your deposit and even an arbitration and conciliation service if a problem can't be solved by other means.

So why not visit our home –www.ggf.org.uk– to find out why looking for the GGF logo helps you to rest easy in your home.

It can even help you to choose your installer with complete lists of members of our two specialist groups, the Conservatory Association and the Window and Door Group.

Glass and Glazing Federation

3 Buy-to-let

Buying residential property to let remains overwhelmingly the most popular type of property investment and it is easy to see why. You have two potential bites of the profit cherry: income from rentals and capital growth on the property itself.

Added to that, there is the big plus that you can buy properties with cheaply borrowed money on a buy-to-let mortgage. It would be difficult to obtain such cheap borrowing for any other type of investment. Also, on paper at least, it seems that you cannot lose, given that there will always be a rental market and that property generally goes up in value over time.

The huge popularity of buy-to-let has been given an added boost in recent years by the proliferation of 'property millionaire' seminars and property clubs, where you buy off-plan properties at a discount and rent them out until you are able (you hope!) to sell them at a huge profit.

But is it true that you simply cannot lose when buying to let? Well, not quite. Success in this endeavour depends on being able to work out your figures very carefully indeed so that you come out on top. There is also the little matter of being able to buy properties that will (a) rent out easily and profitably and (b) sell for a considerable profit in years to come. And with buy-to-let there are very many figures and percentages indeed to take into account, also many hidden costs not immediately apparent. Even buying paint and cleaning materials to smarten up your property adds up.

The big attraction of buy-to-let for many investors is that the projected rental income, rather than salary levels, is used to assess the level of borrowing. This makes it possible for investors to build up an impressive property portfolio very quickly indeed by the process known as 'gearing'.

To start the ball rolling, you have to have some level of cash deposit to put down on your buy-to-let. This will typically be 25 per cent of the purchase price, although some lenders set the deposit as low as 15 per cent. This initial cash is most often raised by releasing equity in the investor's main home and remortgaging, although those prepared to take a very high risk can sometimes stump up the deposit through credit card borrowing.

After one buy-to-let property is purchased, you release equity in that, remortgage, and buy more properties to let. In this way, quite ordinary people with no particular financial acumen have built up portfolios of dozens, maybe even hundreds, of properties, all of which pay their way through the rental income they generate.

But buying up properties at great speed is a little like walking a tightrope in that you have to balance everything out very carefully indeed – and then have a safety net of cash to fall back on if interest rates rise, the boiler breaks down or you cannot rent the place out for love nor money.

Jackie Taylor, a former local government officer who is now a full-time landlord, has amassed a portfolio of 16 properties in eight years, all by mortgaging, remortgaging and gearing. She says: 'I am constantly juggling sums and figures to make it all work and it's very hard indeed. There is such fierce competition out there that your places have to be very smart and very central to attract tenants. Then they may negotiate you down as they have so much choice.

'I have had many sleepless nights, especially as I have had to replace boilers, redecorate and replace kitchens and bathrooms. Some of my properties have not rented out after a few years and I have had to sell them. There is no one perfect formula for success but my advice is that unless you buy a real dog of a property, eventually you are not going to lose.

'You do have to be prepared to hang on to them though, for about 10 years, to see a good return and you may not get a good yield in rent. You always have to think about repairs and maintenance and how you might pay for them.'

To make the enterprise work, you have to number crunch very carefully indeed, taking into account service charges, ground rent, fees to letting agents, cost of renovation, decoration, appliances, furniture and fittings, mortgage repayment, legal fees and stamp duty for buying and all other purchase costs and then set all these against the amount of rent you believe you can realistically achieve.

When all the numbers are computed, the rental yield should give you at least a clear 6 per cent gross yield. Any less than this and you will lose money, at least if buying on a mortgage. It sounds obvious, but if your mortgage repayments are set at 5.5 per cent and the best rental yield you can hope for is 4 per cent, this means you will pay to borrow! The rental yield has to be better than a bank account will produce, otherwise it will be costing you to rent out the property, rather than making anything on it.

The reason you have to work out the figures very carefully is that there are always unexpected costs when letting property, such as rental voids, a sudden hike in service charges (in leasehold properties), an increase in interest rates or a major repair or renovation. The mortgage repayments are far from being the only ongoing cost of a buy-to-let property.

These were the gross figures for rental yields and capital growth on newbuild properties in the year March 2004–5: the average newbuild two-bedroom apartment experienced capital growth of 5.6 per cent; over the same time span, the average gross rental yield of those properties was 5 per cent, making an average total gross return on the investment of 10.6 per cent over one year. These statistics, compiled by estate agents Knight Frank, stated that while the highest growth in that period (capital gain plus rental yield) was 16.4 per cent on newbuild properties, other similar properties in some areas had experienced negative capital growth and had no rental income at all.

At the same time as having no income from rentals, investors would have faced ongoing costs, such as repayments on their loan, service charges (always a fact of life in apartment blocks), council tax and utility bills, thereby adding considerable insult to the injury of nil rent and negative capital growth.

Then the costs of entry and exit from this sector are relatively high. If you sell too soon you can lose an enormous amount of money, rather than gaining, which is the object of the exercise. And as we have seen, there are always considerable costs to buying and selling, whatever your eventual gain. Also, the sums of money involved in buying any property are very large; usually into six figures.

Most investment experts warn that buy-to-let is no longer a get-rich-quick scheme, if ever it was, and that it is unrealistic to expect a quick turnaround on profit. Because of the high entry and maintenance costs of this type of investment, it has to be viewed as a medium- to long-term venture, say 10 to 15 years, before genuine growth and profit can be realized.

In recent years, the emphasis has been mainly on buying new or off-plan properties for buy-to-let investment, on the assumption that they will not need immediate maintenance and as they are smart, new and clean, they will appeal to the increasingly sophisticated and choosy rental market. Mostly as well, these new developments of apartment blocks are in city centres or regeneration areas where workforces tend to be concentrated.

But as with everything in property matters, there is a wide choice of properties which may be suitable for renting out, and also a wide variety of tenants. You do not have to go for newbuild where, when all is said and done, the resale value has not been established on the open market.

Another aspect of buying off-plan is that developers often set the service charges artificially low at first, to attract buyers, and then increase them considerably after all the units have been bought. Further, when a high proportion of units in a new development is owned by investors rather than owner-occupiers, the apartment block tends to lose value. Owner-occupiers may not be interested in buying if they believe a new building is being infested by investors who are only interested in making a profit rather than living there themselves. It is a new and worrying aspect of buy-to-let which the investor has to take on board.

But there are very many property types to choose from. You can invest in upmarket properties in prime areas which appeal to corporate tenants; houses for families or for student occupation; one-bedroom flats for singles or couples; two- or three-bedroom flats for sharers; and properties suitable for social housing. Not all tenant markets operate in all areas, so the thing to do first is thoroughly research an area by talking to letting and selling agents, to see what the market consists of, how much property costs to purchase, and the kind of rents that can be achieved.

Before ever buying a property, it is a good idea to pretend to be a tenant looking for somewhere, rather than going on what developers or agents might say. When actress Annie Hulley decided to start investing in property, she discovered that the rents promised to landlords were very different indeed to the rents actually achieved. She said: 'As a landlord, I was told by agents that I could get £425 a week for a type of flat I was considering buying. But when I pretended to be a tenant looking for a similar flat, I was told £350 a week. It's no good just going on what agents say – you have to work on what you can realistically achieve in any given market.' The other advantage of pretending to be a tenant is that you get to see the competition. You learn what is on offer at specific rents, and how smart or otherwise the properties are. You also hear the spiel given by letting agents, which may be very different from what you would be told as a landlord.

Working out the yield

Before ever deciding on a buy-to-let property, it is essential to work out the achievable rental yield, to see whether it is worth it. A sum of £1,800 a month, or £21,600 a year, sounds a lot of money, but if your property is worth £700,000, that is a yield of less than 3 per cent, far less than you could get with even an ordinary interest account on that amount at the bank.

Assuming for the moment you buy a two-bed flat for £200,000, stamp duty at 1 per cent comes to £2,000; legal costs, say £940; renovation and decoration, another £5,000.

Service charges come in at £1,000 per annum. Your expected rental is £250 a week, or £13,000 per annum. Your gross return therefore is just under 6.5 per cent – about the minimum workable return. Allowing a 10 per cent plus 17.5 per cent VAT letting fee (£1,527.50) and taking into account the service charges, your actual yield now reduces to £10,472.25.

Then you will have to pay income tax on the gain, plus insurance, gas certificate, repairs and renewals.

However, if you are a cash buyer, you will still gain a usable income. If you are buying on a mortgage, you will have to depend on capital growth to come out on top, which is always an unknown.

To qualify for a mortgage, your expected rental return has to be 130 per cent of the mortgage repayment costs. To give a simple example, if the loan costs you £1,000 a month, the expected rent must be at least £1,300 a month. This will give you a rental income of £300 a month – before you pay service charges, letting fees and all the other costs. It is not easy to make a profit when buying on a mortgage, but you should at least aim to break even as well as having some rainy day money for unexpected repairs, void periods or building levies in apartment blocks.

Here again are some simple figures. You put down a deposit of £50,000 on your £200,000 flat, and take out a mortgage for £150,000 payable at a rate of 5.25 per cent. This means your mortgage costs you £7,875 a year, leaving you a rental income of £5,125 a year.

When you take off your letting fee of 10 per cent plus VAT, this comes down to £3,597.50 a year. Take off the service charges, estimated at £1,000 a year, and your income now comes down to £2,597.50 a year. And with these mortgage figures, we have not allowed anything for insurance, furniture, fittings, appliances or incidentals.

As you will see, buying to let on a mortgage gives you pocket money, at best, rather than income. BUT, by the process of gearing, where you use accumulated equity in one property to buy another, the figures start to make more sense. Say you have eight properties all with the same yields and costs, you will be getting an income now of £20,780 a year – just about enough to live on.

By this means, you can see that the more properties you have, the more income you will have. Keeping the same figures, if you have 50 such properties, you will now be getting an annual income of £129,850 a year. This is how property millionaires are made. And anybody can do it.

But with a mortgage, it hardly makes sense with just one property. You have to 'gear' to make it worthwhile, bearing in mind that accountancy costs for 50 properties will hardly be any more than for one property. Also, when you are letting many properties, you can negotiate for good deals with letting agents.

In order to make buy-to-let work, you have to do it on a large scale. The more properties you have, the more the exercise becomes worth it – if you can stand the effort of looking after 50 tenants, 50 properties and all the accompanying problems of the combination of human beings and bricks and mortar – often a lethal mix.

So what about the other aspect of buy-to-let investments, which is the capital gain? Don't forget that when you sell any home apart from your principal private residence, you will have to pay capital gains tax which comes in at up to 40 per cent of your total gain. But the longer you own your properties, the less fearsome this tax becomes because of the process of indexation, whereby your personal capital gains allowance accumulates each year to lessen the amount you pay to the government for selling your property. The spectre of capital gains tax is yet another reason why buy-to-let properties should always be held for 10 years whenever possible.

In the main, buy-to-let works extremely well, even without significant capital growth, so long as three conditions apply: your properties are always, always fully let; interest rates do not rise too much, or they actually come down; and you don't face massive repair bills.

If you die and want to leave your properties to your heirs, you, or rather your estate, will have to pay inheritance tax. Ah – but I hear you asking: can I put all these buy-to-lets into one of those new SIPPs and avoid every kind of tax? Up to a point – all is explained in Chapter 9.

There are now a number of mortgage providers which specialize in buy-to-let, although most of the main lenders now offer this facility. Most buy-to-let investors take out interest-only mortgages, but it is worth comparing rates as, very often, the interest-only period (or other deal) only lasts for a fixed term. There will also be an arrangement fee, a re-arrangement fee if you change your mortgage, insurance, and a redemption fee if you change mortgages or remortgage.

Be aware that every time you alter your original mortgage deal, there will be another fee to pay.

Guaranteed rentals

Many developers are now offering guaranteed rentals on newbuild properties, usually at 6 per cent. The guarantees are for a specific period of time, typically two years after completion of the development. Then you are on your own.

Many landlord associations are not in favour of these guaranteed rentals, for the following reasons: the 'guaranteed rental' does not guarantee that tenants have been found at this rent, or even at all. In reality, this guarantee amounts to a discount on the property and is not any indication that the property is popular with the tenant market.

To make the equation work and to keep inside the law, during the 'guaranteed rental' period you will still be paying service charges, letting fees, your mortgage and the ground rent. Unless you pay all of these, the developers cannot justify their claim of the guaranteed rental.

What you have to ask is: where am I when the guarantee period ends? What hope do you have of finding tenants yourself at that rent or, indeed, at any rent? Before ever agreeing to a guaranteed rental, you must discover what kind of market exists and what tenants are prepared to pay on the open market. You can only discover this by slogging round letting agencies yourself, and not going on the say-so of the developers and their marketing hype.

How the different tenant markets work

There are many classes and divisions of tenants, and you have to consider in advance what type of tenant you are aiming at. Broadly speaking, they fall into the following categories: students; young professionals (singles, couples, sharers); families; older, divorced or separated people; corporate tenants; in-betweeners (those renting while deciding what to buy).

All of these markets have their own dynamics and a property which appeals to the student market, for instance, would be unlikely to suit a high-earning city type, in terms of either the property or the location.

Students

Brian Palacio, a former detective with the Metropolitan Police, decided to invest in the student market in Brighton and Hove when he was invalided out of the Met with a payoff of £170,000. He says: 'I wanted to invest my redundancy money in something useful and also have an interest to keep me occupied. Because of the whiplash injury sustained in the course of duty, I am never going to be a hundred per cent and I had to choose something which would give me plenty of time off. A nine to five job was out.

'My doctors also told me I had to choose somewhere healthy and sunny to live, and also to get out of London. I had already studied with the Open University at Brighton and did two summer schools there. I knew that with two universities and many language schools, there would be a big market in Brighton for student accommodation, and this seemed to be the best bet for me.

'So I started looking at four-bedroom houses and began buying on buy-to-let mortgages. I buy houses in bad condition, renovate them and let them through the university housing office, which regulates rents and conditions.

'The big advantage with students is that there is no council tax to pay and I charge them an all-in amount to cover utilities.'

The rents amount to £65 a week each and Brian works on a 40-week year. As a bonus, his houses are often let during the long vacation to summer school students. He does not make a profit from student lettings, but covers his costs. The real profit, he says, is coming from the capital growth in the houses. Brighton and Hove has the most expensive properties in the UK, after London. Brian adds: 'One of the big advantages of going for the student market is that there is always a ready supply of tenants. The universities provide the students so I never have any problem with filling the houses.'

Brian believes that in order to make the student market work, you have to be hands-on: 'You can't leave it all to managing agents and a lot of agents won't handle students anyway. As you have to be prepared to deal with any crises that crop up, it's essential to be near. I don't think it would work to be an absentee landlord hundreds of miles away, with the student market.'

Most landlords insist on tenants paying by standing order, but Brian believes this doesn't really work with students: 'When you have 12 or 15 students all paying about the same, it can be difficult to check through your bank accounts to see whether they have all paid. I take cheques or cash and have had no real problems with rent. I take one month's rent as a deposit.'

Brian says that if you want an income from letting, don't rent out to students as you are really only likely to cover your costs. The universities and colleges set the rent and won't take you on as a landlord if you try to charge more. But as his houses have already made a tidy sum, it works for him.

A number of companies are now offering student homes as investment opportunities. You will find these companies at Property Investor Shows. Mainly, these student homes are brand-new developments which have been designed to cater exactly for student needs. They cost investors from £88,000 per self-contained unit. The Warehouse, one such company, can be contacted on: 01772 200949.

Young professionals – singles, couples, sharers

This is by far the biggest tenant pool and is in many ways the easiest to operate, as young professionals are earning a fixed salary and know in advance how much rent they can afford.

The secret here is to discover what the average salaries are in a particular location, and then see if your potential investment works financially. Suppose you rent a one-bedroom apartment to a couple in their mid-twenties each earning £25,000 a year, you know that their combined income of £50,000 will mean they can pay around £250–£280 a week in rent. If you set your rents much higher than this, you will simply not attract tenants.

These days, tenants are used to negotiating and slogging around to find the best deal. They will look at around 15 properties before deciding, usually, on the cheapest.

Although an income of £50,000 may sound a lot, remember that many graduates will still be repaying student loans, which gives them less disposable income for rent.

Young professionals like clean, smart, simple flats, usually furnished and with dishwashers, power showers, internet connection and, if possible, some outside space. Having said that, they are not usually keen gardeners and you cannot expect your tenants to look after a garden. Mostly, these tenants do not have cars and do not need garages, but they have to be very near to transport links, near to their work and also to restaurants, pubs and night life.

Corporate tenants

Corporate tenants want very high-spec properties for which they will pay a premium rent. Rents of £3,000 a week are not unusual with this sector, but for that, these tenants want highly designed properties very near to their work. As they work long hours, they will often look for something in walking distance to their jobs.

Mostly, the corporate market is operated by relocation agents who drive very hard bargains indeed. Only enter this highly specialized market if you can afford the high purchase price of the property and the equally high running costs.

In general, as corporate tenants are thinner on the ground than others, it takes 13 weeks to rent one of these properties.

Country rentals

Apart from holiday lets, the country market can be difficult. Letting agent Jane Russam, who specializes in country lettings for Knight Frank, says that a £700,000 country house would yield no more than £1,800 a month in rent.

Country homes must be unfurnished – furnished properties are difficult to let, Russam says, and in addition the property has to have something special about it. The average stay for this market is 13–15 months, and the tenants are most often the 'in-betweeners' who are renting while they look around for something suitable to buy in the area.

Families

This sector wants houses rather than flats, with gardens and near to schools and other facilities for young children. Most families renting are from overseas; there is not a significant rental market among UK families except for those on benefits. Most often, families renting are in-betweeners, who are actually looking for somewhere to buy.

If interested in renting to families, you would first need to discover what, if any, is the family market in your area, what kinds of families they are, and what kinds of rents they are prepared to pay.

Leasing to the local authority or a housing association

Many landlords go for this option because it takes all the worry away from you. Here, you lease your property to the local authority or housing association for a term of, typically, three to five years during which time they simply take it over and you can forget about it.

They will find tenants, paint and redecorate your property, take over all the running costs (apart from service charges in flats) and pay you the rent. They will also guarantee to return your property to you in excellent condition at the end of the lease period. Not only do they not charge you any commission, they may well pay you a golden hello when first leasing your property. This can be up to £5,000 with some authorities and associations, in certain areas.

Very many landlords find this option works extremely well, but in exchange for all this largesse, the association or local authority impose some stringent conditions. A representative will come to your property and assess it for suitability. You have to pay for this. Funnily enough, health and safety standards are far higher here than in other sectors of the market, and you would have to make sure the property had fire doors, smoke alarms, fire escapes and up-to-date electrical and gas installations. You pay for any upgrading the property may require.

Then the authority or association set the rentals. They will offer you so much for a one-bedroom flat, so much for a house – and there is no deviation from this. If you are interested in leasing your property to this sector, first do research as to what is required. Many housing associations provide landlord packs, as do the universities.

Note: when I was considering this option, for me it did not work. The Notting Hill Housing Trust offered me a set rent for a two-bedroom maisonette I was considering buying, but the service charges, which included communal heating and hot water, were far too high to make it a viable proposition. In general, though, yields are far higher here than in the private sector.

Being a social landlord

In some areas, this is the only tenant pool there is, and you have to know you can handle it. Many authorities now pay Housing Benefit directly to the claimant and the days of paying rent straight to the landlord are drawing to a close. The idealistic intention here is to give social tenants more responsibility and choice by allowing them to pay the rent themselves, and operate in the same way as private tenants.

Many landlords, however, find that their tenants spend the rent on themselves and fall into arrears. It is only when the tenant is eight weeks in arrears that you can apply to have the rent paid directly to you, and as the money has gone, there is no way of making up the two months' arrears.

Also, because social tenants have no financial resources whatever, they are not in a position to pay a deposit or for dilapidations. Before entering this sector, make sure you know all the ramifications. Some companies in the North of England find, renovate and sell cheap properties to investors, which are intended for rental to social tenants. These companies also offer to find tenants, but in reality, the operation does not proceed as smoothly as it should. Many tenants in this sector default on rent and then disappear without trace.

Most High Street letting agents do not handle this sector of the market, as it is too tricky.

Property clubs

These are offshoots of the heavily-advertised 'Become a Property Millionaire with little or no cash down' ads you see in newspapers and hear on the radio. What happens here is that you buy membership of a property club, usually at several thousand pounds, for the privilege of gaining access to discounted off-plan properties.

There are two types of property club: one where the club itself buys properties in bulk and sells them on to you, the investor, and the other where you pay a membership fee for access to discounted off-plan properties which have not been bought by the property club.

In 2005, five property clubs were wound up by the High Court for fraudulent practices whereby investors paid several thousand pounds but never got their hands on a property. Rogue investment companies charged naïve investors up to £50,000 for newly built houses and flats at discounts without needing deposits. The problem was, these investors never got their hands on the property – the property club just pocketed their cash. The Department for Productivity, Energy and Industry (a new name for the DTI) discovered that these clubs were simply helping themselves to the money they had taken off investors – who usually raised the cash by remortgaging their main home – and caused them to be closed down.

So does this mean that property clubs, along with timeshare and holiday clubs, are a bad idea and yet another means of separating the gullible and the greedy from their money?

Not necessarily. Although it is estimated that one in six new flats is now sold to a buy-to-let investor through a property club of one sort or another, there are bona fide operators in the game. But always beware of the magic word 'invest' because this always means that you CAN lose some or all of your money, however low the purported risk.

The investment club is usually tied into a mortgage company, and this is where you start paying as, very often, the mortgage deals are not as good as you could get on the open market. But you are locked into them for ever and the investment club may well insist that you use their mortgage providers.

When buying off-plan through an investment club, there is a danger that all the properties will come onto the market at the same time and there will not be enough tenants to go round.

Here are sample figures from one such club, Viceroy Properties, for off-plan properties:

Market price of property	175,000
Discount	26,500
Net price	148,750
Viceroy's fee	4,112 (2 per cent of market price + VAT)
You pay	152,862

Assuming 6 per cent growth over the following year, you have made a gross profit of £33,000. That is without taking into account rental income, which, at 6 per cent of the purchase price, would yield another £9,120, giving you a gross overall profit of just under £42,000 in a year.

The best advice is that until you know how much money you can make from a property, you should not be even vaguely interested in it.

Would you enjoy being a landlord?

It is very important to ask this question, as much of the hype surrounding buy-to-let gives the impression that there is absolutely nothing to being a landlord, and you can just let agents look after everything for you. In fact, the contract remains between you and the tenant, nobody else, and you are responsible not only for your property but also for your tenant.

Both properties and tenants need a lot of looking after and it is emphatically not simply a matter of money in and money out.

Doing it together

Setting up a buy-to-let business is becoming a popular way for couples to join forces and double their expertise. Lee Grandin, of Landlord Mortgages, says: 'Buy-to-let enables couples to build a small business together with relatively little risk. Couples generally are good at working together with, typically, the man handling the finance and the woman handling the interior design, tenants, check in and check out.'

Nearly half of all borrowers with Landlord Mortgages are married couples, and 90 per cent of their most successful landlords are a husband and wife team. Lee Grandin adds: 'It's in their interests to work together because they hope their portfolio will finance a comfortable retirement.'

David and Linda England own three London buy-to-let properties and four in Blackpool, total worth around £1 million. Their rental income of around £50,000 a year more than pays their interest-only mortgages.

Sherron and Patrick Parris own two buy-to-let houses near where they live in North London, which are home to a total of nine people, mainly vulnerable young men. Both former social workers, they now combine building up their property portfolio with housing youngsters who find it difficult to cope in society. This way, they hope to combine work they love with security in retirement.

Dr Nicholas Bateson and his wife Ameer live in London and own a total of 25 properties worth around £3 million. Mortgages come to £2 million, and the rental income offsets the repayments. They do all the work of finding and vetting tenants themselves, thus saving letting and management fees.

The advantages for couples working together in this way is that there is double capital gains tax relief (each individual has a yearly capital gains tax allowance) and personal assets can be exchanged tax-free, which cannot happen with any other type of partnership.

You have to get on well together, though!

Speaking as one who bought a number of buy-to-lets with a partner, I can say from experience that, provided you see eye to eye, it works much better like this than when trying to go it alone, which can be extremely bleak. But – unless each of you pulls your weight equally, this potentially stressful arrangement can lead to massive rows.

Beware the leasehold trap

By far the greater majority of properties bought on a buy-to-let basis are sold leasehold rather than freehold. Most new developments are leasehold properties as they are flats rather than separate houses and, as we have seen, to buy leasehold means that you are never the owner of the property.

Because you have bought a length of time, you have to be very careful that the capital value of your property does not go down as the lease shortens. This is an aspect of property purchase many investors never consider, but if the lease becomes shorter than 70 years, you will find it difficult, if not impossible, to get a mortgage on it. This means you cannot sell the property as it has no resale value.

The same applies to ex-local authority high-rise flats. These are often sold at what seems like an incredible bargain, until you realize they have no resale value, either because the lease is extremely short or because they are on the 15th floor, too high in the sky to get a loan. If you cannot get a mortgage on a leasehold property, assume it is not a good buy.

The only exception to this rule is if you buy for cash on a very short lease, and the rental income will give you much, much more than you could hope for with a bank account. Once the lease is up, you have nothing to sell and you will lose all your capital, but if the rental yield is high enough, you may still come out on top. It is a high-risk strategy, though.

When buying leasehold properties for investment, always make sure that your purchase comes with a share of the freehold. This is the most important question to ask when considering a buy-to-let flat, as otherwise the freeholder sets the charges and levies and you could be seriously out of pocket.

Whenever serious investors are considering buying a flat, they should always ask about service charges, the sinking fund and whether there are likely to be any big bills in the near future.

Be aware that very few newbuild and off-plan properties are sold with a share of the freehold, and this in itself makes the purchase very tricky. These properties do, of course, come with a shiny new lease, and most of these are for 99 years. New properties rarely come with longer leases than this. If you keep the property for 15 years, this lease is getting dangerously near the 80-year cut-off point for mortgages.

Personal story

I started buying flats to let in 1995, and the exercise has served me extremely well. Because I always bought for cash – by downsizing on my main home, rather than releasing equity – the rental income has been all mine. The properties have increased in value and the flats have always been tenanted. As with most people, I have had to learn as I go.

The first flats I bought were very cheap but had extremely high service charges. Also, it was not possible to enfranchise as not enough residents were interested.

I made sure that subsequent investment properties I acquired always came with a share of the freehold, and that the service charges were reasonable enough to allow me to sell the properties if necessary.

The only downside, looking back, is that after a time, your investment flats have to be refurbished as they come to the end of their renting cycle. This usually means they have to be withdrawn from the market as you cannot expect tenants to pick their way around building works.

After refurbishment, you may not get very much extra rent, even though the cost of renovation has been very high. Yet if you don't refurbish, you may not be able to rent the place out at all. These are the figures I was quoted, before and after: one studio flat was being rented out for £300 a month. The refurbishment cost £12,000, after which I could get £410 pcm. Another flat was rented out at £220 a week; again the refurbishment cost around £12,000 and the new achievable rental was £250 a week. Yet another studio flat was rented out at £650 a month. With a new kitchen and bathroom, £8,000 minimum, the rent would be around £780 a month.

A refurbished flat may not, either, sell for very much more than in its grotty state. One of my flats went on the market in its raw state for £170,000; a similar, refurbished flat in the block was on the market for £180,000, but smart as it was, potential buyers considered it too expensive for its size and location. BUT there is a big plus in that the cost of all these improvements can be added onto the cost of your investment, thereby bringing the capital gains tax liability right down when you sell. So, even though a refurbished property may not sell for very much more than an unmodernized one, your eventual profit will be greater because of the lower CGT liability. So – it's even-stevens, one way or another.

The other big plus for me was that a decade after being purchased, all my investment flats were worth far more than when bought and, more importantly, yielded far more profit than a similar amount left languishing in a bank account. Plus, buying, renovating, renting and selling are all exciting activities, whereas just putting money into low-interest-paying bank accounts is boring and frustrating, especially as the interest never amounts to anything.

More than that, the rental on the south coast properties more than paid the running and refurbishment costs of my holiday flat.

Somehow, buy-to-let does work – and the 'property millionaire' seminar organizers know it. Success is a matter of research, research, research, and number-crunching, squared.

Welcome to Blue Property Group
We're here to help you profit from property

At Blue Property Group we win business because we spend time with the client. We focus on two core areas.

1. Off plan property sales.
2. Property Investment Funds/Syndicated Investments.

A Simple Approach

The combined buying power of our investor capital enables the company to buy in bulk, we negotiate significant discounts from developers throughout the UK and overseas.

We conduct detailed research on each development and fully analyse rental and resale values, together with prospects for capital growth.

We offer the investor the opportunity to purchase the property direct or invest via a fund.

Client Satisfaction

We pride ourselves on our attention to detail and focus on client satisfaction; our service can be tailored to your individual requirements.

Maximise returns on your investment

We carry out detailed research on each development opportunity. All have to meet a set of strict criteria:

- The property has excellent growth prospects.
- The local market demonstrates strong rental demand.
- Good prospects exist for potential resale to the local market.
- The developer has a track record of providing quality property.
- Competitive finance packages are available, covering interest payments and minimising the amount of capital investment the purchaser is required to contribute.

Our property investment team aims to under promise and over deliver; this remains constant throughout the entire buying process. We specialise in locating only the very best property investments that meet the above criteria.

Tailored Services

Our clients range from the first time property investor, the first time buyer, professional footballers and established investors.

We can tailor our services to suit individual needs.

We are with you every step of the way, from organising finance and conveyancing, to managing the resale or letting of the property.

Property Selection

Our investors have access to our full research into local markets.

Finance

We select mortgage advisors who can tailor finance packages to suit each investment.

We aim to keep deposits on property to a minimum in order to maximise returns.

Conveyancing

We introduce you to solicitors specialising in the local markets in which we invest.

Property Management

With ISO 9002 accreditation and investors in people status, we can offer a complete property management service if required, individually finding and vetting any tenant, and organising collection of rent in conjunction with Jordans Liverpool.

The Rent-2-Buy Scheme
Bringing Landlords & Tenants together

Are you a prospective property investor looking for a longer term income with no void periods, that is an alternative to a conventional Buy-2-Let investment?

The Rent-2-Buy scheme allows you as a landlord to enjoy a regular rental income during the life of the tenancy, without the worry of maintenance and property repairs, by giving the tenant the right to buy the property at a discount in the future.

Rent-2-Buy brings together landlords who are looking for a long-term tenancy, and tenants who would like to own their own home, but can't afford to save for a deposit and pay rent at the same time.

Under Rent-2-Buy, the tenant agrees to a longer lease and takes over the maintenance of the property, in return for a share of the increased value of the property, and the right to buy the property between the end of the third year of the term and the end of the tenancy.

Rent-2-buy for a Landlord
The Benefits:
- You benefit from no void periods, no maintenance costs and no re-let or interim inventory fees.
- A regular rental stream-if the tenant does not pay they lose the right to buy.
- Even after allowing for the tenant's share in any increased value of the property, it still provides a similar return to a Buy-2-Let investment.
- Your property is let on an assured shorthold tenancy for six years, providing you protection under the 1988 Housing Act.
- If your tenant does not exercise their own option to buy, you can still enjoy the benefits during the term of the tenancy, without giving up a share of the increased value.

If your situation changes, you can:
- Terminate the tenancy after six months by giving the tenant two months notice, but you will have to pay the tenant their share of any increased value.
- Reimburse the tenant's costs in setting up the scheme.
- A payment of one month's rent for each year or part of a year since the start of the tenancy.

Some Frequently Asked Questions
Q. What incentive is there for me, to give my tenant a share of any increased value during the tenancy?
A. You will have a long term tenancy of six years with no repairs or maintenance, rent which can be guaranteed, with no expensive voids, re-lets or inventory fees. You will have a larger secure net income to offset against giving away some of the increase in capital value of the property. Rentals will increase each year in line with the retail price index (subject to a minimum of 3 %).

Q. How does the tenant build up a share of the increased value?
A. When the tenant signs the tenancy Agreement they also enter into a

binding Option Agreement (binding on Landlord and tenant) that gives them 6% of the increased value for each year of the tenancy. The tenant can exercise the option at any time after the end of the third year and their share would be:

After the end of three years	18%
After the end of four years	24%
After the end of five years	30%
After the end of six years	36%

(exercisable after five years and nine months)

Q. When the tenant exercises their option who agrees the current market value of the property?
A. By mutual agreement between you and your tenant, or your agent can assist and if necessary instruct a Surveyor to carry out a valuation and advise both parties of the value. There is a right to arbitration in this option.

Q. If the tenant is responsible for the maintenance and repairs to the property, do I have any obligations?
A. You are responsible for the statutory gas and electricity safety checks. The tenant is responsible for maintaining the appliances in good working order.

Q. Will my rent be secure and paid on time?
A. Under the HomeLet Rent-2-Buy Guarantee your rent is secure if you have the rent guaranteed. (subject to the Rent Guarantee Rules).

Q. What happens if my tenant goes into arrears?
A. Your agent will notify you of any arrears, The HomeLet Rent-2-Buy Guarantee will reimburse you for up to a maximum of six months rent and the tenant loses their rights to purchase the property. HomeLet will take action under the policy to regain possession.

Q. What happens if my tenant's situation changes?
A. Under the agreement the tenant has three options:

1. Any time after six months, the tenant can give one months notice to vacate, but the rights to the option are lost and you can re-let the property.
2. With your agreement, they can assign the tenancy and Option Agreement to another suitable tenant, subject to the usual references.

3. Let the tenancy run for the full term, but not go ahead with the option to buy.

Q. What kind of property is suitable for a rent-2-Buy scheme?
A. A new or almost new property and one that is not older than 25 years old (a House or an Apartment) are best, but a well refurbished older property can also be appropriate. If the property is leasehold you are liable for any service charges (effectively repairs), but they can be passed on to the tenant when the tenancy agreement is drawn up. You may also have some suitable properties in your existing portfolio.

Q. What does it cost?
A. The letting agent's normal fees for letting the property, collecting the rent and managing the property for you, are chargeable and negotiated directly with them.

The Rent-2-buy charges are £705.00 inc VAT, this covers the drawing up of the lease and Option Agreement, and can be offset by the £300.00 option payment that you receive form your tenant. You can also have independent advice from your own solicitor (at your cost).

A typical Example of the Rent-2-Buy Scheme

Buy-2-Let property – current valuation   £150,000
Open market rental value £625.00 pcm   £7,500 per annum

	Yr 3	Yr 4	Yr 5	Yr 6 (last 3 months)
Improved Capital Values @ 5% per annum	£173,644	£182,326	£191,442	£201,014
Tenants Share @ 6% of the growth in value	£4,255	£7,758	£12,432	£18,365
Landlords Receipt on sale	£169,389	£174,568	£179,010	£182,649

To find out more:
Call: **0151 236 3366** or free phone: **0800 073 1119**.
Login in at: **www.blue-properties.com**
E-mail: **info@blue-properties.com**

4 Developing property

Watching amateur developers trying to make money from doing up derelict properties has become a hilarious television spectator sport, especially as they make every mistake going yet, by some miracle never fully explained, end up making money after all.

I suspect that the reason they appear to make money is because not all the figures are factored in. For instance, we never find out how much they have to pay estate agents, how much the repayments on their mortgage or loan cost, and how much capital gains tax they have to pay. Nor, as most of them seem to give up their jobs to do this developing, how much income they lose while 'developing'.

Not everything on 'reality' television is as real as it appears!

But outside the magic rectangle, how easy or difficult is it to make money by developing property?

Once again, it is all a matter of very careful number-crunching. You first have to discover, by diligent research, how much a property in good condition will fetch in a particular area, compared with a similar property in bad or derelict condition. The difference is not always great enough to make renovation worth while.

Then you have to work out the realistic price of developing. Most people completely underestimate just how much it will cost to renovate and how long it will take. You cannot always get builders just when you want them, and often, getting the relevant permissions from the local council takes months as well. Also, councils charge a lot of money (plus VAT) for giving planning permission.

Then there is the cost of the loan or mortgage to take into account, plus the buying and selling costs. Also, when you own a property, you become liable for council tax, service charges if you have bought an apartment, and utilities. These charges continue right up to the day you complete your sale.

Apart from this, you have the always unknown factor of house price fluctuations. There may be a sudden collapse in the market which will adversely affect the sale price of your development, however lovingly you have restored it.

Before ever developing a property, you have to consider how long you could keep it going if it took a year or more to sell. I once had two flats on the market for nearly a year, with no interest whatever from potential buyers. Then, weirdly, they were both sold the same weekend. You cannot make people buy a property, and if the market is not there – well, it's not there. Sometimes you just have to hang in there until the right buyer happens along.

Getting started

The first thing you have to do is target an area just starting to come up. This is identified by at least a few houses in the street having smart front doors, tidy front gardens, and expensive curtains, blinds or shutters at the windows. Another sign of regeneration is late-registration cars parked in the road.

One way of discovering a hotspot is to look at areas just next to those which have already come up. For instance, when Holland Park, W11, got too expensive for most people, buyers started looking in W14, W12 and W9, all backing onto Holland Park.

When I first bought a house in Richmond, Surrey, the surrounding suburbs such as Twickenham, East Sheen and Teddington were much cheaper and vastly less desirable. Nobody who was anybody would dream of living in Twickenham. But now, Twickenham and East Sheen are just as expensive as Richmond, although in my view nothing like as glamorous. Barnes, also in the borough of Richmond, has become ferociously expensive, as well.

To take another area I know well, when I first bought a flat in Worthing, West Sussex, nobody wanted to know. This dull, dismal town, Brighton's poor, plain sister, was full of decrepit old people and nursing homes. But then Brighton and Hove became a city and prices there soon went out of the price range of ordinary buyers. They came ever further along the coast – and discovered Worthing. Now, although it would be an exaggeration to say that Worthing rivals Brighton for style and flair, it is certainly getting there. Professional developers have targeted the town and are building high-spec new developments there; the first high-spec residences for 200 years, since Worthing first became a resort in the reign of King George III.

As a result, trendy shops are coming to the area, restaurants are opening up and, so I am told, the night life is improving.

Why is this all happening in Worthing? Simply because Brighton, apart from its high prices, is full up. There is nowhere for future developers to go in Brighton, and they are being forced further afield. Even Bognor Regis, long a joke town, is finally getting high-spec new apartments, for the same reason. When expensive areas are full up, or too pricey for the ordinary buyer, the place next door starts to be colonized by the people who would have bought in the trendy place, if they could have afforded it.

Regeneration has already happened in Littlehampton, 10 years ago a dismal seaside town with little to offer. There are now many expensive seafront apartments, a marina, and interesting little shops and restaurants. In fact, swathes of Britain's long-neglected coastline are being enthusiastically rediscovered. Huge developments are going up in Eastbourne, Torquay and Hastings. Whitstable, once a very ordinary little town full of cheap housing, has now become trendy and expensive. But with all these areas, somebody had to take the plunge and be the first.

When developing for profit, be wary of houses that have been on the market for a long time, say a year, as this indicates there is not much profit, if any, to be made from developing. Houses and flats that can be turned round quickly for profit are snapped up very quickly indeed. There are a lot of people in this game, looking all the time!

England's for Sale

Recently, a broadcast on the *Tonight Programme* with Trevor Macdonald exposed one of this country's biggest ever windfall payouts! Thousands are set to benefit from this and some could even become millionaires. What is it all about?

Better health, longer life, immigration, divorce and higher standards of living mean an ever increasing need for housing, creating a very real issue that needs addressing as a matter of urgency. The government forecasts that if current building rates continue over the next fifteen years there will be a 1.4 million shortfall in the number of homes required to meet our increasing demand.

The reality is that this country is facing a housing crisis the likes of which we just haven't seen before. It has become increasingly clear that the existing urban, brown field land traditionally used for building residential housing on is simply not in sufficient supply to allow the projected demand to be met. As there is limited urban brown field availability, the shortfall will have to be met by developing new land – meaning green belt.

Deputy PM John Prescott has thrown his considerable weight behind the proposals, stating repeatedly that the increased demand for property and affordable housing should be met by developing selected parts of the green belt. And indeed this government has approved nearly half of the development proposals in England on green belt lands over the past four years.

This has generated a relatively new industry to capitalise on an already well established theme. There are now a number of companies offering green belt land to private individuals, and they are claiming to offer possible returns that seem to defy the laws of investment mathematics. Of course Landbanking itself is nothing new. It has been used very successfully by developers and property companies for generations, often delivering spectacular gains. But it has proved tricky for the private investor to take part and benefit from the spectacular gains that result from effectively choosing a prime development site. Issues of cost, land availability and the lack of expertise to identify viable plots are the most prominent reasons for an amateur to steer well clear.

However, you can now work in tandem with the professionals, simplifying the whole process for yourself and at the same time using their expertise to choose the best possible land available. We spoke to one such company, called The English Land Partnership, who gave us an interesting insight into this fascinating subject.

Senior partner Ian McCallum explained: "For years landbanking has been out of the reach for the 'ordinary' man in the street. By its nature its been considered too risky and pricey all round. We are solving these problems by expertly selecting most strategically located land that lies on the direct path of inevitable urban development, before it receives planning consent for residential development. The land is then, metaphorically speaking, sub-divided into smaller, affordable plots and these are then sold on to the private individuals. When the site eventually obtains a change of use to residential the land value obviously increases dramatically, leaving each purchaser with potentially healthy profits." The potential benefits could be huge, literally measured in the 100's of %. Very nice work if you can get it.

How does it work? The purchaser chooses a plot in a Site with the advice of a Landbanking Advisor; his choice being determined by the length of tenure he is willing to hold as well as by the funds available. The plot is then taken off the market and optioned in his name. He then receives the Freehold Title Deed directly from the Land Registry with his name as a full owner of the land. As the land selected by the Landbanking Advisor is Prime Development land, its natural value could grow yearly by 10% to 14%. So as an exit strategy, the investor can sell his land to a third party with the accrued benefit to himself; the Landbanking Advisor can put it back on the market for him or he can wait for the term to conclude and benefit from the projected 300% to 600% profit on his land.

And the downside to such schemes? Well the most obvious of course is that a change of use is not granted, leaving the owner holding an (expensive) piece of field. But as the land is strategically located he will still benefit from the potential Organic growth of his land. Time is also an issue, not to mention tying up capital without any guarantee of success. Ian McCallum again: "Buyers should ensure the land they buy is suitable for future development, and that it lies 'in the path of progress,' if you will. I've lost count of the number of agricultural fields I have seen touted as 'investment land,' when it's often got no chance of being developed. Stay well clear of such sites, take professional advice, and as always use common sense."

McCallum claims many of his clients are landbanking to compliment their existing portfolios, and it would appear that as an interesting and hassle free alternative to buy-to-let or that ever decreasing pension pot, land may well have a place in today's portfolios. Spectacular gains could be made. Indeed English land increased in value by 926% over a twenty year period to 2002. But as in any other section of the property market there really can be no guarantees. Still it is a case of how to turn a crisis into an opportunity for you. Good luck.

Then ask yourself: is this property just dated, or a total wreck, bearing in mind that wrecks can soon turn into a money pit. Sometimes, just stripping wallpaper off will bring down a whole wall. In one very dilapidated flat I bought, I daren't even risk taking off the wallpaper, but just papered it over with lining paper, then painted it.

If you are new to developing, it is better to go for something that simply needs updating, without incurring planning permission, rather than a total wreck which will need the whole complement of planners, architects, project managers, building trades, interior designers, landscape gardeners and the entire professional team.

The thing to look for when renovating or developing is rarity. Pretty Victorian and Georgian houses will always be worth renovating, as no more will be built, and they were the last attractive type of bulk housing to be erected. Edwardian, thirties and subsequent housing tends to be extremely ugly. But not all old housing stock is well built. The Victorians and Georgians were well used to jerry building, to putting houses up quickly, and in any case, the kind of building materials used in those days is no longer available.

Then areas ripe for regeneration or rapid growth have, in themselves, to have something special. Obviously in Britain there is a limited amount of coastline, and figures from the Land Registry show that seafront homes have increased in value far more than any other type of housing, since 1990.

Otherwise, an area has to have natural beauty, or be very near offices, factories or other significant places of work. Or it has to be an area specifically targeted for regeneration such as Gateshead, next to Newcastle on Tyne. When I lived in Newcastle, most of Gateshead was extremely run down. Now it is vibrant, attractive and buzzy.

An area will not come up simply because you have bought a dilapidated house there!

Areas next to existing hotspots will also never be the next big thing unless they can offer facilities such as good schools, good transport links, good shops, good restaurants and lack of crime.

Particularly lack of crime. In fact, high crime rates are probably the biggest reason nowadays for areas to be shunned by people with money and taste – the sort you need to attract to your newly developed property. People will only buy in a surrounding area if that area can offer a good lifestyle in itself – not just because it is next door.

After targeting an area and maybe a property type, you have to see how it can make you money, not forgetting that there are significant costs in buying and selling, however much the value of the property increases in the meantime.

The next thing, again before you buy or ever make an offer, is to get some ballpark figures from builders as to renovation costs. Mainly, these estimates will not involve painting and decorating. It is not worth doing a place up cheaply and badly, as it will always lose out on survey if it has serious damp, subsidence or needs a new roof. If buyers cannot get a mortgage, they will not be able to buy, and they will only be able to get a mortgage if the lender approves the property for the loan in question.

Then there is the garden to think about, plus presenting the house to your target market. Everything costs, and adds up, and when time is important, costs can soon mount up. When renovating your own home, you can get things done gradually; when developing for profit, you do not have the luxury of time.

When doing costing, always round UP the figures rather than down. Also allow for council tax, utilities, interest on the loan and incidentals such as new windows, a new front door or new locks, plus, as always, service charges if buying a leasehold apartment.

It is also worth going into some local agents and finding out how quickly places are selling, how long they hang around, which kind of properties are the most popular, and whether designed properties go for significantly more than those in their raw or dingy state.

The only way to property develop, on an amateur scale, is to undertake meticulous research. You have to know for sure that you can add significant value.

Here is a case in point: when the conservatory extension on my house was finished, the beige carpet was in a terrible state and badly needed replacing. My dilemma was that most of the other houses in the street had also gone up into the roof, making them four-bedroom, two-bathroom homes, rather than three-bedroom, one-bathroom properties. If I was going up into the loft, there would be no point in replacing the carpet until the work was finished, whereas if I replaced the carpet, I would not want to ruin it by embarking on a loft conversion. It was a seemingly insoluble dilemma, so I called a local estate agent for advice. She said: 'If you go up into the loft, you will have to put your house on the market for £700,000 and in that street and without a garden, you will struggle to find buyers at that price. But at £650,000, without the loft work, you will find it easier to sell.

'Also, although the carpet looks dingy to you, it looks fine to a casual viewer, if you are going to put it on the market. Plus, if your buyers want to go into the loft, they can do that themselves at a later stage.'

That conversation convinced me that it would be a waste of my time, money and effort to do a loft conversion, as it would actually make the house harder to sell. At the time I had not really thought of selling it anyway, but doing the loft conversion was going to make it too expensive for buyers, if I was going to get my money back plus make a profit on the conversion.

I sold the house anyway, and was glad not to have to face extra work and expense. Other owners in the street who had gone up into the loft found they simply could not get any more money for their properties than I got for mine – and some of these owners were professional property developers or at least, builders. Whenever contemplating improvements, you must discover, by studying the current market, whether they will actually add value, over and above what the renovation actually costs.

Finance

Unless you have the money sitting in the bank, you will have to get a loan or mortgage and the most obvious way of raising the money is to release equity in your main home and remortgage. If you do not already own a home you will have to buy the property on an ordinary mortgage, which might be difficult if you do not ever intend to live there yourself and are just developing. You will almost certainly have to find a large deposit.

And do not forget that remortgaging comes at extra cost. You have to pay a fee to remortgage and may also have to pay a penalty for withdrawing early from the original mortgage.

The television property expert Alvin Hall advises against borrowing from family or friends, which is often recommended on expensive property seminars for people with no cash resources of their own. It is never a good idea anyway to borrow the deposit to buy property as the interest repayments are too high to make it worth while financially.

You can now get specialist loans for bridging, investment and refurbishment; in fact, finance for all types of property improvement such as developments, conversions, buy-to-sell and buy-to-let. Again, it is a matter of working out the interest payable and adding this onto the other costs, before making an offer. You also need to discover how much it costs for a short-term loan such as a bridging loan. Mostly, short-term loans for investment and refurbishment have much higher interest rates than ordinary mortgages, which are payable over a long period, usually 25 years.

The reason short-term loans are more expensive is that, over 25 years, you pay an enormous amount of interest on a mortgage. Although it seems a cheap loan, interest adds up over such a long period, and mortgage lenders, peculiarly enough, do not like to forgo any tiny bit of interest due to them.

So expect that borrowing will be much more expensive for developing or investing than when buying to let or buying your own home.

Which improvements add value?

In any street or any area, there is always a ceiling, a maximum that people are prepared to pay. If you are selling one house and buying another, it may not matter too much if you take a low offer on the house you are selling, and make an equally low offer on the one you are buying, as the two things even out.

When developing, this doesn't happen. You have to maximize your profit in every way you can, and do not want to put yourself in such a position that you have to accept a low offer. In areas of low wages, that ceiling may be very low, so it makes sense not to decorate or refurbish it beyond what the market can afford. If considering developing in a particular area, it is worth finding out beforehand what the average wages and salaries are, and what the average mortgage is, as well. When my son Will and his family were looking at three-bedroom houses in Peckham, London SE15, with a view to buying, they found that they were all on the market at around £250,000. At prices between £245,000 and £250,000, they were soon snapped up; a house on at £275,000, much larger than the others and with a big garden, lingered on the market for many months. When Will offered £250,000 the offer was gratefully accepted right away. From that, you can learn that £250,000 was the most buyers were prepared to pay in that area – mainly because although targeted for regeneration, Peckham and Nunhead still have a very long way to go before they become expensive and chi-chi.

One reason for the prices sticking at this level was that the only interested buyers were young families and first-time buyers who were very limited in the amounts of money they could raise. And the significance of the £250,000 limit was that stamp duty thresholds increase at this amount. Where the upper price limit nudges dangerously close to a change in stamp duty thresholds, there is little chance of buyers offering over the amount where they would have to pay more to the Treasury.

Where prices are way above these thresholds anyway, the stamp duty amount is not a decisive factor. Buyers interested in a £1 million-plus house are not that concerned about stamp duty levels.

But where there is no hope of attracting higher-level buyers to an area, there is little point in developing to beyond the limit – as nobody would pay it. Richer people would seek out trendier areas anyway.

Note: if an area gets a bad reputation for having a high crime rate and street violence, this will damage its reputation for many years after this is no longer the case. A bad reputation sticks to areas for very many decades, and it is hard to reverse it, whatever the reality.

Where there is a profit margin, the following improvements will add value: power shower, central heating (essential – NEVER put in horrible storage heaters to save money), new kitchen and bathroom and, most of all these days, offstreet parking. People will pay a lot, do a lot for offstreet parking, especially now that most built-up areas have restricted parking and in any case, very few urban areas have allocated parking. In Brighton, for instance, it has become almost impossible to park, and in some areas of London, garages and off-road parking spaces are changing hands for £100,000 or more, so valuable have they become.

Gardens are an asset for some sectors of the market. They are essential for young families, but very optional indeed for singles, young couples or even older couples.

Renovating and developing are great fun, which is why so many people like to do it. I find renovating totally addictive and just love it. But sometimes I have to be aware that, by renovating, I am actually pricing the place out of the current market, and there is actually no way of making a quick profit.

The real problem with amateur developing is the need to sell on quickly, as the only real way to make money is to be able to hang on until the market is at its peak for selling. Some people worry that by the time their property has reached its ceiling price, the décor will no longer be so fresh and new, especially if they are forced to rent it out in the meantime, to cover running and loan costs. In an ideal world, you would buy a wreck and then just sit on it until the market was ready, then renovate. Most ordinary people could not afford to do this, but it is how big property developers make their money.

Many very rich property developers I know buy sites, or derelict developments, then wait years before putting them back on the market.

Buying land

The plethora of television programmes about property development has made many people imagine that the only way to 'develop' is to buy a tatty old home that you turn into something wonderful. The great majority of shows have concentrated on this aspect of developing because, again, it is something everybody understands, and it is visually interesting.

But property development can also be about buying land for development; land on which nothing has yet been built. Here, you buy a stake in the land which then increases greatly in value when houses are built on it. You as the investor do not buy the actual houses, or plots on which they will be built, but only the land.

Over the past few years, a number of companies have sprung up offering land investments. One glossy brochure, for United Land Holdings, makes the point that as values have climbed steadily over the years and they are not making any more land anywhere in the world, the actual earth on which the homes are built is becoming an attractive investment in its own right.

When approved for development, land once used for agricultural purposes can increase greatly in value. The ULH brochure goes on to say that as there is so much resistance to building on greenfield sites, the value of land which is available for building simply keeps increasing in value.

ULH offers land which is as yet undeveloped but situated next to existing developments. In other words, you buy the field – or part of the field – next door to a new estate. Thus building land is collectively owned before ever building work starts and when the developer buys the land, each investor gets their share of the already inflated price.

At least that is the idea. The only thing is that you may have to hang on to your investment for many years before cashing in, as planning permission can take a long time to achieve. ULH concludes by saying it is seeking investors for 'long-term investment', without saying how long term it is likely to be.

As with any other investment, you are taking the risk that the land will eventually be approved for building on; otherwise, it is not likely to increase greatly in value, especially if there is no profitable use to which it can be put in the meantime.

The way it works is that the original landowner takes investment advice before a sale is made, and makes sure they sell at a profit. They will also try to seek a slice of future profit when the land is used for building.

Land with development potential is usually sold with uplift. This technical term means that the original landowner receives a proportion of any future increase in land value if planning permission is achieved. The value of residential land has increased by 926 per cent since 1985, and presently, over 3.2 million new homes are required in the UK over the next 18 years. Companies such as ULH buy tranches of land and then try to interest investors in theoretical parcels of it. You buy a 'share' in the land in much the same way that you might buy a share in Marks and Spencer, for instance, in that you do not own an actual slice of the real estate, the clothes or any of the retail goods, just a share in any profits the company might make.

ULH also makes the point that the richest people in the country are usually landowners or property developers. Well, you can't argue with that as it is demonstrably true!

Here are some figures: in 1983, land in Inner and Outer London cost £759,000 per hectare; 20 years later its value had risen to £5,493,000 per hectare. Land in Wales in 1983 cost £85,000 per hectare; in 2003, its value had risen to £980,000 per hectare.

But it is all a complicated matter. You cannot just go somewhere in the UK, buy a field off a farmer and then guarantee to make a huge profit when houses are built on this land. Although the UK is undergoing a massive residential expansion, and new housing seems to be going up everywhere, it is not quite what it seems. The focus in many parts of the country is on affordable housing, and providing homes for key workers at rock-bottom prices. Areas on which building is likely to take place can only be in those places that can sustain significant increase in population. Brighton, for instance, is 'full' and there is a serious problem with water shortages. This in any case limits the amount of new housing that can go up in the area, whether it is 'full' or not.

There also have to be good enough roads to take the extra traffic, schools, hospitals, public transport and other facilities.

Katherine Lewis, senior partner at Hayden James Land Acquisitions, believes that buying land as an investment can be very difficult if you are doing it on your own. She says the secret of successful investment in this daunting sector – hedged in as it is by political considerations, protests by residents and pressure groups, vested interests by local councils and possible shortage of essential facilities such as water, gas and electricity (or the difficulty of laying pipes) – is to use a land banking company which offers land plots for sale and releases freehold title deeds to the plots. You as the investor need to know that all the necessary services will be laid on, as well as planning permission for profitable building.

'Land banking' is the term given to the strategic acquisition of land parcels in advance of expanding urbanization.

These are some of the things you need to know if interested in investing in land (which saves you all the hassle of actually buying or building a house for investment):

In the UK, it is now law that on many, if not most, sites, around 28 to 32 per cent of a development should be allocated to affordable housing. The idea also is that no specific development should become a cheap housing ghetto, but the prime-price housing should be mixed in with the 'affordable' or cheap housing. New developments in future must consist of mixed housing and not just detached four-bedroom homes with beautifully landscaped gardens.

So far as location is concerned, the land must be next to an existing development, as this is how new developments work. As an investor, you need to know that the land is highly likely to be developed for proper residential use.

You also have to know that the roads and highways will be able to cope with increased volume of traffic. Also, how is the site being sold – for investment, or self-build? In the main, self-build cannot be considered primarily an investment. Although you may make money, you must not be seen to be self-building primarily for profit.

Buying land as an investment only works when the entire site is sold to one developer, rather than dozens of individual self-builders.

You must also know what the projected timescales are. Although these are notoriously elastic in the building trades, experts in this business advise that timescales vary from 8 to 20 years in the future. So you could be looking at a long time before your investment pays off.

Then, before signing up with a land company, you need to know that the projected returns are based on true market values rather than land values. The market value is the value once the affordable housing, services, roads and so on have been deducted from the return.

It is also essential to know whether the local sewage works can cope with the extra population in the area. If the capacity is considered insufficient, the projected development will not be allowed to proceed until the plant is upgraded and expanded. The costs of upgrading the sewage plant will also affect the final market value.

So – a lot to think about, especially for amateur part-time investors.

Other questions you must have answers to include: does the development company use a local planning team? Local knowledge is important when trying to build a rapport with local departments.

Are you provided with an individual freehold deed for each plot of land purchased? If the land company only registers your interest in their books, you could end up with nothing if the company goes bust.

Is each project self-funding? You need to know who is going to pay for planning consent, at £200,000 minimum.

Financing the investment is also complicated. Most land companies retain financial experts who will advise on the best means of financing the investment. Options include a fixed-term loan and remortgaging.

As we said earlier, when one type of investment has reached its peak, the smart money goes on to another type of investment. Investing in land, rather than the actual housing, is relatively new, at least so far as the ordinary, small-time investor is concerned, and definitely worth considering at times when it is becoming increasingly difficult to make significant profits from ordinary developing, given the very high cost of purchasing developable properties in the first place.

Caution!

Very often, huge returns are promised when buying agricultural land for future housing developments. A large field that costs £100,000 in its raw state can be worth £2 million-plus once planning permission is granted, say promoters of these schemes which, typically, parcel up a couple of acres into small plots for investors putting up between £5,000 and £10,000 each. Exhibitors at property shows are currently pushing this investment option hard.

But unless you know for sure that planning permission has been, or soon will be, granted, you are advised to stay away from the hype. Otherwise, this is the most speculative type of property investment of all, with a very high failure rate if permission is not granted, or not likely to be granted within your lifetime. Without such permission already in place, the land remains virtually worthless.

Buying at auction

Ever more people are buying investment and development properties at auction, especially as there are now a number of mortgage companies offering specialized 'auction finance'. The usual offer is of 70 per cent of the valuation or purchase price, whichever is the lower, or 100 per cent finance with proof of additional security, such as a large amount of equity in your main home.

Cash deposits are not allowed in auction sales, because of the risk of money laundering, and all finance must be in place beforehand. The time between making a successful bid and having to complete the deal is usually 20 working days, and as most mortgage lenders take far longer than this to process a deal, you would need to find out in advance whether you can borrow the amount of money needed. And don't forget that most auction properties need work after purchase, and you would have to find the finance for renovation as well as the purchase.

You have to hand over 10 per cent deposit of the hammer price immediately after the sale, plus the auctioneer's fee of, typically, £175.

By far the greatest majority of properties bought at auction are those which need some work – usually a lot of work. Either that, or they are repossessions, or contain sitting tenants paying a peppercorn rent, who can never be evicted. There is usually some significant reason why a property goes up for auction, which is that it cannot easily be sold any other way. It is rare for auctioned properties to be in the most desirable areas, as well, which could limit the pool of future buyers or renters.

Very many professional builders and developers buy at auction, so you are competing against skilled and wily operators.

Again, on television, we have seen amateur property developers buying at auction who then find they cannot make any real money at all once the property is theirs. You need to know just how much you can get on the open market for a developed property, as costs can easily run away with you. Also, people get carried away by bidding at auctions, where the 'guide price' given on the catalogue is usually the starting, rather than the finishing, price. Very often there will be a reserve on the property, which is about the same as the guide price. So always expect to pay more than the price listed in the catalogue.

Most catalogues have a little 'plus' sign next to the guide price, which is your indication that the hammer price is expected to exceed the catalogue price. If the hammer price wildly exceeds the loan or mortgage you have secured, you will have to find the finance in another way, usually by a horribly expensive bridging loan. There will also be another arrangement fee to arrange any extra finance.

Example: Robert bought a totally derelict studio flat at auction for £46,000. It was so derelict it did not even have an electricity supply or a working toilet. The flat was in a listed building, so required listed building consent as well as ordinary planning consent.

Although the studio looked easy enough to modernize and renovate, in fact it turned out to be a terrible job. Robert was prevented by the council from starting work until all the listed building consents were in place, and this took months as the applications had to be sent round to every resident in the block and also posted on lampposts in the area.

Another complication was that wiring and cables for the whole building ran through the flat. Instead of boxing these in, Robert cut through them, thereby cutting off the entryphone and telephone systems for the entire building. BT charged £3,000 for repairs.

All the time work was not proceeding, Robert had to pay service charges on the flat plus interest on his loan. In the end, the work cost £15,000, excluding decoration, furnishings or appliances, bringing his total outlay up to £61,000. Add on another £5,000 at least for other costs and we are up to £66,000. Such studios, in good condition, fetched between £75,000 and £80,000, so for all that work and effort – by the time the permissions were through and the flat was finished – Robert had owned it for six months, and would get, at best, a clear profit of £10,000.

If he rented it out, at, say, £400 a month, this would bring him in a gross rent of £4,800 a year. Take off service charges (£800), letting fee (£564) and mortgage or loan repayments, and it is hardly looking like a good investment.

Don't forget either, that council tax becomes payable on an empty or uninhabited flat after a period of time. Councils vary in their time limits but eventually you will have to start paying, even if the property is still unfinished.

By contrast, John and Diane Edwards, featured on the television series *Homes Under the Hammer*, have successfully bought two properties at auction, both in Wales. The first one cost £24,500 to buy, and they spent £5,000 on materials for renovation. Two years later, the property was valued at £70,000. Their second auction property cost £32,000 and they spent £8,000 on renovation. That was valued at £50,000 a year later.

The secret of making money from cheap properties bought at auction is, the couple believe, to do most of the work themselves and treat it as a business. John says: 'We will take on projects only if the figures add up. When buying at auction, I ask the agent for the "out" price – what the house would be worth when renovated. I then work out how much it would cost me to do it, and that fixes my limit.'

Buying at auction is always fun and exciting, but seasoned operators in the game stress that it is not a soft option. The competition from other bidders, the need to work out very specific figures, including interest payable on short-term loans and the cost of renovation, all have to be carefully calculated before making a bid. It is always a good idea, if you are new to auction buying, to attend a couple of sales as a spectator, before attending for real.

Also, always view the property before making a bid. Auction sales do have viewings, but they are usually block viewings, for a couple of hours or so only. It is rare that agents will take time to show you individually round a property coming up for auction.

When buying at auction, you will need to provide identification, such as: current passport, full UK driving licence, HM Revenue and Customs Tax Notification or Firearms Certificate (!). You will also have to provide evidence of your permanent address with a council tax bill valid for the current year, original mortgage statement from a UK lender, a utility bill issued to your address within the last three months, or again, a full driving licence, although you cannot produce the driving licence for both requirements. You need two separate acceptable documents.

So what can you get at auction? There is, nowadays, the whole range of property, from houses with vacant possession, to flats with and without vacant possession, to land, with or without planning permission, garages, flats above shops, commercial property, sites for development, ground rents, freeholds, property both in the UK and overseas, timeshares, newbuilds, and land with planning permission for use as holiday homes.

It used to be the case that only terrible properties were sold at auction, but now sellers have realized that they can often get MORE at auction, either from bids on the actual day, or sealed bids beforehand, than they can on the open market.

A friend put his garage, sale value through estate agents around £7,000, up for auction, where it went for more than double as a result of fierce bidding for this very rare product in a built-up area.

Conversions and change of use

Many people, on seeing a large derelict property on the market, immediately think: conversions. Although there is certainly a lot of money to be made from turning a large derelict house into flats – professional builders are doing it all the time – it is difficult for the first-time amateur to work out all the costs involved. Also, such projects almost always go over schedule and over budget.

In general, big conversion jobs are something best left to established firms of builders, as you not only need planning permission, but have to assemble a professional team who will, between them, be able to do everything required and also work their way through the maze of planning requirements. Then you have to liaise at an early stage with a firm of estate agents, who can start to market the conversions, starting with the show home, and proceed to sell the rest off-plan. It is a daunting prospect for the well-meaning but inexperienced property investor. The best advice is: start small, and if you are successful and discover a flair for this hands-on type of investing, proceed from there.

The first thing you have to think about is how you would fund such a project; secondly, and vitally, is there already outline planning permission?

A good tip is that you should never buy a derelict property such as an old pub, or farm outbuildings, with the idea of turning them into apartments or habitable homes, without knowing for a certainty that planning permission has been, or will be, granted. Do not ever expect that permission will automatically be granted. Councils are peculiar animals, as I know from my long fight with Richmond Council to get permission for two parking spaces – which were already there – in front of my own house.

Tip: whenever trying to get planning permission for a project, always make an appointment to *see* the council official concerned. Do not try to do everything by letter. Once the council planning people actually see and meet you, they can change their minds, particularly if you have good plans already drawn up – NOT scrawled on the back of an envelope, and can put a good case for permission being granted. It's often assumed that local councils are just faceless organizations, but this is not true. Once you get a human being on your side, it's amazing what they will agree to.

This is particularly important if you are considering turning former business or commercial premises into residential dwellings or holiday homes, as it can be a long, hard struggle to persuade councils that you are going to turn a former eyesore into something beautiful and useful.

Listed buildings

There are around half a million listed buildings in the UK, which are subject to special rules and planning consents that make them more difficult to develop and renovate than other properties.

To address the specific problems of listed buildings, Peter Anslow founded the Listed Property Owners' Club in 1994. For a fee of £55, members can access information sheets, legal and specialist advice, specialist insurance and a bi-monthly magazine. The Club will also advise on grants and matters such as VAT, which is zero-rated on some aspects of renovation, but not others. For instance, if you want to put in new alterations in a listed building, this is zero-rated for VAT, but repairs and maintenance – an ongoing task with listed buildings – attracts VAT. It is the other way round from what it should be, but there you go.

There are grants available for improvements to listed buildings; we, the residents, managed to get two improvement grants for a listed building from the local council, and there are also lottery grants available. But they are rare, hard to come by, and you have to be able to put forward a very good case indeed.

The Listed Property Owners' Club can help you round the maze of improving these buildings. They can be contacted on 01795 8449398; e-mail: info@listedpropertyownersclub.co.uk.

Letalert The only reliable National database of bad tenants.

One of the main reasons why a tenant can afford to default is because renting offers mobility without commitment, and this poses problems when chasing arrears. Many serial defaulters will move from landlord to agent, "saving" thousands of pounds in rent whilst leaving the Landlord equally thousands in debt. In fact, recovering the arrears becomes the least of their priorities as the task of evicting the tenant now takes precedence over all other considerations.

Your first port of call may be one of the many specialist tenant eviction companies that have sprung up in recent years. The fact that so many of these companies now make a lucrative trade from such activities only goes to highlight the extent to which this problem has now grown.

These companies claim that the first warning letter sent out to a troublesome tenant is normally heeded by a tenant, at a cost of well over £100. It may be true, but if the tenant decides to wait for eviction, then the debts will only mount up.

So wouldn't it be better to serve a notice before the start of a tenancy rather than later and have the power to stop the tenant from securing new accommodation in the event that you may have to evict them?

Well, a company called **Let Check**, has come up with one of the most long awaited and sought after solutions for the lettings industry. Having been running for under a year, it offers a solution aptly named "Letalert™."

Letalert is a searchable database of tenants that have been in arrears or in breach of their contract with a previous landlord or agent. But the solution doesn't stop there. Their proactive approach helps to provide a deterrent to would be defaulters by engaging and issuing warning notices at any sign of trouble thus ensuring that their database has fully complied with all the relevant laws and legislation.

It works by attaching all County Court Judgements, Local Authority Orders and Tenant Evictions to the tenant's personal ID numbers, such as Passport and National Insurance. By this way, searches are quick and accurate, so there is no need of asking the tenant for their previous landlords address.

The process is simple and straightforward. When you have found your tenant, using either a stand alone Letalert solution or with a Let Check reference check that includes the let alert solution, after checking the tenants ID and noting the Passport, National Insurance Numbers, the date of birth and full name, you will need to register the tenant on Letalert for a small fee, either on-line at **www.letcheck.co.uk** or by phone on **08712 77 00 88**. A search of the letalert database is then conducted and if no adverse information is returned, the tenant is registered. At this stage, a letter of notification from Let Check is sent out to the tenant at the new letting address, detailing the service terms and conditions.

During the course of the tenancy, if the tenant fails to keep up with the rent, all you have to do is to contact Let Check and they will write to the tenant, warning them of the consequences of non payment. If in the event that court action has to be taken by you, then any county court judgements or orders obtained will be attached to the tenant's ID's and the tenant will then be permanently placed on the letalert database.

Another advantage of this service is the fact that tenants stay on this register until all the debts are discharged, unlike a County Court

Judgement which is wiped clean after 6 years, regardless of whether the debt has been cleared or not. And, they will remain listed for a further period of 5 years after the settlement of the debt. Of course, if a tenant was subsequently found on let alert but had since cleared their arrears, the landlord would have the opportunity to make a decision on the suitability of the tenant, taking into account the circumstances and time taken to clear the previous debt.

And whats more, if the tenant that is listed on letalert wishes to make any payments in the future to the landlord, then these can be paid via Let Check. The account is then updated immediately and any payments made are forwarded onto the landlord. So even if you move address, you can be sure that Letalert will still be working for you.

In such a short space of time, Let Check has registered over 8,000 Landlords and a growing number of Letting Agents that use Let Check Referencing and Letalert solutions. A few companies have recently started to proclaim to offer a similar service but fall well short of this, by allowing Landlords to write comments on a tenant that may well be untrue. With Data Protection laws continually tightening, landlords must be careful when leaving remarks or references in the public domain that could lead to litigation if they cannot be substantiated. With Let Check's approach, a record of all communication between Let Check and the tenant is recorded before they are listed on Letalert.

Emmanuel Nkwenti, Head of Marketing, commented, "the industry was crying out for a solution that would provide a cost effective answer on tenants in rent arrears and in breach of contract but at the same time one that also ensured the integrity of the data collected was compatible with their own standards and complied with current legislation. This third party, independent approach, ensures just that."

5 Holiday lets

Holiday cottages and holiday lets are very different from buy-to-let in that they are considered a commercial business, rather than unearned income. Also, there are very different arrangements concerning tenure, since holiday lets are not considered housing, as such.

Holiday lets, tax-wise, fall into much the same category as having a car-hire or boat-hire business.

With buy-to-let, you are entering into complicated landlord and tenant regulations, which do not apply with holiday lets. Even so, there are stringent tax, insurance and letting considerations; most holiday let companies issue fat books of rules and regulations to owners which must be complied with before they will take your cottage onto their books. Some of these are legal requirements, such as health and safety matters, while others are simply operating rules to ensure the smooth running of the business.

Some people find that it is easier to invest in holiday lets than buy-to-let, since the considerations of unpaid rent, evicting bad tenants, problems on return of tenants' deposits, whether to furnish or not, simply do not arise, as you are providing somebody with a holiday, not an essential roof over their heads. You could, theoretically, let the same property as a holiday let or an assured shorthold let, but the two types of stay come under completely different rules. Holiday lets are a specialized business and it is rare for the same agents to handle both types of business, although this is now starting to happen.

Holiday lets are always fully furnished, all the rent plus deposit is taken upfront, and the length of stay is clearly spelt out in the letting agreement. Once the letting period has expired, the holidaymaker simply leaves. You, the owner, provide everything and the guest hands over a wodge of money in return. Obviously, there are rules regarding breakages and damage, and these are set out in the agreement, but when damages occur, the deposit, or part of it, is simply not returned. It is unusual for holiday lets to get into long wrangles and legal disputes, and this is another reason why some people prefer the quick turnover of holiday guests to the hassle of long-stay tenants.

In order to count as a holiday let, a property cannot be let to the same person for more than a month, it must be available for holidays for 140 days a year, and actually let for at least 70 of these days. The same tax and investment rules also apply to caravans, mobile homes and park homes let out on a holiday basis. The main difference between holiday cottages, and caravans or mobile homes, is that the former increase in value over time (you hope), whereas the latter depreciate fast. As such, with caravans, recreational park homes and (static) mobile homes, or immobile homes, all the value of the investment is realized in rentals; with bricks-and-mortar cottages, you have two possible investment streams.

For most owners, there are two ways of playing the holiday lets game: you either buy purely as an investment, or you buy the place as your own holiday home and make it pay for itself when you are not in residence yourself. Because it is difficult to make a good income from lettings alone, most owners take the attitude that the lettings will enable the cottage to cover its costs, be available for their own use, and appreciate in value. But if you go through a letting agency, which most cottage owners do, you will find it is not available for your own use during high season – the very times you might want to use it yourself. Many agencies will even not take your cottage on if you want it yourself during high season, as that is when they, as well as you, make most of the yearly income.

Some agencies may even charge you for using your own cottage! In general terms, if an agency takes over your cottage, it will not be available for your own use between May and September.

Many people imagine holiday cottages to be sweet little secluded hideaway gingerbread houses, with thatched roofs and roses round the door. But these days, the holiday lettings business includes designer apartments, modern bungalows, terraced houses in towns and almost any kind of property – so long as it is situated in a place where people want to take holidays.

The term 'cottage' is used very loosely, and can encompass grand mansions and huge farmhouses as well as studio flats suitable for one or two people.

In recent years, the holiday lettings business has become extremely sophisticated and streamlined and if you are interested in this kind of investment, you can get advice on where to buy, how to finance the purchase and how to furnish and equip it for maximum return.

Marsdens Cottage Holidays have been operating in North Devon since the early 1970s and have the whole holiday lettings business down to a fine art. They will advise on every aspect of the business, including what to purchase – so long as you are interested in North Devon, of course.

Director Janet Cornwell said: 'We can advise on the best areas to concentrate on, depending on whether you want the cottage purely for business or partly for your own use. We are in touch with most local estate agents, and can say whether a particular property is likely to prove a good holiday let. Once we take on a cottage, we take it over. We can find housekeepers, gardeners, plumbers and other tradespeople, as we all live in the area ourselves, and we also give a star rating to your cottage depending on how it is furnished and what facilities it offers.'

As with hotels, the more stars, the more expensive the cottage.

The star rating, from one to five, does not depend on the size of the property, but how coordinated, comfortable and 'designer-y' it is. For instance, a cottage awarded one star will be in good condition, but there may be signs of wear and tear and the furniture will not necessarily be new or coordinated. Crockery and cutlery may not match. A five-star property, by contrast, will have new, expensive and coordinated soft furnishings and carpets. With a one-star property, guests may not be met personally but will be told where to find a key; with a five-star property, guests are personally greeted on arrival and there will be a welcome pack consisting of fruit, flowers, groceries and possibly wine or champagne.

Most reputable holiday cottage agencies in the UK belong to the VisitBritain (VB) organization, which was formed in 2003 by the merger of the British Tourist Authority and the English Tourism Council. Their officers will come to inspect holiday cottages and give them the appropriate rating, using standard tests applicable to every cottage.

The idea of VB is to 'build the value of tourism by creating world-class destination brands and marketing campaigns'.

Janet Cornwell says that the more beautiful parts of the UK remain highly popular with tourists and also families who do not want the hassle of travelling abroad. Another huge advantage of holidaying in the home country is that you can take your pet. Most UK holiday cottages allow pets, so long as they are well behaved, and this is a major plus for pet lovers. Because schools do not now allow children to take time out for holidays during term time, school holidays are almost always fully booked. Holiday cottage owners who do not want children in their cottages have to buy properties which are unsuitable for families. There is a lot of emphasis in all the brochures on what type of cots, bunk beds or other equipment for small children is provided – and if you want to discourage families with small children from staying in your cottage, you simply do not provide these items. But it may be more difficult to exclude pets, especially if the competition allows them.

Purchasing and financing a holiday cottage

You first need to ask yourself whether you are interested primarily in investment, or in purchasing a cottage for your own use. Secondly, are you primarily concerned with rental income or capital growth? It is not always possible to obtain both from a holiday cottage. Some investors like to break even, and pin their hopes on capital growth, while others do everything they can to maximize the rental return.

As with other property purchases, there is a wide variety of mortgages you can take out for your holiday cottage, and buy-to-let mortgages are available, provided you are not going to use the cottage yourself, as a second home. You just need to make sure the place can be self-financing through rentals.

The other thing to bear in mind is that there is an increasing market for high-quality cottage accommodation, to let primarily to couples rather than families. These people are normally interested in short breaks, maybe as short as two days. The upmarket holiday cottage is becoming ever more popular, although agents say that high capital value and fabulous furnishings are not always reflected in extra rental yields.

Marsdens, for instance, can provide income projections for cottages in their area once they inspect a potential purchase. They point out that the more individual and unique a property, the more likely it is to let well. As with everything else concerning property investment, successful holiday lets are all a matter of sussing out the market, and then buying appropriately.

Most holiday letting companies advise borrowing money rather than using your own capital to purchase. The reason for this is that you can get tax relief on mortgage interest payments, repairs and replacements – even losses. And if the rentals cover costs, why use up your own money, which then becomes unavailable to you? You will, of course, have to find a cash deposit of, typically, 20 per cent of the purchase. Marsdens say that many of their owners and potential owners are suspicious of mortgages and like to own the place outright, if they have the capital available. But this is not always advisable for tax reasons.

Holiday letting income is treated as investment income but, unlike buy-to-let, it is treated as earned income for income tax and certain capital gains tax purposes.

In order to count as income, the lettings must be on a commercial basis and carried out with a view to making a profit. Losses may be set against other taxable income and certain capital expenditure also qualifies for tax relief. Loan or mortgage interest payments are allowable in full, and you can also use capital gains tax rollover relief and business relief on a property let for holiday purposes. You cannot do this with ordinary buy-to-let.

Because holiday lets are treated differently from other types of property investment, it is advisable to take advice from a specialist accountant before proceeding with a holiday lettings business. You would need to know, as an investor, whether it would be more profitable to go for holiday lettings than ordinary lettings. Because it is a specialized business, accountancy fees may be higher, as you are now running a bona fide business, even if you only have one modest little holiday cottage in your portfolio.

But obviously, as with any property investment, all rental income receivable has to be set against the costs of purchase, agency fees, refurbishment fees, council tax and utility bills. In most circumstances, you as the owner will be responsible for all bills, and you must also provide not only the television, satellite and cable services where applicable, but make sure there is a valid television licence covering the property as well.

The rental income from holiday lets is an all-in fee, minus the agency charges of around 20 per cent. In most circumstances, the tenants do not pay any extras apart from their rent, although in some circumstances, they may pay for extra cleaning or house-keeping.

Investment pointers

When buying a holiday cottage for investment purposes, the matter of supply and demand is all-important. Obviously holi-daymakers flock to the popular spots, where there are already likely to be lots of holiday cottages available, and where there is fierce competition, prices may come down. On the other hand, if buying in a remote, little-visited area, you may find it hard to attract enough visitors to make the investment worth while.

Many developers are now concentrating in holiday areas, and are building high-spec apartment blocks, often right on the seafront. While these make wonderful holiday apartments, you must check first to see whether holiday lets are allowed. Most residential leases do not allow holiday lets, as these are considered a business, rather than housing. So before ever buying a beautiful high-end apartment for holiday lettings, make sure you do not fall foul of the lease.

It is up to the owner to make sure holiday lets are allowed in apartments, as public liability insurance will be required before holiday accommodation can be taken on by agents. Public liability insurance, insisted on by holiday letting agencies, indemnifies you the owner for up to £2 million, and is applicable only to businesses.

Interior design

Thanks to all the makeover programmes on television, even holidaymakers, let alone buyers, are now expecting a far higher standard of comfort and design than in the past. Many items considered 'luxury' at one time, such as dishwashers, power showers and ensuite bathrooms, are now expected as a matter of course, even in a one-star property. Marsdens insist on a minimum three-star rating before they will take a cottage onto their books.

VisitBritain has compiled a comprehensive, not to say virtually indigestible, guide to star ratings for holiday accommodation, which even lists the type of cutlery and level of cleanliness a property must possess to be awarded a certain rating. For instance, a cleanliness rating of 68 per cent achieves a three-star rating, whereas for a five-star rating, the cleanliness level would have to be 90 per cent or above. Assessors, says the VB brochure, 'ignore their own individual personal tastes and judge the quality by way of benchmarks'.

Here are the current standards for the average three-star rating, just to give an idea of how detailed VB is in its assessments:

▊ All double beds must have access on both sides (ie, not to be pushed against walls); the exterior must be well-maintained but can have some weathering; there must be easy access to parking with a well-maintained surface (ie, not up a muddy track); there must be a good first impression with no noise level discernible; there should be evidence of attention to detail regarding cleanliness, clean and fresh surfaces and soft furnishings and carpets cleaned on a regular basis; there must be six coathangers (not wire) for each guest; kitchens and bathrooms must not be carpeted and laminate or wood floors in living areas should have rugs on them; toilet brushes must be provided; all kitchen equipment and appliances must be thoroughly cleaned and smell fresh when guests arrive.

■ There should be a 'good range' of pictures on blank walls in living areas, good quality flooring and underlay for carpets. Tiling should have clean grouting and wooden floors must be in good condition. Curtains should be lined and 'not watermarked'; furnishings should be coordinated and furniture be of good quality. There must be a table large enough for all guests to dine comfortably. There must be a range of sofas and chairs and a general fresh and airy atmosphere.

■ There must be plenty of table lamps and floor lamps, and automatic, thermostatically operated heating. Beds may be of 'older style' but in good condition and all mattresses firm and not soggy. Bedding must be coordinated and pressed. The bathroom(s) must have coordinated sanitaryware, a shower, good shelf space for guests' belongings, a fixed razor point and light adjacent to mirror. Finally, all items in the cottage must be free from damage or marks.

Phew! But that's not all.

So far as introductions and management goes, a three-star service would include a picture of the cottage to be sent beforehand and a letter of introduction; welcome beverages must be provided, such as tea and coffee set on a tray; where bed linen is provided, beds must be made up before guests arrive. Tourist information and places of local interest should be provided, plus lists of places to eat. There should be a 'good range' of up-to-date magazines provided, also games and detailed guest information such as local churches, shops, chemists and pubs.

If a cottage is also your own holiday home, many items may not be 'compliant'. As with buy-to-let, they have to meet certain minimum standards by law, never mind the appearance of the cottage. Upholstered furniture must comply with regulations concerning flammability, and any furniture manufactured before 1988, when the new regulations came in, may not pass muster. So don't be tempted to furnish your holiday cottage with hand-me-downs from aged relatives; at least, not if you want to rent it out for income. All furniture and bedding in the cottage must have a permanent label on it stating that it complies with 1988 Fire Safety Regulations. Fire blankets and fire extinguishers must carry the appropriate British Standard; smoke alarms should be fitted and fire extinguishers serviced annually.

These regulations become even more stringent when it comes to children's equipment such as bunk beds, high chairs, cots, pushchairs, or play equipment in the garden. If you are not sure about any equipment you can ask your local Trading Standards Officer to inspect; in any case, agencies will not take your cottage onto their books unless it complies in every detail with current regulations.

A one-star cottage could have cheap unlined curtains, whereas a five-star cottage would need to have lined and interlined floor-length curtains with tiebacks and a matching pelmet.

Obviously, as with buy-to-let, it is all a matter of catering for the right market, depending on the clientele and what they are prepared to spend. There is not much point in designing and equipping a holiday cottage way beyond what the market requires or can afford. If you over-design it could frighten some people off, as they will be terrified of marking or soiling the plush furnishings.

Case study

Marion Mathews and Renske Mann bought a holiday cottage in bad condition in the quaint North Devon seaside town of Appledore. They bought it on a mortgage which was covered by rental income on an existing buy-to-let property in London.

However, as usually happens, the renovation had cost far, far more than the original estimate and by the time it was finished Marion and Renske were out of pocket. They reluctantly decided to try letting out as a holiday cottage, which was not their original intention, and were pleasantly surprised to discover that their holiday home, which sleeps five, was in great demand.

'At first I was not keen on the idea of letting it to strangers,' says Marion. 'But after we had let it, through a local agency, for a couple of weekends, we got used to the idea and realized we could easily use it ourselves and let it out to holidaymakers. Now it is fully booked for much of the year, and we book ourselves up a week or a couple of weeks between holiday bookings.'

As Marion and Renske are now both retired from work, they can visit the cottage out of season. 'The agency don't like you to book it up yourself during the high season, but obviously if there's a cancellation, or a gap between bookings, we can use it ourselves or lend it to friends.'

The cottage is about 200 years old, right on the sea wall and so has a stupendous view overlooking the harbour. There is no garden, just decking outside, so no garden maintenance. The cottage has three bedrooms, one with ensuite, a very large open-plan living room with picture windows looking out onto the sea, a large dining area, and small kitchen at the front. It is fully furnished (all from Ikea!) and has wooden floors downstairs. The cottage is trendy, designer-y, fully equipped and everything is new. It lets out for around £500 a week in high season, and is booked for about 20 weeks a year.

Marion says: 'The rental income is paying the mortgage and the cottage is now entirely paying its way. I wouldn't say we are making a profit, but we are certainly covering costs and the good thing is that the cottage is occupied for much of the year. We thought we would mind strangers using it, but find it is no real problem at all.'

One thing Marion and Renske were certain about is that they wanted to use an agent which did everything. 'Some agents just put your property on their website, which doesn't work if you are not around yourself. The local agents we found do the whole thing, down to cleaning and making the beds, and we just leave it to them. They did insist on public liability insurance and would not take on a property without it.'

The other aspect to be aware of, says Marion, is that competition is hotting up with holiday lets and most holidaymakers have plenty of choice. Therefore, standards have to be high in order to get bookings.

'We would not do holiday lets as a pure investment,' Marion added, 'as the returns are too low. The awful climate in the UK means that there is a short high season, and the competition in popular areas keeps the prices low.

'On the plus side, we are covering the costs of a beautiful holiday cottage which we expect to appreciate in value as it is very old, very special and right on the seafront.

'We are looking at a 10-year time span, by which time, with any luck, the property would have increased significantly in value. You have to own a property for that long before the investment pays off. In the meantime, we are getting a lot of pleasure from it and enjoying our jaunts down to Devon between bookings.'

Investment extra

Marion Mathews and Renske Mann own three properties which are all producing income: a five-storey house in Holland Park, London W11, which they restored from a wreck; a modern two-bedroom apartment in Brook Green, London W14; and the Devon cottage.

The Holland Park house has an art gallery downstairs, let on a commercial rent to an art dealer; the modern apartment is rented on an Assured Shorthold Tenancy; and the Devon cottage is available for holiday lets.

Marion, formerly editor of a beauty magazine and Renske, a PR director, can now enjoy a civilized and comfortable retirement.

They have also taken advantage of the Civil Partnership legislation, meaning that they can leave the properties to each other without incurring inheritance tax. For this, same-sex partners have to formally declare that a Civil Partnership exists.

Holiday lettings overseas

More or less the same strictures apply to holiday lettings in other countries, where you can either try to make money from dedicated holiday accommodation, or cover some or all of the costs of your home overseas by renting it out when you are not there yourself.

By far the greatest number of home owners overseas finance their home in the sun by borrowing against their UK home, and then try to cover the running costs and mortgage with rental income.

The problem here is that nowadays so many people have homes in the sun that fewer people want to rent other owners' villas or apartments than used to be the case. Increasingly, people have their own homes, which they are also trying to rent in high season. There are also so many new homes being built in popular places such as Portugal, Spain, Greece and Florida that it is becoming ever harder to break even, let alone make money. When the market has been flooded with new properties, everybody will inevitably get a smaller slice of the cake.

Also, in most overseas locations, as with the UK, you will not be able to get rental income all year round. In Portugal, for instance, you might get 22–26 weeks a year once your property is well known and you have started to attract repeat business.

Just to give an example: a three- or four-bedroom, three-bathroom villa with a pool in the Algarve, Portugal, might bring in up to £2,000 a week in high season. Outside July and August, you might need a heated pool to attract guests, and this means extra costs.

On average, if your villa is popular with guests, you might make around £10,000 a year from lettings, with about £5,000 left after expenses. You will also, in Portugal and most other countries, have to pay extra insurance and pay extra to maids and other staff during high season.

In Portugal, most owners will be banking on capital appreciation, although in Greece in 2005, house prices actually went down. But over the long term, these fluctuations usually correct themselves upwards.

With buy-to-let, the uppermost consideration in every investor's mind is making money. But with holiday lets, the pure investment side may take second place to being able to afford that place in the sun, or that place to retire to one day.

Caravans, mobile homes and park homes

These cater for a different kind of clientele from the holiday cottages business, given that caravans and mobile homes have to be situated in parks, rather than being hidden in secluded valleys. In most cases, they cannot be regarded as permanent homes and in any case, as they are all on sites, agreements have to be entered into with the site owner who may provide facilities such as toilets, shops, restaurants, bars or leisure activities.

As such, you would have to obtain permission from the site owner to keep your caravan or park home on the site and enter into a legally binding agreement. Insurance cover is also different from that for holiday cottages, which can, if necessary, be used as a permanent residence. If you intend to rent out your caravan or (static) mobile home to holidaymakers, you will need public liability insurance as well as contents insurance and rebuilding insurance should the home burn down.

Caravans and park homes have always had a more down-market image than holiday cottages, due to their being situated on sites, but in recent years, this element of the tourist industry in the UK has grown faster than any other.

Are caravans and park homes good investments?

There are two kinds of park homes: holiday homes and residential homes. In general, holiday homes would depreciate in value in much the same way as a car, and the only investment angle would be from the income you receive from letting the place out. Not all parks allow lettings to others, so when thinking about a park home from an investment point of view, you would have to check with the park owner to make sure lettings are allowed.

Some holiday homes are built to withstand the British winter, while others are for summer use only, and the park would be closed down in the winter. Park holiday homes are not considered 'property' in the same way as other homes, but are intended for recreational use only.

The other type of park home is the residential home, which is intended as a home and not meant for holidays. In most cases, you would not be allowed to rent out a residential park home for a holiday. Most residential parks are 'age exclusive' and there is usually a lower age limit of 50 or 55. Children are not allowed to live in these parks, although they may come to stay for short holidays.

Both holiday homes and residential homes on parks are prefabricated, in that they are built in their entirety at the manufacturer's and then deposited on the site, where they will remain. Both types of homes have to be licensed by the local authority, and both types will incur a yearly pitch fee.

But whereas the holiday homes decrease in value over time, residential park homes follow exactly the same pattern as other types of residential property in that they can appreciate in value, and follow booms and busts just like property not on a park site.

John Buston, spokesperson for the British Holiday and Home Parks Association, which was formed in the 1950s, says: 'Residential park homes act just like ordinary bricks-and-mortar homes, except that they are primarily intended for retirement. Owners like them because the park provides a semi-secure environment and there is also a social life available in the park.

'These homes intended for permanent living are following an American pattern of retirement living, and for the individual they can definitely be an investment, as you can sell your park home in exactly the same way as any other home. These homes are built for permanent use and many these days are extremely luxurious. There is also security of tenure with the residential homes.

'Where the homes are intended only for holidays, parks do their utmost to discourage permanent residence. You would pay council tax on the residential home but not on the holiday home. Local councils make stringent checks to make sure nobody is illegally using the holiday home as their main home.'

The third type of park home is the timber lodge. These look like log cabins, and many are built for permanent residential use. Timber lodges tend to be more expensive than other types of park home and the residential ones can easily cost as much as a bricks-and-mortar home as they are built for winter conditions to Scandinavian standards.

Although holiday parks and park homes have a lingering 'trailer trash' image, those in the industry assure me that this is way out of date and there is now a distinct cachet attached to the more luxurious park homes on beautifully designed parks. 'On some of the best parks, there is a long waiting list,' says John Buston.

VAT

In theory, holiday homes attract VAT as they are considered a business. In reality, your turnover would have to exceed the VAT threshold (£56,000 pa) before this applies, and it is very unlikely that one or two holiday cottage rents would ever come up to the VAT threshold. You would have to be charging £1,000 a week and guarantee to have the holiday let fully booked all year round to rake in this amount.

But if you have a large number of holiday homes, VAT might apply. It is an investment consideration if you are thinking about building up a large holiday let portfolio. A VAT registration for holiday homes cuts both ways: on the good side, it means you can reclaim VAT on agency charges, repairs, renewals and anything else pertaining to the business which attracts VAT; on the bad side, you would have to charge your guests 17.5 per cent more for their stay – and this might put you out of the competition as far as other, similar or identical holiday cottages are concerned.

Very many holiday home owners and holiday let companies work to very tight margins, because of the fierce competition. One holiday home owner in Devon told me that he was having difficulty making ends meet because so many of the local farmers were now offering holiday accommodation at cut-price rates.

HM Revenue & Customs produce a leaflet: Hotels and Holiday Accommodation (VAT notice 709/3), which you can download from their website: www.hmrc.gov.uk, and which gives useful information on the ramifications of VAT for this particular type of business.

6 Commercial property

The prospect of investing in commercial property used to frighten off the averagely timid residential investor.

In fact the very word 'commercial' was offputting in itself, reminding potential investors of boarded-up shops, dismal business parks on bleak sites and grim offices with dirty windows, stained grey carpet tiles and vertical blinds.

But we are all getting braver now, investing in all kinds of property, and commercial property is the latest such product to attract ordinary, everyday investors who are looking to broaden their horizons and, with any luck, make more money. Also, the fact that commercial property has been allowable for inclusion into a SIPP since 1989 has made ever more people who want to avoid paying tax consider this option.

Around 75 per cent of those who have already invested in residential property are now looking at commercial properties with a view to diversifying their portfolio, expanding their skills base and also, giving themselves another interest. Long-term investors are starting to get tired of residential buy-to-let as they think: been there, done that. In general terms, commercial property is less hassle than residential property, requires less commitment of time and energy and often has higher returns. In addition, these returns are guaranteed for maybe a 10-year period, during which time there will be several rent reviews in an upward-only direction. Some commercial leases are for as long as 25 years, which saves the problem of having to find new tenants every six months or so.

Other attractions of commercial property are that there is no work for the landlord once the premises have been bought and rented out. There is no maintenance, no decorating, no looking after the tenants and their problems, no renovation or updating. The tenant, not the landlord, is responsible for the upkeep and decoration of the premises. Most commercial leases stipulate that even if the property is let in dreadful condition, it has to be returned in excellent condition, under the terms of the 'full repairing lease' the tenant signs at the outset.

Some people believe that commercial units are more predictable in their yield than houses and flats, which are driven by supply and demand. But yet, there are many empty shops, empty office premises and abandoned business park units which once housed thriving businesses. So – there are no absolute certainties.

It is true that, in the past, small-time investors hardly ever considered commercial property, as it was more difficult to understand, and just did not have the attractive vibe of residential property. In the old days, it was a way for the rich to get richer and avoid paying punitive income tax rates. Most rock stars, premier-league footballers, Hollywood film stars and other mega-rich people have for a long time invested in commercial property, on the advice of their accountants. They have interests in recording studios, business parks, retail outlets and other non-glamorous premises. Sex, drugs and rock 'n' roll is not all sex, drugs and rock 'n' roll. It's about hanging on to serious money as well, and investing in commercial property for significant gain.

But now, just as overseas property has come within the scope of the average person, so has commercial property. Both types of investment have been made easier in recent years by the availability of suitable mortgage products for business or investment purposes, aimed at the small-time investor or purchaser.

One of the major reasons people rushed to invest in residential buy-to-let in the first place was because housing was something they all understood. After all, everybody has lived in a house or a flat, maybe both, and everybody has had experience of renting or buying. Therefore, to make the leap into investing in residential property was not all that strange or unknown. Also, in buying their own homes on a mortgage, everybody had in some sense invested in property, even if they were not doing it primarily for financial gain.

But commercial property – necessarily less appealing than a lovely new flat where you have seen the beautifully designed show home – was, for many, a foray into terra incognita. Would we be reduced to letting out our retail premises to a charity shop? Would we be buying office space nobody wanted? Would all the businesses housed in our premises suddenly go bust, leaving us with a white elephant? And whereas with residential property we could pick and choose our tenants, with commercial premises we might not have a choice as to what kind of business would be carried on within.

There is also, with commercial property, none of the potent satisfaction of renovating, decorating and presenting the place to appeal to renters or buyers. Tenants of commercial premises are usually themselves responsible for doing up the shop, office or business park in their own way.

However, more investors are now overcoming their initial distaste and taking the plunge, typically starting with small offices and retail shops, and if all goes well, expanding into small business parks or light industrial units. Such investors are attracted by the capital appreciation and usually higher yields of commercial property, without all the accompanying baggage of thousands of years of landlord and tenant law to grapple with.

But first of all, what is the definition of commercial property? For the purposes of this chapter, it is defined as any premises which are used solely for carrying on a business and are not used or intended for any kind of residential purpose. A guest house or hotel, for instance, where you are living on the premises yourself, comes into a slightly different category which will be discussed in Chapter 7.

David Whittaker, founder of Mortgages for Business, which arranges mortgages for all kinds of non-domestic purposes, explains all:

'The typical new entrant to the commercial property sector is an experienced buy-to-let investor who has been in the business for about a decade and now wants to diversify.

'This kind of person is nervous of investing in greenfield sites, for instance, or multimillion-pound new office developments, but has become thoroughly versed in residential buy-to-let and has maybe started looking at flats over shops, then started thinking: why don't I buy the shop as well?'

When first venturing into commercial property, it is important not to stray too far from your existing skills base or your geographical base. 'If you have a couple of residential buy-to-lets on the south coast, you might think about diversifying into retail shops. After all, you know the area already, you know which types of shops succeed and which ones don't last and you know the kind of people who live and shop in the area. You might not know much about these things in a totally unknown area.'

It is also important, at first, not to stray too far outside your financial comfort zone. 'If you have been used to buying rental properties for £150,000 each, it is not too far out of your orbit to buy a commercial property for £200,000. You should always buy within your existing comfort zone as once you step outside your range of skills and enter an unknown world, you stand to lose money. As a general rule, you should never buy into assets you know nothing about, as they have a habit of turning into a nasty liability.

'You should not invest in anything which feels totally unfamiliar.'

David Whittaker emphasizes that as residential buy-to-let is not a get-rich-quick scheme, nor is investing in commercial property. 'As with residential investments, you are looking at a 10–15-year time period for your investment to pay off,' he says.

There are very many advantages of commercial property investment over residential, not least the fact that with commercial property, you are not taking on board complicated laws concerning tenure, some of which go back to the Doomsday Book. When a tenant moves into rented residential accommodation, that tenant has rights, simply because they have now been housed and you cannot just make a person homeless. Also, residential tenants can only move into a property which has already passed all the health, safety and fire regulations, which has an up-to-date gas certificate, and where the furniture must be compliant with the latest regulations.

None of this applies to commercial property. It is up to the tenant to make sure the premises comply with any health and safety rules. And all you as the commercial landlord do is to collect the rents, quarterly in advance.

Also, you will insist on a deposit of, typically, three months' rent. Plus, you the landlord are not responsible for maintaining the property.

So how do you get started? First of all, you get the particulars of a commercial property up for sale, in exactly the same way as with a residential property. If the premises are already occupied, you ask to see the business accounts. If the business is a limited company, you can search records at Companies House, as company accounts are then in the public domain.

Otherwise, you get on to the accountants. If the business is not a limited company, they may refuse to let you see their accounts. 'Then you have to look at the general appearance of the business, the cars of the directors and employees, and judge for yourself whether it is a prosperous concern that can pay the rent,' says David Whittaker.

The next step is to look at the lease. If you are very new to buying commercial premises, it is essential to take the lease, which will be part of the vendor's pack, to a suitably qualified commercial lawyer who will give it an expert reading. You need to know from the lease who pays the rates, and whether the rent is an all-inclusive amount or excludes certain rates and other costs.

The lease, in this instance, will not be the lease on the property, but the lease issued to the tenant of the business premises. In normal situations, the lease will be for a period of 10–15 years, as opposed to the six months of an Assured Shorthold Tenancy.

If, on the other hand, the building is empty, you need to know how long it has been empty and what the usual rent on the premises would be. If there is only normally a six-week gap between tenants, then you can expect to be fairly certain that it will rent out again. If, on the other hand, the shop or office premises have been boarded up for many years, there may be a problem with renting these premises out. If retail businesses blow up and blow down within a year, and nothing lasts very long, you may be best advised to walk away.

There may be no passing trade, there may be too much competition in the area, the location may be crime-ridden or too far away from the town centre. There may be all sorts of reasons why businesses in those premises do not succeed and, as with residential buy-to-let, a lot of preliminary research is required.

Before proceeding, you need to know the market very carefully indeed, and not be tempted to buy a boarded-up building in an unknown area or unknown town.

Supposing you decide to buy a particular retail shop or suite of offices. You now need to know the percentage yield in rent that you can expect. 'The more blue-chip the company, the tighter the yield and the harder they negotiate on leases,' says David Whittaker. 'If you are renting to a new interior design company or wine bar, for instance, you would expect a yield of 10 per cent, at least, and for the tenants to sign a lease of 10 years. But if you rent to Boots, for instance, who are unlikely to go bust in the near future, your yield may only be 5 per cent, and the lease they agree to sign may also be only five years. But you can be pretty sure they are not going to go out of business, and you have much more security than with, say, a new and untried restaurant.

'As a landlord, there is much less hassle than with residential property, but negotiations can be more protracted when there is a rent review. The tenant may have 10 years' security of tenure, but they may negotiate hard to keep the rents down, even though they will go up by a certain amount. The tenant agrees to ever-upward rent reviews, but can argue about the actual amount.'

Mortgages

Mortgages on commercial property are no different from buy-to-let mortgages on residential investments. Typically, you the landlord would have to find 20–25 per cent of the purchase price in cash, and then get a 20-year mortgage on the rest.

As with residential buy-to-let mortgages, the repayments come from the rent, and the mortgages are granted on the ability of the tenant to pay rent, rather than your own income or assets. Commercial mortgages tend to be at a slightly higher rate than residential mortgages, typically 1.2 per cent over base, compared with 0.9 per cent over base for residential mortgages.

But the market is now becoming competitive, as commercial mortgages aimed at the small investor are getting more stream-lined, so as ever, it pays to shop around.

In most cases, you would have to present a business plan, as the lender needs to know that the money is safe. Domestic mortgages are relatively easy to determine as you are going to be living there, but with commercial property, there are a lot of considerations that need to be addressed, such as: what kind of retail outlet or business will rent these premises, and how much profit/turnover will they be able to guarantee? Some mortgage lenders exclude fast-food outlets, restaurants or any business operating anti-social hours.

Mostly, a lender would have to have a fairly clear idea of the type of business envisaged in the premises before agreeing to lend money to purchase. They are naturally keener to lend when there is already a blue-chip tenant in situ than with a new, untried and uncertain business.

Much commercial property is now bought at auction, and you can get fast-track loans for these, as well. There is usually an arrangement fee of around £500, and there may be other costs involved in buying at auction.

So why do users of retail outlets, office premises or business parks not buy the property themselves, rather than renting from an outside landlord?

David Whittaker explains: 'For a shop owner, their money is tied up in stock. If they have £100,000 to spend on their new business, they are going to want to buy wine, clothes, furniture – whatever they are going to sell – rather than wanting to tie it up in the real estate. Similarly, in the case of business parks, where there are many little outlets trading in what I call Janet-and-John businesses, where there are one or two employees manufacturing teddy bears, for instance, they do not want to put their money into a building where it becomes unavailable to them to run their business. Such people do not want to put capital into the premises, but concentrate on selling their goods. All profits and assets will be ploughed back into the business. In most cases, it makes more financial sense for them to continue paying rent to a landlord.

'Many people renting office space, similarly, do not want to put capital into the premises, but into the business.'

Tax implications

Rental profits from commercial property are taxed in the same way as any other rental income, whereby you pay income tax at either 22 per cent or 40 per cent, depending on overall income level. If you set up a company, you pay corporation tax at rates ranging from 0 per cent to 32.75 per cent, with the average that most people pay coming in at 19 per cent.

You do not get an annual 'wear and tear' allowance of 10 per cent on commercial property as on residential property that is rented out but instead, you become eligible for a series of capital allowances. These can be set off against your other income if you have not made a rental profit in that year. These capital allowances are usually available only on the fittings, rather than the main fabric of the building.

With commercial property, you are taxed as with holiday lets, where you are assumed to be in it for profit. Therefore, it is not considered unearned income as with residential buy-to-let, even though in most cases it is far less work than renting to residential tenants. But there you are.

Capital gains

This is a major advantage of investing in commercial property, as there is the prospect of a 75 per cent capital gains exemption, known as 'business asset taper relief', allowable after owning the property for two years. In order to qualify for this exemption you must have let out your property to what is known as a qualifying trading business. Examples of this type of business include any kind of trade carried on as a sole trader, partnership or unquoted company. Where your tenant is a quoted company, this relief does not apply.

Stamp duty

This is much the same for commercial property as residential property, except that (at the time of writing) exemption for commercial property transactions is £150,000 rather than the £120,000 for residential property.

VAT

You have the choice as to whether to charge VAT on top of your rent. If you do, you can recover VAT on costs and expenses which incur this tax, such as building, renovating and redecorating costs.

Charging VAT on commercial property rent is usually known as 'exercising the option to tax'. If your tenants themselves are registered for VAT (which in a business, they almost always are) then everybody can recover this tax. The problem comes when tenants cannot recover VAT, either because their annual turnover is too low or, more likely, because their business or profession does not attract VAT, such as an NHS medical practice.

The stumbling block here arises when you do not initially charge VAT on the rent as you cannot change your option, once it has been exercised, for another 30 years. One way round the complicated VAT option is to charge a higher rent – say 17.5 per cent above what you would normally charge – to include VAT, rather than charging it on top. This always assumes, of course, that you will be able to get the higher rent.

Lease premiums

This is a lump sum payable to you in consideration for granting the lease and only applies to commercial property.

Clearly, in order to start investing in commercial property you need the services of a good accountant conversant with this type of investment. It is more complicated initially than residential investment, but once up and running, should not cause day-to-day concerns.

Flats above shops

The government has been trying to interest people in buying flats above shops and been successful, up to a point. Flats above shops are usually cheaper than dedicated residential property, and investing in a flat of this type is very often the starting point for investing in commercial property. Sometimes you have no choice but to acquire the commercial premises at the same time as the flat.

Flats above shops are often in excellent locations, and are usually cheaper because you have no say in what type of shop sets up below the flat; if it is an Indian restaurant, a betting shop or off-licence, your residential flat may continue to be worth less than other flats of the same or similar specification.

Many people buy flats above shops in the belief that eventually they will be able to turn the shop into a dwelling, and thereby make a killing. But beware – in most cases you would not be allowed to do this. It is one reason why shops below residential flats often stay boarded up for years. Nobody wants to take on the shop because they cannot see how to run a viable trade there, yet the council will not give permission to turn the shop into another flat.

Note: If a property has a commercial lease, or part commercial lease, and you do not use the commercial part for carrying on a business, you could be liable for enforcement action from the local council. In some cases, leases state the kind of business which must be carried on in the commercial part of the premises, such as a café, general store, grocery, chemist, or whatever. Take advice before attempting to deviate from the provisions of any commercial lease.

Case study

Many years ago, a couple I know bought a totally derelict house in London W11. The upstairs of the early Victorian terrace was a residential flat on two floors, and the downstairs was a disused dairy. They said: 'Originally the big advantage for us was that buying the property enabled us to live in an area where we probably could not have afforded a whole house, as commercial properties are usually worth much less than residential ones, and it's easy to see why.

'Having commercial premises below a flat spoils the look of the residential property and also means more people are coming and going. In our case, we have a reliable tenant who runs an upmarket art gallery and who pays us a rent which covers all of our overheads for the entire property.

'Commercial tenants are far less hassle than residential tenants, and our tenant does all the repairs and paints the gallery regularly, so it always looks good.

'So far as change of use is concerned, you are unlikely to get permission to convert to residential use. When we put our house on the market once, we tried to get permission for change of use from the Royal Borough of Kensington and Chelsea but were refused. Local boroughs get more money from business rates and also like the idea of shops, art galleries and restaurants to bring people to the location. Our advice is: don't ever bank on getting permission to convert to residential use as you are more likely than not to be refused.

'Our property would be worth around £400,000 more and be much easier to sell if we could convert, but we can't. When we tried to sell, most of the people who were interested wanted to convert the place back to a whole house, like the others in the row. But they kept coming up against blank walls. It can also sometimes be difficult to get a mortgage for a part-residential, part-commercial use.

'But it works both ways. Because our place is partly commercial, we did not pay as much for it in the first place.'

As with holiday lets, owners of commercial premises have to take out public liability insurance. You may also have to present a business plan. One of the problems that my friends faced with buyers when they tried to sell their West London house was that there were restrictions on what type of business could be carried on there, as any new venture could not be in direct competition with existing businesses. There were already enough restaurants, antique shops and interior design shops, so a new business had to offer something different. It would have been possible to rent the place out as an alternative health clinic, hairdresser's or similar service, but the premises were deemed too expensive for this kind of business to succeed.

The art gallery presently runs on the ground floor and basement is obviously ideal and here my friends have been lucky. But anybody buying commercial premises or, in particular, a unit consisting of a flat and a shop, might find it difficult to let the shop as a going concern. The shopkeeper has to be certain there is enough of a profit margin from having premises in any particular area.

Commercial premises abroad

Increasingly, British people are seeking ways of buying property abroad which generates an income, and living over the 'shop' while renting out the retail premises to shopkeepers or office workers is one way of doing this. It can be difficult to acquire business premises abroad, especially where local laws differ from those of the home country.

In Spain, for instance, if you buy a business you take on the tax debts, if any, of the previous owner; in France, buying commercial property may involve purchasing shares in a holding company.

It can also be difficult to raise finance as British mortgage lenders are not keen to lend money on commercial property in other countries. You can of course – in theory anyway – get a commercial mortgage in the country where you wish to buy property.

British people have started to invest in commercial properties in other countries, but as with residential property, it can be difficult to establish title and also understand laws concerning foreign investment. This has not prevented British investors who already have holiday homes overseas from investing in shops, cafés, wine bars and other concerns which they do not intend to run themselves, but just take the rents from the tenants. Although it sounds risky, mostly it seems to work, but you would need a good bilingual commercial lawyer to help you through the process.

Syndicated property purchase

As I know from experience, it can be extremely bleak going it alone when buying investment property. This bleakness is intensified a million fold when buying commercial property, for although it can be quite interesting going to look at office blocks or retail enterprises with your friends, it is depressing going to look at these unpromising edifices by yourself.

As investing in commercial property is also something of an unknown factor for many ordinary investors, the sensible thing can be to purchase commercial property through a syndicate. Here, a group of people, say between 5 and 15, each pool their resources to invest together in commercial premises. The syndicate (often successfully formed through a group of friends who already know and trust each other) can then purchase a single property or a group of properties, which may be offices, retail, warehouses, industrial buildings or leisure centres.

Each person would invest, say, £50,000 minimum. Then the syndicate can jointly borrow up to three times the amount invested; the loan is secured on the property and the rental income receivable. In a typical syndicate, each property is bought with a 7- to 10-year time span in mind. There must obviously always be an exit strategy and properties bought in this way must have resale value.

Once the properties are sold, the profits are returned to the syndicate. There should also be protection for any member who needs or wants to exit early.

There are companies that specialize in this kind of thing, or you can go it alone and manage the whole thing yourself. One huge advantage of buying commercial property in a group is that you can amass pooled expertise; clearly, you would need to team up with people who are all equally dedicated and who can all put some expertise into the pot. One member may have previous experience of running a retail business, another may know the area well, another may have links with local councils and planning departments, another may be a qualified accountant or lawyer.

Whether you decide to have your syndicate professionally managed or whether you believe you have enough expertise to do it yourself, it is vital to have a legally binding document drawn up before you proceed. Sounds obvious, but very often friends just think they can trust each other and then, a long way down the line, discover this is just not so.

Property unit trusts

This is a way of investing in commercial property at a distance and may suit those who do not want all the hassle of coping with this type of property themselves. The trusts invest in the shares of commercial property companies listed on the Stock Exchange, as well as investing directly in offices, retail and commercial premises such as business parks.

There are three main funds: Aberdeen Property Share, New Star Property and Norwich Property. These funds have in the past given investors spectacular returns of 15–60 per cent, and believe that even with a downturn, annual returns of 7 to 10 per cent can be expected.

Most financial experts continue to believe that investing in commercial property is generally less risky than residential property, but if there is a crash, can you get your money out quickly? The funds, believe City analysts, are generally well managed and may suit somebody who likes the idea of the gains possible on commercial property, but is not keen to get their hands dirty themselves. Analysts also advise investors not to put all of their faith – or money – into these trusts, but only a proportion.

In an article in June 2005, *The Guardian* money pages gave these investments three stars, out of a maximum of five.

7 Setting up a B&B

It is becoming ever more popular for people who are tired of living in cities or going to their stressful jobs to 'retire' to the country or a popular tourist area with the intention of running a B&B or small guest house to give a desirable lifestyle as well as earning enough income to keep body and soul together.

Of course, the secret of lifestyle success when running a B&B is to choose a lovely house in a lovely area which is not absolutely overloaded with cheaper competition and which has a steady turnover of polite, well-behaved guests.

So, if the idea of buying and running a B&B or small guest house attracts you, what do you need to know?

Hugh Caven, managing director of Walbrook Commercial Finance, which has been arranging finance packages for the B&B industry for 20 years, says: 'The B&B industry is thriving and a lot of people want to get into it. But in order to make it work – and before ever making an offer on a place where maybe you have had a wonderful weekend – you need to do intense research.'

Firstly, you need to find a location that appeals to you and where you can envisage living. The next thing is to discover the typical occupancy rates of B&Bs in that area, and the kind of market available. 'Ideally, you would need 75 per cent occupancy all year round to make it work financially,' says Hugh Caven.

'If you choose a place where there is only holiday trade, you might find yourself without bookings for most of the year, and then you are hectic for about two months in the summer.

'Our offices are in Tunbridge Wells, where there is both tourist and commercial trade. This means that a good B&B will have occupancy all the year round, and if you choose somewhere like this, you have a head start on somewhere that has only summer holiday trade. The trick, when assessing whether a particular place is a good buy, is to link occupancy and room rates. Obviously, if you are only charging £10 a night, you will have your work cut out to make it pay.'

Unless you are a cash buyer, you will have to go to a specialist mortgage broker, such as Walbrook, for the finance. They will want to see existing profit and loss accounts for the past three years of the place you are considering buying, plus a detailed business plan from you as to how you are going to achieve or increase existing turnover.

The main way that a B&B goes up in value, when you come to sell, is if you can improve its profitability. And how do you do this? There may be too much competition around to put room rates up very much, so the only thing is to concentrate on increasing the occupancy, by making your B&B irresistible and head and shoulders above the competition. (BUT – beware the VAT trap, see later.) Running a B&B can be a fabulous business, but you have to get it right. The B&Bs that survive are those that attract year-round trade. This means that the business can survive a poor holiday season because of bad weather, for instance.

'Many people coming to us for finance say they will improve the profitability by doing evening meals,' says Caven. 'In my view, this is a mistake and almost always leads to disaster. Most people don't like to have dinner in the same place they have breakfast and if you've ever watched three lone guys having dinner in an otherwise forsaken guest house dining room, you will know there are few bleaker scenes imaginable. It's horrible.

'Unless you have a master chef and can offer gourmet meals in a proper restaurant you open to the public, you won't be able to make it work. Then you would need a restaurant licence and may have to attend a catering course.

'The only way that offering evening meals works is with the coach trade, where old age pensioners buy a package that includes the coach travel and guest house, with virtually nothing else to buy. And that really is at the very lowest end of the market.'

KBSA – YOUR FIRST CHOICE WHEN INVESTING IN A NEW KITCHEN

The Kitchen Bathroom Bedroom Specialists Association (KBSA) covers all four homes interest sectors to ensure quality of product, service and installation for the consumer.

KBSA members are specialist retailers who are monitored regularly to make sure they continually meet the organisation's stringent criteria. All KBSA members have been trading for two years or more and offer a complete design and installation service.

The KBSA runs a consumer helpline (**01905 726066**) and provides a comprehensive advice pack for customers who make a complaint against a member.

BUYING A NEW KITCHEN – SOME KEY GUIDELINES FROM THE KBSA

- Never accept a quote for the design and installation of the kitchen until a retailer has visited your home.
- Never pay a deposit of more than 25 per cent of the total contract value and make sure you get a written payment schedule.
- Always visit the showroom before choosing your kitchen to check out the quality for yourself (all KBSA retailers have their own showrooms with permanently fitted displays.)

To find out more and to order a free copy of the KBSA booklet,
'The Dos and Don'ts of Buying a Kitchen',
visit the KBSA website **www.kbsa.co.uk**

KITCHEN•BATHROOM•BEDROOM
SPECIALISTS ASSOCIATION

Setting the Standards

PEACOCK BLUE
BED AND BATH STYLE

Luxury and style at its best, specialist mail order company, Peacock Blue have been providing fine bedlinen, bathroom linen and accessories for the last 7 years. If colour, texture and quality are what you are looking for to update your home or treat your friends and family with this Spring, you are bound to find something to delight you in their new Spring 2006 Brochure. Their latest range boasts a wide selection of desirable designs and beautiful colours, including simple vintage chic bedspreads, gorgeous quilts, soft woollen blankets, fluffy towels in a wide range of colours and stunning bathroom accessories to make the home of your dreams. Super soft pure cotton bedlinen are their speciality as well as the best value and quality fitted and flat sheets, duvets and pillows…all essentials…and all of this delivered direct to your door!

Ordering couldn't be easier, either request a brochure on **0870 333 1555** or view their products online at **www.peacockblue.co.uk** with delivery straight to your door, you could transform a bedroom and bathroom in no time at all! You can also visit their shop which is situated on 201 New Kings Road, London, SW6.

Order before 1st May 2006 and Peacock Blue will give you **10% off** your first order. Simply quote **PB002** when ordering to take advantage of this offer.

If you are interested in running a B&B, you should buy an existing business rather than trying to start from scratch, as the chances are you will not be able to get proper finance for a start-up where there is only potential, and not actual, trade. This is apart from any planning permission considerations, and in conservation areas, or national parks, it is difficult, if not impossible, to obtain planning permission for yet another B&B.

There is also the fact that B&Bs change hands very quickly indeed, and the average stay in one place is three to five years, when they are on the market again. So the chances are that it would not take you long to find an existing B&B for sale in your chosen area. The rapid turnover is not, Hugh Caven points out, because the businesses have failed, but rather because the couple running the place are retiring or splitting up.

Around 99 per cent of people buying B&Bs are couples, either same-sex or heterosexual. It is very rare for a single, lone person to be interested in this kind of investment.

Another factor favouring couples is that one partner can be mainly responsible for the B&B while the other continues their existing job. This means that the turnover can be kept below the VAT threshold because there is another source of income.

The couple trap

The vast majority of B&B businesses are bought by couples who believe they would love to work together. But after a few months of being joined at the hip, they often discover they are unable to work together after all. They may start working together at 5.30 in the morning, and are still together at 11 at night.

Another reason why B&Bs frequently come back onto the market is because of illness. There is a high level of illness in the industry, mainly because the couple running the B&B drain themselves by working too hard. They may think they can't afford staff, or they can't find staff, and so do all the work themselves. They discover that running a B&B is not the doddle they imagined it was going to be.

It is also very common, so I am told, for one half of the couple to fall in love with a member of staff, where staff are employed, and go off together.

So – as with establishing a buy-to-let business, you need to be reasonably certain, if you are a couple, that you will be able to work together day and night, and enjoy never, ever being separated. Working together in this way can also be stressful when you are trying to establish a new business, especially in a brand-new area.

Almost all of Walbrook's customers are first-timers and almost all are couples. And it is the ending of the relationship, rather than the failure of the business, that brings the B&B back on the market after a very few years.

Markets and buyers

There are several distinct markets in the B&B industry, and in many cases, they would not overlap. The places of outstanding natural beauty and the national parks attract mainly holiday-makers who want a high standard of accommodation – apart from the hikers, who are happy to bed down in a dormitory-type overnight place.

Then there is the commercial B&B which caters for workers away from home who, again, need somewhere quick, easy, simple and cheap to bed down for the night. This type is not dependent on holiday seasons.

Finally, there is the upmarket B&B catering for people going to a wedding or other big party, or having a quiet weekend away where they need ensuite, hairdryer, ironing and other hotel-type facilities. This type of B&B would also attract year-round trade.

Another market is coming to the fore, and that is in putting up grandparents who want to visit, but not stay with, their children and grandchildren. Increasingly, grandparents are booking into a guest house instead of staying with their families, either because they have got used to peace and quiet, or because their families have no spare rooms.

Depending on number of rooms, an establishment designated a B&B can cater for one or two guests, or up to about 20 people. They can be in beautiful places or right in the middle of busy towns. You as a potential buyer have to think hard about the way you want to enter this market, and what kind of guests you would be happiest to accommodate. B&Bs can also be basically overnighters, or places where people stay for up to a couple of weeks.

Then, what kind of buyer are you? Most estate agents selling B&Bs say there are two distinct types of buyer: the couple coming up to retirement who want a gentler lifestyle but either do not want or cannot afford to retire just yet. These are the 'lifestyle' buyers where maximizing income is not the prime consideration.

The second type of buyer is younger, and eager to make a very successful business of the enterprise. This buyer wants a proper income from the B&B, not just a way of paying costs and maybe affording a new car or a foreign holiday every year or so.

Research

The first thing is to research the chosen location, to establish that there is a year-round, or at least, good enough trade available or potentially available. If there is a very tight season and no real way of attracting guests outside these times, you are probably not going to be able to improve the profits significantly. It is also a good idea to visit both the planning department of your local council and the tourist office, to establish how many visitors the place gets each year, and whether there are any big businesses either coming to the area shortly, or about to close down, which might affect potential trade.

Improving profitability

This is the first thing any lender will want to know, when they study your business plan. As we have seen, most first-timers believe they can increase the takings by serving evening meals, but this is unlikely as, apart from the dismal prospect of guests eating by themselves in an otherwise deserted dining room, most towns with any substantial B&B trade are full of pubs, wine bars and restaurants anyway.

There are several ways of improving profitability when taking over an existing business: updating the décor, introducing mini-bars (and other bars), having a professional-looking website, and putting ensuites in every room.

Hugh Caven reckons that, of these, improving the website is one of the most fundamental. 'In today's world, a professional, up-to-date website is vital, but many B&B proprietors have amateur, home-grown websites that may be three or four years out of date.'

It can be expensive to update the décor and for this reason, many new proprietors leave this as it is until trade picks up and establishes itself. Very many people buy with very tight cash flow and there is simply not enough left over for renovation and updating. Mostly, as B&Bs are bought as a going concern, you would have to work out how much you could increase profitability by renovating and upgrading the appearance of the place. Could you charge more for rooms? Could you get more occupancy?

The next thing to consider is the bar – or serving alcoholic drinks. Many B&Bs do not have liquor licences but again, this is not only a potent source of profit but also a way of attracting more guests. Hugh Caven recommends mini-bars in each room, and a bar in or near the dining room which is open, say, from five to seven in the evening. 'Many guests, especially those working during the day, like to get back to the guest house, have a drink at the bar, then have a shower and change before going out in the evening. I advise my customers to buy a B&B where there is already an established bar, rather than buy without one. Again, it is what guests want these days.'

An important task is to make sure that every single bedroom has an ensuite. Again, Hugh Caven says: 'This is absolutely essential. If rooms do not have an ensuite, you are going to have to charge much less, which means you tend to get the backpacking trade.'

Most existing B&Bs have some, but not all, guest rooms with ensuites. Here, if you find a place that interests you, discover whether it is possible to put an ensuite in the rooms without one. Otherwise, walk away as the rooms without ensuites are going to be difficult to let year-round. Obviously, they can always be let when everywhere else in the area is full.

So these are the main considerations. If, after a few years, you want to move on from the original B&B and you have increased trade, you will be able to sell on at a profit. If profit has declined during your occupation, you may find it difficult to sell at all.

Here are a couple of ads for B&Bs taken from the monthly magazine *Bed and Breakfast News*:

Cross Lanes Cottage, four star Silver award B&B at foot of the Chiltern Hills, Oxon/Bucks border. Accommodation comprises: 2 double and 1 twin room all ensuite, luxurious lounge and well-stocked garden with fruit orchard. Owners' accommodation includes 2 large bedrooms with bathrooms, office and sep. family/TV room. All B&B rooms to be sold intact to include: carpets, curtains throughout, china, bedlinen, towels, everything needed to begin immediate trading including dining room, fully furnished with antique furniture. Price £780,000.

Fordside, four star. Semi-detached Edwardian house, situated in Buxton, very close to attractions, Peaks and Dales. Comprising: 4 guest bedrooms (3 ensuite), owner's bedroom and private lounge. Private parking. Fire Certificated. The house has not been run as a B&B for three years but would take very little to establish as a thriving business. Price £410,000.

These two highly typical advertisements are aimed at owner-occupiers who need to know that there is private accommodation as well as guest accommodation. As such, you can expect that the sellers will already have complied with all existing regulations concerning hygiene, health and safety, and have all permissions and licences, including television licences, in place.

Information you would need from the seller would include: price of rooms in high and low season, cost of business rates, if applicable, plus any extra insurance needed, such as public liability insurance, and whether the place can be run by, say, a couple, or whether you would need to employ extra staff. You would have to pay any staff the minimum wage, at least.

You would also need to know about laundry arrangements, as these are easily the most potentially problematic areas of running a typical B&B with a quick turnover of guests. Who does the ironing? How many sets of bedlinen do you need for each bed? Is there a commercial laundry available nearby?

The two ads above do not state that the B&Bs are licensed to sell alcohol; so the assumption is that they are not. This is something you might want to alter straightaway.

Before making any kind of offer, you would also need to know how the price of the property compares to other, similar sized properties in the area just used as a private residence.

In general, private houses are more expensive, so by taking on the B&B, you should be getting something of a bargain. You would also need to know how long it has been on the market, and what sort of interest there has been from other buyers.

Finance

Assuming the place is nicely ticking over, the next step would be, before putting in an offer, to go to a finance company which specializes in mortgage packages for B&Bs and guest houses, and see what they have to offer. Even if you have enough cash to buy outright, it is probably preferable to go for finance, as with this option you have to prepare a business plan and let the lender have sight of all accounts, plus you hope that the B&B occupancy will mean the premises are self-financing. Finance is arranged on the basis of income from the B&B rather than your existing salary or cash at the bank.

In general terms, you would need to find 30 per cent of the deposit minimum in cash before any mortgage offer could be made. The lender would then determine whether the offer would be mainly residential, or mainly commercial. This depends on the proportion of space used for the owners as compared with that set aside for guests.

In general, if 40 per cent or more of the accommodation is used by the owners, you would obtain a residential mortgage, but if the percentage favours the guest accommodation, you would be offered a commercial mortgage.

Supposing the place needed a lot of updating, you would have to negotiate a mortgage similar to that used by self-builders, where you would get stage payments until the place was ready for occupation. Throughout this period, you would typically go for an interest-only mortgage, after which the capital repayments would start. Ideally, as with any other accommodation provider, the yearly turnover would more than cover the mortgage, meaning that you are living rent- and mortgage-free in a beautiful house in a fabulous location.

You should also go and look at the competition, maybe staying in a similar guesthouse yourself, to get a feel for the way the business works. You will also have to think about whether or not you welcome children, and if so, whether you are going to provide family rooms or any particular facilities for children or babies such as high chairs or cots. Also, would you welcome pets? There are 'pet-friendly' hotels, and if you would welcome a well-behaved cat or dog, you can certainly charge a premium, as it is always difficult to get your pet looked after for a few days.

There are many more issues to consider when setting up a guest house, however small or modest, than renting out a self-catering holiday home. For instance, you may well have to get planning permission for change of use; there may be parking considerations; you may have to provide some kind of disabled access; and if you want to serve alcoholic drinks, you will have to go through a lot of legal hoops to be granted a licence.

For purchase and renovation, the Cumberland Building Society, for example, will lend up to 70 per cent of the market value at any one time. Money for renovation can be drawn down in stages, as with self-build projects, and for extending or improving existing premises. Then you would have to provide a business plan, with projections of occupancy level and takings for the next 12–18 months.

The Cumberland Building Society, which specializes in finance packages for guest houses and hotels, says that although very few new guest house and B&B business are being created, there is a very active market in purchasing existing places and renovating or improving them. By far the greatest number of requests for finance is to increase the number of ensuites, ideally so that there is one to each bedroom.

VAT

This is a highly problematic area which stymies very many B&B proprietors. Briefly, the situation is this: if your turnover (not profit) is £60,000 or more (in 2006) you become liable for VAT at 17.5 per cent. Estate agent Haydn Spedding, of Colliers Robert Barry, who specializes in selling B&Bs in the Lake District, says: 'Maximizing income is not always the criterion, as if you go over the VAT threshold, you will have to charge more for rooms and services and this may put you above the competition, without necessarily being able to offer anything better. You are up against people who are not charging VAT.

'The trouble is that in the B&B industry, there is very little you can claim back on VAT, which makes it a tricky tax to deal with. There is no VAT on food, for instance. If your turnover is between £60,000 and £150,000 a year, you can opt for the flat VAT rate of 9.5 per cent, and this can come in handy if you have a renovation or upgrading programme on which you can reclaim VAT.

'For this reason, a lot of buyers like to keep their turnover just below the threshold, which means they will probably have six or fewer guest rooms. If you have 14 to 20 rooms, you will almost certainly go over the VAT threshold.'

Haydn Spedding recommends talking to an accountant about the VAT and turnover situation in advance of making an offer or drawing up a business plan.

Legislation issues

VisitBritain's Pink Booklet – the highly detailed bible for existing and potential 'accommodation providers' – states that even if you are only intending to offer simple bed and breakfast in your own home, you may still need 'change of use' planning permission. It is also very likely that any house will need at least some adaptation or alteration before it becomes suitable for guests, and whenever you admit strangers to your property, you have to abide by health, safety and fire rules, and make sure all furniture complies with existing regulations.

You may also be required to take out extra insurance, and in any case, mortgage lenders must be informed, as the home is now being used partly as a business and to make money.

You must also inform the HM Revenue and Customs. It is simply not worth taking the risk of just offering accommodation and breakfast without invoking officialdom.

Business rates

If you are offering accommodation in return for money, you may have to pay business rates instead of council tax. Naturally, business rates are higher. In some cases you may not have to pay business rates, if the premises are very small and can only accommodate up to six people at a time, and you are yourself living full time on the premises. But before ever advertising for guests, you must speak to your accountant.

Just to make matters more complicated, it is possible you will have to pay business rates on the part of the house used for guests, and council tax on the part you use for yourself.

Business rates are calculated on the possible rental value of your property, the way old-fashioned 'rates' used to be calculated. Again, you would need to contact your local council at an early stage to discover what these business rates are, and how they might affect what you are thinking of charging for bed and board.

Fire safety

This is of the utmost importance and can never be ignored. The best thing to do, at an early stage, is to ask the Fire Brigade to come round and advise on fire precautions, unless there is a fire certificate already in place, as you will need a valid fire certificate in order to run the premises as a guest house. This regulation does not apply if the guest house can take a maximum of six guests, excluding those living there permanently as family, but including any residential staff.

Current legislation means that you are allowed to burn six guests, but not seven. If buying an existing business and considering extending, or adding to the number of guest rooms, a fire certificate would be needed.

You will also, as with holiday lets, be required to take out public liability insurance, and insurance companies may interpret the 'six bed space' rule very strictly. Ordinary household policies do not cover use of your premises for business purposes.

It is as well to wise up on all these aspects before ever advertising for guests and, if buying an existing business, ask about insurance matters. In any case, your mortgage lender will need to have sight of these documents before arranging the mortgage.

HOW TO MAKE A COOL PROFIT FROM YOUR HOT PROPERTY!

Sub-Zero refrigeration and Wolf cooking instruments are the ultimate in cooking and cooling, combining stunning good looks with professional performance.

As the must-have kitchen appliance of discerning A-list celebrities and celebrity chefs such as Gary Rhodes, Madonna and Sting; Sub-Zero and Wolf will give your developments the genuine 'wow factor', offering you the edge over your competitors, when almost every development these days is branded, 'luxury', whether it really deserves the title or not.

Sub-Zero and Wolf have recently been seen in some of the most exclusive developments and are in huge demand by uber-developers Candy & Candy and Finchatton London.

Think of American appliances and you traditionally think big – however, Sub-Zero offers a choice of design options and sizes to suit any space - big or small. From the classic 1219mm wide stainless steel fridge/freezer to under-counter refrigerated drawers – space or the lack of it, no longer becomes an issue when designing in the very best in refrigeration.

A selection of beautifully designed wine storage units completes the Sub-Zero product range. Offering the perfect two-temperature-zone, humidity-controlled environment and providing an elegant solution to long and short-term wine storage.

The Wolf range of cooking instruments complements Sub-Zero's product range perfectly and includes built-in electric wall ovens, gas and dual fuel ranges, as well as a choice of cook-tops and integrated domino units from electric steamer and fryer to gas wok burner.

These 'Kitchen Ferraris' feature every conceivable futuristic convenience from pyrolitic self-cleaning ovens to revolving control panels. And surely nothing can surpass the downdraft ventilation system which rises effortlessly from the counter top when required and descends to finish flush to the counter-top when it has effectively performed it's job!

For more information contact Juliette Raine at The Westye Group Europe on **0208 418 3800** or visit **www.westye.eu.com**

430 WINE COOLER & 695 SIDE-BY-SIDE

Catering

It can be a much more complicated matter to offer meals in your establishment than to set up self-catering units, as you will need licences to operate your business. Just about all premises which offer food and drink to outsiders for profit will have to register with the local authority. The only exception to this rule is if you have no more than three bedrooms for the use of guests, and are offering tea and biscuit-type refreshment only.

In any case, you should contact your local environmental health department for advice when considering offering catering services, however basic. There are very many regulations which must be complied with, and you never know when an inspector may call, especially if you are operating under the auspices of local or national tourist organizations. Recent scares concerning food poisoning, for instance, have meant that the Food Standards Agency has now issued strict guidelines for handling cooked meats, and preventing cross-contamination from raw foods. There is a 10-point hygiene plan for ensuring food safety in catering establishments, available from the Food Standards Agency, Ref: BEL.

Liquor licensing

If you would like a bar area or are offering evening meals, then you must have a liquor licence in place. In general terms, it is worth going for a suitable liquor licence as you will attract more trade and may also be able to charge more for accommodation. Places with drinks licences are vastly more popular than those without.

There are several different types of licence available: full-on licence; restaurant licence; residential licence and restaurant and residential licence; occasional licence; and occasional permission. Here, you have to decide what type of service you would want to offer regarding liquor, then go to your solicitor to handle your application, as it is a complicated matter whereby procedures must be followed to the letter.

In general, licences are granted to a named individual by the liquor licensing department of the magistrates' court. The licence, once granted, allows the licensee to sell alcohol in named premises. If you have not had previous licensing experience, you may also be required to attend a one- or two-day course run by the British Institute of Innkeeping at a local college.

You have to apply to the relevant licensing session in writing (known as Brewster Sessions), giving 21 clear days' notice. If applying for a new licence, you will need to attach plans of the premises and the location, plus display a notice at or near the premises where the application may be seen by passers-by. And don't forget that neighbours may object.

A notice also has to be placed in the local newspaper. You may be granted, or refused a licence, or, in the case of new premises, you may be granted a provisional licence by the licensing justices. If you are setting up a new guest house, it is best to apply for, and obtain, the provisional licence before you start on renovations or adaptations.

Your local court should have all the papers and documentation you need, and the clerk there may well give advice. But as this is a complicated legal procedure, it is worth using a solicitor conversant with licensing laws. There are also strict regulations about selling liquor to children, or allowing children in bar areas, so if you are setting up a family guest house, this also has to be taken into account.

Television licences

Most overnight guests want television facilities, and here you would need a special Hotel and Mobile Units Television Licence. You should always take out a hotel licence if providing television sets for the use of guests. The fee for the licence is determined by the maximum number of guests and if no more than 15, the licence fee is the same as the standard licence; this goes up for each additional five rooms. In most cases, this covers television watching by owners and staff.

If you want to play music as entertainment, you will also need a Performing Right Society Licence.

Regarding use of guest telephones, there are no regulations concerning how much you are allowed to charge guests for telephone calls. These days, as most guests have mobiles, telephones in bedrooms have become less necessary. Many small guest houses nowadays just have payphones in the hall where you can make outgoing calls but not receive incoming calls.

Unless the guest house is very large, it is probably no longer worth bothering with telephones in guest bedrooms. You may have to think about whether you want to provide internet access for guests, especially if you are catering for commercial trade.

So far as the law is concerned, your guest house is considered either a 'hotel' or a 'private hotel'. Most often, a small guest house will be the latter, and it means you can pick and choose your guests – you do not have to accept just anybody – and people have to book in advance. If you run a 'hotel', by contrast, you are not allowed to refuse a guest unless you believe that person will be a nuisance to your other guests.

Disabled access

This is a bugbear for all who wish to offer rooms to guests on a profit-making basis. In general, the Disability Discrimination Act applies to you if you provide any sort of accommodation in return for money. The best thing here is to contact your local council to see what, if any, adaptations you may need to make to ensure your establishment is usable by disabled people. In most cases, you would have to make the place wheelchair-friendly. Even when buying a going concern, it is worth checking with the council to ensure that your disability provision meets current requirements.

If running a small guest house, obviously the disabled facilities you may be required to provide will be less stringent than if running a five-star hotel. If you are offering bed and breakfast with only two bedrooms, you would not be expected to carry out extensive building work to provide wheelchair access to these rooms.

Furniture and fittings

As with finance packages, there are specialist companies offering 'everything' for the B&B proprietor. Out of Eden, for instance, is a mail-order company specializing in everything for the guest-house proprietor from soap and toiletries to beds, bedlinen, signs ('Thank you for not smoking', 'Do not disturb'), and menu holders and wine lists. Catalogue from sales@outofeden.co.uk.

Those with high aesthetic standards have to bear in mind that furnishings suitable for your own home may be completely inadequate for a guest house, which gets much harder wear. Also, guests staying for only a night or two may not be so choosy as for a permanent residence. Because you are running a business, you may have to go for brighter colours or more lurid patterns than you would ideally like, as these are harder-wearing and do not show the dirt. In particular, carpets in common parts must be extremely hard wearing and resistant to marks.

Starting from scratch

Many property investors would like to turn a private house into a B&B but this is fraught with difficulties, particularly when it comes to getting a mortgage, as you could not get a commercial mortgage for a business which does not yet exist, and a residential mortgage would not be forthcoming for purchase or renovation of a building which will have a change of use from residential to commercial.

TOP QUALITY FURNITURE, BATHROOMS AND KITCHENS – DIRECT FROM THE MANUFACTURER AT UP TO 50% OFF NORMAL SELLING PRICE.

Operating out of warehouses in Essex, **You're Furnished** sells furniture, bathroom ware and made to measure kitchens 'direct from the manufacturers' – it's a distinctly no frills operation, simple showrooms, no commissioned salesmen and no high street overheads – you just view and buy – at up to half the price you might pay on the high street.

There is a wide range of branded furniture very competitively priced, sofas in a large selection of fabrics, dining tables & chairs, bedroom furniture, bathroom ware and much more.

For kitchens, the buying process is also pretty simple – you can visit the showroom (recommended that you book an appointment) and bring a plan of your existing kitchen for the designers to work with (£50 fee payable), or bring a kitchen design for **You're Furnished** to quote against (free); alternatively, a designer can come to your own home to help plan your kitchen (for a cost of £150 subject to geographical restrictions). There are over 100 door styles to choose from, traditional and modern, with a vast array of wooden, laminate, high gloss and even hand painted finishes. Island units, wine racks, pantries – almost anything is possible.

The bottom line is that a kitchen you might pay 20-25k for at certain high street retailers can cost around 10-12k. Better yet, you can have your kitchen delivered within two to six weeks – again, because you are buying direct from the manufacturer.

Open 7 days a week. 10am to 5pm Monday to Saturday, 12noon to 4pm Sunday.

For kitchens and bathrooms:
Network House, Waltham Hall Industrial Estate, Bambers Green,
Takeley, Essex CM22 6PF Tel: 01279 870036
Email: yfk@btconnect.com www. yfk.moonfruit.com

For furniture and bathrooms:
Unit One, Waltham Hall Industrial Estate, Waltham Hall Farm,
Bambers Green, Takeley, Essex CM22 6PF Tel: 01279 815028

For furniture:
Unit 4, R/O 14, Cambridge Road, Stansted, Essex CM24 8BZ
Tel: 01279 815028

If, however, you already own the property and would like to turn part of it into a B&B, you would first have to contact the local council to see if planning permission is likely to be granted. The next step would be to submit detailed architect's plans and get in some quotes for the work. But raising finance for this would be difficult, so the only real way is to have the money to do it yourself. Obviously, expensive loans can be raised, but before ever entering on such a project, see whether planning permission would be granted in the first place.

Very many councils are not keen to give planning permission for new B&Bs or small guest houses as this increases parking difficulties. There might also be problems with neighbours, if the area is mainly residential.

It is becoming ever more difficult to change the use of any building, whether this was originally residential or commercial. Obviously, I would not recommend this course of action, but, there is nothing to stop you doing the conversion secretly 'on the black' and then applying for retrospective planning permission, as one way round the restrictions increasingly being used.

Ratings

All B&Bs are now liable to have a diamond rating, going from one to five. This rating means that the establishment has been inspected, and is also regularly inspected. Briefly, a one-diamond rating means that the establishment is acceptably clean and tidy and offers a full English or continental breakfast. Two diamonds indicate a greater emphasis on guest care; three diamonds indicate comfortable, well-maintained bedrooms and quality items for breakfast; a four-diamond establishment has high quality furniture and excellent customer care; and a five-diamond place has very high quality furniture and outstanding customer care.

Those who are just starting out can gain an 'entry level' rating, which can be upgraded when the business is more established.

And finally...

Estate agent Haydn Spedding says that the B&B industry is intimately affected by politics and government policies. 'In the 1990s, people were getting out of B&Bs because they realized they had made a huge gain on their premises, so they were selling them and pocketing the proceeds.

'Most people buying into B&Bs sell their existing house to do so, and the business also becomes their home. But now, people coming up to retirement are buying B&Bs to give them a few more years in employment whereby they can build up their pensions.

'All sorts of things are likely to affect the business, such as charging for roads. If this comes in, are people going to pay £500 to drive up to Ambleside for a £100 holiday? There will always be a market for the B&B but it will always keep changing. The B&B market is far more liable to change and fluctuate than the hotel market, so buyers have to be very sure about what they are getting themselves into.'

PURE Luxury Radios

A recent survey by the patent office placed radio second after the bicycle on a list of favourite inventions, and this much-loved medium is having a real revival at the moment with the arrival of digital radio, which has become one of the must-haves in consumer electronics.

PURE Digital makes the nation's favourite radios including EVOKE-1^{XT}, the world's most popular DAB radio. A UK company using UK technology, PURE's milestones this year have included shipping its half-millionth radio in March and seeing its EVOKE-2^{XT} win What Hi-Fi Sound and Vision Radio Product of the Year. PURE's mission is to reach across all product categories with its DAB technology – a process which this year has ranged from the PocketDAB 2000 portable pause/rewind DAB radio and the Oasis ruggedised radio, with much more to come in 2006.

The DAB transmission standard provides high quality, interference-free digital audio without the hiss, crackle and fade of AM/FM broadcasts. Fast autotune locates all available DAB stations and users simply select stations by name. New stations are spreading across the country – for example in London you can receive over 50 digital stations – and up to twice as many stations are available in many areas as via FM. The radio's display shows station name, date/time, scrolling text with news, sports results, song titles and more. What's more DAB radios with a clock display automatically adjust for summer/winter time.

The latest generation of PURE radios significantly improves digital radio battery life – by over 100%. We've also introduced a wider selection of radios which are rechargeable, such as our PocketDAB 2000. For owners of our EVOKE-2^{XT} and EVOKE-3 radios we've introduced a new rechargeable option. The ChargePAK C6 recharges in-unit to provide convenient DAB portability.

With PURE's ReVu pause, rewind & record functionality you can now control broadcast audio just like CDs or MP3s. An electronic programme guide (EPG) enables you to browse programmes for a single station or all programmes on at a particular time, and to select them for scheduled listening or recording, much like a PVR box.

Amazingly advanced features aren't just limited to expensive boxes either. For just £130 you can have ReVu, MP3 playback, USB PC connection and EPG with PURE's Bug radio. £199.99 will get you PURE's top of the range EVOKE-3, or put ReVu radio in your palm with PocketDAB 2000.

The high-quality audio, wide range of extra features, and greater choice of content has revived radio, and it is no longer seen as the poor relation to digital TV.

www.pure.com   Tel: 01923 277488

8 Buying property abroad

I often used to see a neighbour of mine outside in the street cleaning his car. One day, after a few years of briefly acknowledging each other, we got into conversation, as is the British way.

'Terrible weather, isn't it?' my neighbour offered, looking up at the unrelieved grey cloud blanket overhead in what was supposed to be the height of summer. 'Still, doesn't worry us much. We're off to Cyprus for a fortnight at the weekend.'

'That sounds nice,' I said. 'Have you got a villa or apartment there?'

'Not yet,' he said. 'A few years ago I bought some land...' My hitherto taciturn neighbour became expansive. It turned out that he had bought a large tract of land in Northern Cyprus for £2,000 and eventually hoped to build four villas there. Like any professional developer, he was biding his time, and waiting until Northern Cyprus joined the EU. He did not seem concerned. 'It could be five, seven, years, even longer.

'Still, it's only a couple of grand. Worth taking the risk. The thing about Northern Cyprus, the Turkish part, is to make sure of the title. In many cases, the title is disputed and you never know who really owns it. We bought the land through a friend of a friend, and we shan't start building until the Turkish part of Cyprus is harmonized with the rest of Europe.'

Southern Cyprus, of course, joined the EU in 2004 but, at the time of writing at least, no date has been set for the Northern, Turkish part to do likewise. My friend also pointed out that Famagusta, on the border, is littered with abandoned and derelict hotels built in the early sixties in the expectation of a tourism rush which never came when the Turks invaded Cyprus in 1964.

My car-cleaning friend knows he has taken a risk but it is one that may eventually pay off handsomely. In the meantime, as he nudges towards retirement, he has an exciting project to keep him occupied.

At one time I would have been flabbergasted, not to say Famagusted, at this ordinary-seeming middle-aged man being a property expert on Northern Cyprus. Not any more. As we talked, my new friend told me about people he knew who had been snapping up apartments in Bulgaria for £10,000 each, investing in Croatia, buying up car-wash franchises in Poland, investing in safari parks in Africa, and other such exotica.

I just think that the newfound enthusiasm of British people to snap up foreign property as an investment is a miniature version of the same mercantile spirit that took us adventuring on the high seas and led to us conquering and colonizing vast tracts of the world in earlier times. Then as now, the main purpose of the endeavour was to make money.

At one time, people bought property overseas mainly for the purposes of realizing a dream, and to have an exotic bolthole. But increasingly, property investors are looking abroad to expand or even start their investment portfolio – and the name of the game is profit, rather than enjoying a leisurely lifestyle in the sun.

The expectation is that much of 'abroad' offers greater long-term capital growth prospects than the home country, and when looking to invest, as with anything else, there are many options to choose from.

These include: emerging markets; beach destinations; existing or mature markets; long-haul destinations; golfing properties; European cities; and ski destinations. Some overseas markets may offer more than one of these possibilities. For instance, an emerging market such as the Czech Republic also offers skiing; other such markets may also be beach destinations, long-haul destinations or golfing locations.

At the time of writing, existing or mature markets include Florida, Spain, Portugal, Turkey, France, Italy and Ireland. Emerging markets include Bulgaria, Croatia, the Czech Republic and Shanghai, and long-haul destinations include Australia, the Caribbean, South Africa, New Zealand and Phuket.

When investing in property abroad, what is the main purpose of the exercise these days? According to a survey by the Homebuyer Show in 2005, just over 25 per cent of investors were after long-term capital gains; 21.24 per cent wanted a holiday home; 20.35 per cent were interested in short-term holiday lets; 15.93 per cent wanted a possible retirement home; and 7 per cent were interested in renting out their property to local residents. Only 2 per cent were considering short-term corporate lets.

So how can you tell whether your desired spot has investment potential? One obvious appeal is a budget airline, although these are notoriously subject to going bust. Property experts maintain that wherever there is a low-cost airline, the property buyers soon follow. Another is existing or potential membership of the EU and yet another plus is a wide range of leisure facilities such as sport, children's entertainment and water activities. And of course, good weather is always a prime attraction.

BUT BEWARE! The most popular overseas locations, at least for Brits, are hot, dry places. Coming from a cold, wet country, we long for reliably hot, dry weather. But any country which is both hot and dry is also very liable to have a chronic water shortage. In Spain, for instance, where there is an insatiable demand for private swimming pools and golf courses – which of course have to be watered regularly – there are also often severe water shortages. Desalination plants, which are used in places where it virtually never rains, are extremely expensive.

The more developments that go up, the greater the demand for water, yet a prolonged drought could wipe out much of the value of any investment. And rainfall is not something anybody, even the cleverest property developer, can control.

The water situation could be one of the most vital considerations you need to know about when considering investing abroad. You would also need to know by how much property has gone up in recent years and whether the indications are that such growth is likely to continue. You also need to know the situation regarding mortgages, and what happens about taxation.

Finding the perfect property and the perfect exchange rate when buying abroad

Buying a property in another country is very involved. Not only do you have to deal with different legal and tax systems you also have to pay for it all in a different currency to your own. This means that if you are not careful and do your research when it comes to foreign exchange your newly found property may cost you a lot more than you thought, or it may even become too expensive for you due to fluctuations in the exchange rates.

The actual money transfer might not seem that important to you in comparison to everything else to do with the property but you stand to gain – or lose – a lot depending on how you send your money abroad. For this reason, it pays to invest a bit of time in finding the best way to go about it.

Transferring funds can be a costly exercise with several factors that can affect how much money you will receive. These include:
- transfer fees
- exchange rates
- market fluctuations

Transfer fees
The fee charged for international transfers varies from provider to provider and can be as much as £35 in the UK. On top of that it is quite common for the receiving bank to take a fee as well. Look into what kind of fees you are charged – there are some companies like UKForex who don't charge any at all on larger payments.

Exchange rates
Some banks and foreign exchange companies not only charge large fees they offer poor exchange rates as well, hurting your wallet every time you transfer money internationally. Maximising the proceeds of your transfers allows you to stretch your funds further which may pay for some extras such as new furniture for your property or perhaps even some renovations. You can only achieve this with a competitive exchange rate and good advice. UKForex offers corporate rates to individuals to help you get a good result on your transfer.

Market fluctuations

The foreign exchange market fluctuates every second so the actual cost of your property calculated in Pounds from when you start thinking about buying the property to when you actually make the payment can be vastly different. In a falling market your Pounds will be worth less in terms of the currency you are converting to and conversely, in a rising market your funds will be worth more. This means that your property in reality goes up and down in price, and can even move out of your price range.

The risk of market fluctuations can be managed in many ways. The easiest and most popular is the use of a forward exchange contract (FEC). An FEC is an obligation that allows you to buy or sell a specified amount of foreign currency at a fixed exchange rate (agreed upon now) for settlement at a specified future date – it's a kind of "buy now – pay later" contract. The forward contract effectively "locks-in" the foreign exchange rate for a future date, eliminating the effect that fluctuations may have on the proceeds of your transfer so in effect you are fixing the cost of the property in Pound terms.

What to think about when choosing an FX provider

It is in your financial interest to explore the various alternatives when transferring money internationally as it could result in thousands of Pounds in savings. The best thing to do is compare services and consider such things as:

- Differences in exchange rates, transfer fees and receiving bank fees
- Transparency of prices - is the provider open about their margins?
- Ease of use
- Access to experts who can help you over the phone
- Can you choose the time of conversion yourself?
- Access to hedging tools such as Forward Contracts
- Is the foreign exchange company you are dealing with licensed and regulated?

Speak to a dealer at UKForex about your deal, perhaps find out more about FECs or to arrange one. You can reach us 24-hours a day on **0845 686 1950** or visit us at **www.ukforex.co.uk**

Information supplied by UKForex		www.ukforex.co.uk
Telephone	UK	0845 686 1950
	International	+44 2072 973 438
	Email	dealers@ukforex.co.uk

buying a property abroad?

You find the PERFECT property ...
We give you the PERFECT exchange rate

For more information, call us on 0845 686 1950 or visit us at www.ukforex.co.uk

Investing in property abroad is always risky, but many overseas property experts believe that the only real way of making a profit, either with existing or mature markets, is to buy off-plan or newbuild apartments or villas in places that are on the up and up. It is almost impossible to make money from buying a romantic wreck and then lovingly restoring it yourself.

It is usually the case that the new developments are most likely to increase in value, although in Eastern Europe investors are also looking at old-style apartments dating from before the communist era. Most investors believe the communist-bloc apartments themselves are best avoided.

But in any case, in order to make a profit there has to be a thriving rental or holiday market as, unless people actually want to be in the area, you are wasting your money.

As with UK property, there are two main ways you can hope to make money: from rental income and from resale.

Most investors would hope for both types of gain, although this may not always be possible. If you are mainly interested in rental income, you would need to determine the popularity of the place as a holiday destination or resort, and what attractions, including weather, are on offer. You may have in mind a beachfront property, a ski chalet, a golfing villa or apartment, or a place with huge attractions for children. But there has to be something that makes people want to flock to the area.

You would also need to know how long the rental season lasts. In some countries or cities, there may be year-round letting potential, but in other locations, the season may be extremely short.

Then there is the vexed question of competition. If there is huge competition, this will inevitably bring down prices, and you may discover that your wonderful villa or apartment is either empty, or will only rent out at a rate far too low to cover costs, let alone make a profit.

To give an example, many investors who snapped up cheap-seeming properties on Sunny Beach in Bulgaria, where many developments are going up, managed to rent their apartments out for just six weeks in the year, at around £200 a week. Therefore, although they may have only paid £30,000 for their apartment, the gross rental return was just £1,200 a year, or 4 per cent. The net rental return, after advertising, cleaning and management costs, would be about half this – hardly enough to cover the mortgage and service charges on the apartment.

There are also no low-cost airlines flying to Sunny Beach and in 2006, a return flight to and from the UK would cost around £250; over £1,000 for a family of four, before villa or apartment costs. You can get a vastly cheaper package to Spain, for instance – and the weather is likely to be much better as well, as Bulgaria has a short sunny season.

It's not that I have anything against Bulgaria; I am just using it as an example of how careful you have to be when considering investing in somewhere that seems not only exotic and sunny, but cheap. At the time of writing, Bulgaria is being talked up as an investment hotspot, but there is massive development going on, at the same time as the tourist industry is not well established. Some investors have already had their fingers burnt in Bulgaria, and got out.

Cheap is cheap for a reason; it is high risk. And the newer the market, the longer you would have to hang on to your investment before it produces the hoped-for returns.

Beware also the 'guaranteed rental' trap. One company advertising new and off-plan apartments on the Black Sea in Bulgaria was offering a 7 per cent guaranteed rental – for six months. Guaranteed rentals are also a feature of many new developments in Portugal.

Note: almost all off-plan developers now offer inspection trips, guaranteed rentals and discounts for early buyers. It all sounds good, but never forget that developers are all in the business of making money from you, the investor. Never buy unless all the figures stack up, and there is not just a genuine rental market, but a guaranteed resale price as well.

You particularly need to know, as with the home market, whether there is a real rental demand, and whether you could get that 7 per cent (or whatever is offered) on the open market when the guarantee period finishes. Not all these 'guaranteed rentals' mean that the place is actually rented out.

As a general rule, it is not easy to make a profit on rentals from holiday apartments anyway. You would be lucky even to cover your costs in most places, simply because there are so many similar apartments, and very many companies offering huge discounts you may not be able to match. The only exception to this is Italy, where there is little speculative development, and many beautiful, tastefully restored villas which appeal to the upmarket lover of Italy.

The bog-standard family wants somewhere sunny, cheap and easy to get to for a holiday – and this market has a great deal of choice.

Other questions you must ask yourself (or ask an objective overseas property expert with nothing to sell you) include:

- How easy or difficult is the buying process?

- How easy is it to get a mortgage?

- What are the costs of buying?

- Are there any local taxes to pay?

- Are there restrictions on UK nationals owning property in the country?

- Do you have to form a company in the chosen country?

- How easy or difficult is it to establish title?

- How long would you realistically have to wait to see a good return on your investment?

- What is the situation with paying tax on rental income?

- What about inheritance tax and capital gains tax?

All countries have different rules, even within the EU. And, as ever, when investing in property, the eventual profit you may make is not just a matter of looking at the purchase price and the selling price, but how much it costs you to buy, and how much it costs you to sell, bearing in mind then when thinking about 'abroad' you have to include the costs of getting to and from the place, as well as all the entry and exit fees, local costs and taxes.

Finance and mortgages

By far the greatest majority of people who buy abroad finance the purchase either by downsizing on their main UK home, or by remortgaging, to free up the minimum 20–25 per cent of the purchase price needed before being granted a mortgage. There are now very many mortgage options for buying abroad, but across Europe they all work broadly on the same principle, which is that they are available for up to 75 per cent of the purchase price.

To set up the mortgage, you will have to pay an administration fee to the lender, plus a valuer's fee (non-refundable), legal fees, land registry charges and the notary's fees. The notary, a legal personage without an exact equivalent in the UK, usually acts for both buyer and seller, and has to examine and assess all relevant paperwork for the sale to proceed. You are also responsible for the lender's legal fees, so need quite a lot of spare cash to complete the sale.

As with obtaining a mortgage in the UK, lenders have to know your exact financial position, and will assess your ability to pay the mortgage. If you are hoping to cover the mortgage by renting out the property, they will have to be satisfied that enough of a rental market exists.

Buying property abroad on a mortgage gives some checks on the purchase, as lenders will not advance money for a complete ruin. At least, so one hopes!

In many countries, there is high VAT levied on new properties, so you would need to know whether this applies. It has just been introduced in Cyprus, for instance.

Tax matters

There are no reliable figures to show how many overseas investors rent out their overseas homes without declaring the income, but a new EU Directive requires banks throughout the community, plus the Channel Islands, Isle of Man and other tax havens such as the Cayman Islands and Gibraltar, to disclose the identity of account holders to their home tax authority.

If you have been receiving income from a foreign property, but have not declared it to the HM Revenue and Customs, there will most likely be an investigation which could go back many years, and result in large fines and possibly other penalties.

These rules do not apply to companies or trusts, only to individual account holders. If you have funds in an overseas bank, they will not reveal your identity without your consent, so if you receive a letter asking to reveal this information, you can be pretty sure that a tax investigation is under way.

Either this, or the bank will automatically deduct a withholding tax of 15 per cent from your account.

At the time of writing, banks in Hong Kong and the Bahamas are not included in this Directive, but it could only be a matter of time before it actually becomes impossible to evade tax on foreign investments.

The best advice, as ever, is not to take the risk but to make sure all income received from overseas properties is declared.

As ever, take advice from a good accountant conversant with foreign tax matters before going ahead with an investment.

Profitability

The wise investor also undertakes extensive research when it comes to the possibility of capital growth. For this, you would have to know the average resale prices of similar properties in the area. If very many new developments are going up, you are unlikely to make a profit on resale for a very long time, as who would buy a two-year old apartment or villa at a premium price, when they can get a brand-new one at a discount?

On the other hand, it would be hard to lose out on a beachfront apartment, ultimately, simply because there are limited areas of seashore, as opposed to inland. But if buying right on the beachfront, you would need to make absolutely certain that there is no possibility of a huge building going up in front of yours, obscuring your view and decimating the value of the place.

Private, gated developments are also unlikely to lose value, although it may take a long time for them to realize their full potential. As in the UK, it is usually the case that you have to hold the property for at least 10 years to make a decent profit on resale. A friend with a property in Boca Raton, Florida, held onto it for 11 years before it became profitable. In that time, the value of the house went down before it went up again.

There is huge development going on in many popular resorts and destinations, whether new or established, such as Croatia, Bulgaria, Cyprus, Spain, Dubai, Portugal, France, Florida, South Africa, Shanghai and Australia, and very many of these developments are specifically aimed at the foreign investor. They tend to be heavily marketed at investor shows, where cheap inspection trips are on offer.

Beware of these. Before enthusiastically signing up for an apparently cheap fly 'n buy trip, you need to know about the developer's track record and whether it is a good idea to reserve off-plan in the belief that you can make a significant profit on resale. In Florida, many investors are 'flipping', which means they sell their off-plan property on completion, without ever having lived in the place. Many investors also hope to do this in Spain, but first you would have to be sure that the property will make you a handsome profit in that timescale.

As with the UK, property prices in other countries are subject to fluctuation, and the presence or absence of cheap airlines, international airports, exchange rates and economy upturns and downturns can all make a dramatic difference in a very short time. A cheap airline going bust could wipe out all your investment, for instance. There are always many unknowns, and it is impossible to have a crystal ball to foresee them all.

Because 'abroad' is a big place, and to describe everywhere in detail would take a big book in itself, here are a few examples of popular markets outside the UK. For a fuller picture, see the author's *Complete Guide To Buying Property Abroad*.

Existing markets

Spain and France continue to be the most popular 'abroad' countries for UK nationals, with Florida now coming up close behind. In 2003, £57 billion was taken out of UK property, and most of this money went into buying properties abroad, with Spain and France the top favourites for investment.

Prices in Spain rose by 17 per cent in 2004, in spite of predictions of a major cooling off. Demand for France also remains strong, in spite of much competition coming now from newer entrants to the overseas market. Paris and Nice are well-established hotspots, attracting much foreign investment, and apartments in these two cities are popular with the rental market.

One reason why France and Spain continue to be popular, apart from their being known quantities in many ways, is that the buying process is now well established. In emerging markets such as Croatia and Bulgaria, it can be difficult to establish title, and because these markets are relatively new, nobody knows what might happen when these former communist countries get properly on their feet with a market economy.

In countries which have the euro, you can now get a euro mortgage whether or not you have a euro income.

Portugal

Portugal is a mature market, with – some believe – still a long way to go before it reaches saturation point. The overwhelming attraction of Portugal lies in the sporting facilities, particularly golf. Investors are advised to look for developments which have championship quality golf courses, not just ordinary ones. There are many huge new developments going up in Portugal, where the entry level is higher than Spain, and the whole place seems to be more upmarket.

The most popular buys are new, lavish apartments with private swimming pools in gated developments right next to a wonderful golf course. Guaranteed rental schemes are a particular feature of new developments as a way of hooking investors, and as ever, investors have to be sure there is a genuine rental market once the guarantee period ends.

Leaseback deals are also heavily marketed. Here, you buy a room, or suite, in a hotel, on a lease, and it is rented out for you, with some of the profits coming back to you. With most of these schemes, you are allowed to use the room yourself for a certain number of weeks. It can cost into six figures to buy one of these deals so again, you would have to do a lot of number-crunching and ignore the glossy brochure to see if it makes sense from an investment point of view.

Lengths of lease vary, and can be from 5 to 99 years, depending on the deal.

Emerging markets

Eastern Europe

Much of Eastern Europe is considered an 'emerging market' because, although there have been some spectacular property price increases since the fall of communism, most experts believe there is still more to come. However, this does not mean that unprecedented riches will automatically be showered on anybody who invests in Eastern Europe. Because many countries have not fully established themselves since communism, nobody really knows what will happen in the future, and whether all this foreign investment will continue to be welcomed, especially when the idea is not to benefit the country concerned, but the individual investor.

For every potential investor, there is a lot of homework to be done. Chris Howard, managing director of 4:you Property Partners, plc, believes that assessing the pace of change is an important factor. But it can be difficult in some Eastern European countries to access good information about price trends and economic growth. We are used to being able to access such figures in the UK, United States and established European markets, but in some of the newer entrants to market economies, as opposed to communism, such figures may not be available or, if available, unreliable.

The most contentious issues surround legal title and ownership and whether foreign nationals are actually allowed to own property, or whether you have to form a company in the chosen country. There is also the fact that in many of these new market economies, the profession of estate agent is not established at all, and you have to rely on websites which may not be particularly reliable.

Property developer Alan Goss has decided to invest in the Czech Republic – but only after undertaking massive research. In 2005, he bought a 1920s apartment in Brno, the second city after Prague, which he has rented out to Czech law students. Alan's partner is Czech, which obviously helps with language problems, but before ever investing, he drew up a factsheet giving details of population, neighbouring countries, age demographics, population growth, GDP, currency, literacy levels, type of government, national holidays, temperature variation, official language and international airports.

In other words, he carried out the most thorough research that it was possible to do, before deciding to take the plunge. His first purchase cost £46,000 and he is now negotiating for more properties, with a view to investing in the native rental market.

Emerging Eastern European markets which are welcoming foreign property investors include Croatia, Poland, Estonia, Hungary, Latvia, Slovenia, Lithuania and Bulgaria. Do not, whatever you do, lump all these countries together and imagine they are all identical, just because they are all former communist countries. They not only have their separate identities, pluses and minuses, but their emerging economies are very individual, as well.

Most property experts believe the Eastern European countries have a long way to go before they reach their peak, investment-wise, but you could have a long wait.

Dubai

Massive new developments are going up, some the last word in luxury. But many property experts believe that the Muslim Sharia laws, which mean that women cannot inherit property, for instance, will have to be changed or modified to fit in with Western ideas, before investments there become profitable.

South Africa, Australia, China and New Zealand

These rapidly emerging markets are worth looking into, as foreign investment is being actively encouraged. Again, these places are heavily marketed at property fairs, with inspection trips usually offered as part of the deal.

Cyprus (on the cusp of emerging and mature)

Cyprus, which joined the EU in 2004, is highly popular with UK nationals and it is easy to see why. Because of British occupation, Cyprus has a definite 'British' feel and many people speak English as well. Their laws are based on British laws, so are not too difficult to understand.

Since 2004, property developers and investors have been targeting Cyprus in the confident expectation of a huge property bonanza. In contrast with, say, Florida, it is not possible to build and build because Cyprus is an island with only a very limited amount of land available for development. The small size of Cyprus is one of the main factors beckoning investors. Because it is hot and dry, there are also fears about water shortages, and this as well is limiting development.

The official currency is the Cyprus pound, worth 1.15 British pounds. Eventually, the island will probably go over to the euro.

Local banks can offer mortgages of up to 75 per cent of the purchase price over 15 years, with interest rates typically 2.5 per cent above the UK rate. The Cypriot government must normally approve foreign purchases, but investors tell me this is only a formality.

Purchase tax is 3–8 per cent, depending on the price of the property, and stamp duty is also payable on a sliding scale.

If you stay in your Cyprus holiday home for more than 182 non-consecutive days in one year, you may have to pay Cypriot income tax. Most non-Cypriot residents pay 5 per cent, although it can go up to 30 per cent. You may also be liable to pay tax on any rental income.

Since joining the EU, property prices in the South have enjoyed 15–20 per cent annual growth. Lettings for residential and short-term holiday lets have increased as ever more property management companies set up on the island.

EU membership has also meant more work and investment opportunities, more budget airlines and vastly more developments, from simple studios to magnificent detached villas with their own swimming pools and wonderful sea views. You could also buy a 100-year-old stone house with character, although by far the great majority of UK purchasers buy off-plan. The most popular tourist area is around Paphos, very heavily developed now, and entire village developments are going up in the area, most of which are expected to be sold to UK nationals. Golf is a big draw, as with many sunny spots in Europe.

With apartments, all tenure in Southern Cyprus is freehold. There is no such thing as leasehold, and this is another plus as when you buy a leasehold property abroad – as in the UK – there is usually a head freeholder who wants to make money out of you, the leaseholder, and you may not have much control over service charge increases and swingeing levies. Whenever buying leasehold property in another country, pay close attention to the terms of the lease and ask for explanations of any clauses not fully understood. An apparently cheap apartment can become very expensive when you have to pay your share of exterior decoration, for instance, or landscaping the grounds.

When it comes to the Northern (Turkish) part of Cyprus, the situation becomes complicated, as when the Greek Cypriots fled the Northern part after partition in 1974, whole villages were abandoned. In some cases, it may not be known who actually owns the derelict properties, or the land on which they sit.

So far, Northern Cyprus is less populated than the South, it tends to be poorer, and there is much unemployment. On the plus side, property is also cheaper than in the South, and there are many beautiful areas, including some of the island's best beaches. If interested in buying into Northern Cyprus, which, along with the Southern Greek part, is being heavily featured at property investor shows, the most important aspect of the purchase is ensuring that there is a clean legal title, and that nobody will come and claim it after you believe you have bought.

Putting foreign property into a SIPP

In 2003, Chancellor Gordon Brown announced that residential property, both in the UK and abroad, might in some cases be eligible to put into a self-invested pension fund, and so attract the tax breaks that pension funds generally enjoy.

Then without warning on 6 December 2005, this facility was withdrawn, four months before it was due to be implemented. The result is that residential property abroad can no longer be put into a SIPP. Technically it can, but because there is no tax advantage, there is no point.

In hindsight, many commentators noted that putting a foreign home into a SIPP would have been very inflexible, as buyers would have only been able to access the rental returns upon retirement, and the SIPP might have to fund the investment for many years before the pension scheme would pay out.

What you can still do, if you wish, is to buy into a property fund whereby you invest in property for your pension fund, but it is not self-invested. Property funds allow investors to buy a spread of property, although they do not own the property themselves, so the individual control which the SIPPs would have allowed will be lost.

Experts also warned that the cost of putting overseas property into a SIPP was so high that in most cases, it would not be worth it. It seems unlikely that the sudden withdrawal of the SIPPs facility for overseas property will have a significant impact on investing abroad. However, it is now not possible to wrap up residential foreign property investments, such as second homes and buy-to-lets, in a pension fund.

Church End Library

Tel: 020 8359 3800
Email: church.end.library
@barnet.gov.uk

Borrowed Items 29/12/2019 16:32
XXXXXXXXXX6861

Item Title	Due Date
* Herbal remedies handbook : more than 140 plant profiles : remedies for over	19/01/2020
* Conducting your own court case	19/01/2020
* The complete guide to investing in property	19/01/2020
* Making a small claim in the county court	19/01/2020

* Indicates items borrowed today
Thank you for using this unit

Last word on buying abroad

If you are buying purely for investment, you have to do a lot more number-crunching than if buying that dream place in the sun.

The best advice is to go to the place where you are interested in investing, get to know it, get a 'feel' of the place, do all your homework regarding demographics, infrastructure, political set-up, healthiness or otherwise of the economy, before ever making a down payment. All too many people get carried away at property shows, and sign up for a wonderful-looking off-plan apartment they have only seen on the internet. That, of course, is the idea!

And also never forget that once the property is yours, wherever it may be, it becomes your responsibility. You are responsible for repairs and upkeep, for paying service and maintenance charges and local rates and taxes. You cannot just buy a property abroad and forget about it, as with a stock or share.

Easy *Living in Cyprus*

Did you know that Cyprus is now number 4 on the places most people would like to live? Since joining the EU in May 2004, demand for property is escalating as it is now possible to work as an EU citizen and increasingly more of the younger generation with families are moving to live and work in Cyprus.

However Cyprus is no exception to the pitfalls. When looking for and buying property it is imperative that professional advice is sought to avoid any potential regrets. Always use your own lawyer who will work for you and not the vendor.

There are an abundance of developers vying for your business, that makes it a difficult decision. Always use an agent that has a licence and is registered with the government. **All agents selling property in Cyprus have to have a qualification and a registered number. Ask to see the certificate before you even look at any property with them.** Do your homework before you leave the UK. Use people who will specialise in finding you the property you want, not what someone wants you to have!

The most economical way to buy is *off-plan*. Re-sales attract premium prices but good ones can be rare. Prices are highest in Paphos, less in Limassol and less again in Larnaca with Ayia Napa and Protaras being on par with Limassol. However Ayia Napa and Protaras due tend to close during the winter months as they are manly tourist areas.

If you use the experience of **www.living-cyprus.com** for *free*, you will find it invaluable. As the founders explain:

> *"Living-Cyprus.com was set up because we suffered what many others did and still do trying to find a property. Arriving in Cyprus with a dream, people just wasted our time which was precious as we only had 14 days to view and choose a property. Quite by chance we found an established estate agent, licensed and in business since 1945. They escorted us to view only properties we specified in our budget, assisted us with negotiations for changes we wanted and introduced us to a solicitor. In fact the process was made so easy and enjoyable we wished we had met them when we first arrived in Cyprus. We left Cyprus very happy people."*

www.living-cyprus.com work in partnership with these people and all the reputable developers and vendors and have many satisfied clients (see the website for details). Living-Cyprus.com are a specialist organisation, based in England, experienced in helping people who wish to purchase property on the idyllic island of Cyprus. The company has long established relationships with all the major developers, along with a database of properties on the re-sale market.

Property facts

Buying property in Cyprus is safe if you follow the guidelines. The process starts with finding the property, paying the reservation fee and signing the contract. Surveys are not usually carried out as new properties must be built to strict building regulations and earthquake standards. The contract is registered almost immediately with the Land registry in the buyer's name, even if all the money has not been paid. This ensures the property cannot be resold without the buyer's signature. Application must still be made to the council of ministers for permission to buy property but this is usually a formality carried out by your lawyer.

Property transfer tax is payable to the government once the title deeds are issued, usually about 1 year after taking possession. This is at variable rates; upto CY£50,000=3%, next CY£50,000=5% above CY£100,000=8%. Therefore a property bought for CY£150,000 would attract transfer tax like this, CY£50,000 at 3%, next CY£50,000 at 5% then 8% on the remainder.

Example property prices

Here are the starting prices in a variety of areas. These prices refer to properties of a high construction quality. No doubt there are properties selling for less, but not for the same quality.

Villas: 3 bedroom villa with a private pool, from CP160, 000-CP100, 000.

Terraced Houses: 2 bedroom terraced house with a communal pool, from CP65, 000-CP75, 000.

Apartments: 2 bedroom apartment in a complex with a communal pool, from CP48, 000-CP80, 000.

So whenever you decide to move abroad, Living-Cyprus.com are there to help in any way they can to make the whole experience a stress free, enjoyable one, making for Easy Living in Cyprus.

Contact: Website: **www.living-cyprus.com** Email: **info@living-cyprus.com**
Telephone: **0845 095 6409** or International: **+00357 99663493**

Exchange rate movements tamed

There can be few things more infuriating when buying an overseas property than seeing a fantastic exchange rate but not being ready to take advantage of it. All too often we hear stories of international property buyers whose costs spiralled because the exchange rate moved the wrong way before they were ready to complete the purchase.

We have to be extremely tactful to avoid tears and tantrums as we explain how these buyers could have bought their currency when the exchange rate was right but delayed the physical exchange of funds until their payments were due or until their funds were available. If only they'd known about forward contracts, things could have been so different.

Managing the risk of currency movement is rather simple really, as long as you have the right tools for the job and the right assistance to make those tools work for you.

Whether buying a new build property with a series of stage payments or awaiting the completion on a resale property, the only way to remove all risk from exchange rate movement is to buy the necessary currency on forward contracts.

A forward contract is an agreement made to buy a set amount of currency for an agreed delivery date at a preset exchange rate. This means that whether the exchange rate rises or falls after the contract has been agreed, the buyer and seller are not affected.

This can be done for a single lump sum or for smaller amounts to coincide with the staggered payments usually required for new property purchases. Many international property investors use forward contracts to guarantee their expenditure in Sterling rather than leaving themselves exposed to the changes that two year's worth of exchange rate movements can inflict upon the cost of stage payments for a new build property.

Of course the rate could rise but where there is an equal chance that it could fall and diminish your investment return, is there really an argument for taking an unnecessary risk?

David Johnson is an FX Consultant with Halo Financial Ltd, a specialist foreign exchange company providing expert currency exchange services to both companies and private individuals. If you are at the start of buying an overseas property or in the process of buying currency to pay for a new home, it is never too soon or too late to save money on foreign exchange. Halo Financial can be contacted on **020 7350 5474** *and their website can be viewed at* **www.halofinancial.com**

More Currency
Less Worry

Why offshore?

Planning Offshore Operations: where to go, and, why go there?

What are the key factors that smart people and businesses usually consider very carefully when looking for with a suitable offshore company location?

3 They will require the offshore company location to have the right characteristics in the following major areas:

- no burdensome taxation,
- ease of company administration,
- adequate company confidentiality,
- excellent political stability,
- well established rule of law (preferably a familiar legal system), and
- excellent communications, in a reasonable time zone.

3 They will also usually be looking for significant assistance in the professional administration of the company (company secretarial administration – annual renewal of the company, any reporting requirements, etc.), and total long term confidentiality regarding all matters concerning their offshore company.

3 They may need significant additional assistance in operating their offshore company, depending on how it is used; key areas of assistance include:

- accounting and audit functions,
- banking operations,
- trade services (letters of credit, trade negotiation and payment, insurance, shipping, funds transfer, etc.)

The resolution of the first set of points above will determine which offshore country to choose. The resolution of the next 2 sets of points above will determine which corporate services company to choose. Normally the experienced offshore operator will buy his offshore company from the same company chosen to supply the required ongoing corporate services.

Hong Kong: Is often used by companies with major trading volume with China and the Far East. The address is not so provocative to home country tax authorities. More compliance is required here, trade financing is a routine activity with the banks here.

Singapore: is often used by companies with a specific need for operations in South East Asia, centred on or around Singapore.

British Virgin Islands: is the most frequently used of all offshore locations: it is the lowest cost, has the lowest compliance requirements, and is ideal for all types of offshore operations.

Bahamas: is very often used for offshore banking, insurance, and trust operations.

The Cayman Islands: is very popular as a leading offshore banking center.

The Isle of Man: is very often used to enable lower cost trade and personal services operations with the EC.

Jersey: is often used to enable lower cost trade and personal services operations with the EC.

Panama: is most often used for ship operations.

Mauritius: is often used in a way that is very similar to BVI: as a lowest cost, lowest compliance, general-purpose offshore center.

The Cook Islands: is often used for Pacific based operations as a low cost, low compliance, offshore location for trading and personal services operations.

The rest of this section will set out a basic description of the characteristics of major different offshore locations to enable you to understand them better. Following this, a direct consultation with us (which is free) via phone: **00 33 468 81 62 17**, e-mail: **fpmanagement@wanadoo.fr** for a meeting to discuss your needs should complete this process for you.

Summary: main characteristics of some major offshore locations:
Summary tables of these characteristics follow. After these tables we will give a deeper discussion of the group of major offshore jurisdictions which we see requested most often by our clients.

These tables are intended to give you some idea of the

different requirements for disclosure and financial reporting that are imposed by the various offshore locations. These requirements can change from time to time, so you should check with us before making any final decision regarding choice of jurisdiction.

Pacific Rim & European locations table						
	Hong Kong	Singapore	Cook Islands	Western Samoa	Jersey	Isle of Man
Stability	High	High	High	High	High	High
Legal System	English Common	English Common	English Common	English Common	English Common	English Common
Beneficial Owner Disclosed	No	No	No	No	Yes	No
Tax on offshore profits	No	Yes if remitted to Singapore	No	No	No	No
Annual Return	Yes	Yes	Yes	No	Yes	Yes
Annual Audited Accounts	Yes	Yes	No	No	No	No

Caribbean, Atlantic Ocean and Americas locations						
	BVI	Bahamas	Cayman Islands	Bermuda	Nevis	Panama
Stability	High	High	High	High	High	High
Legal System	English Common	English Common	English Common	English Common		Spanish Civil
Beneficial Owner Disclosed	No	No	No	Yes	No	No
Tax on offshore profits	No	No	No	No	No	No
Annual Return	No	No	No	Yes	No	No
Annual Audited Accounts	No	No	No	No if waived	No	No

To help you to get the additional information on each of these locations, plus some other locations, please visit our web site **www.wwmdirectory.com** and just click on the flag of the country you wish to review.

9 SIPPs

It is generally accepted that as a nation, we do not save enough to give ourselves a comfortable retirement. But it is difficult enough to save any money out of taxed income, unless you are extremely rich. My grandparents, along with most other people of their generation, saved hard out of earnings to be able to supplement their old-age pension in retirement. But today, by contrast, most people live on credit and borrowings rather than being able to put money away for a rainy day. Many of the over-50s, even, are deeply in debt even though they are approaching retirement and coming to the end of their working years.

In fact, for many, the whole idea of saving has become completely theoretical. Most people believe they do not have enough money to get by day to day, let alone save.

Added to that, even those who have saved or put money into a pension fund have often seen these savings eroded through inflation or bad management of the pension fund. It is with retirement, or a nice nest-egg, in mind that people have been investing in buy-to-let, holiday homes or properties overseas since easier mortgages became available from 1998. The idea was that by the time retirement was reached, either the mortgages would be paid off and the rents would actually count for something, or, alternatively, the investment properties could be sold for a substantial capital gain which would give a welcome boost to retirement funds.

One of the reasons so many people started investing in buy-to-let was dissatisfaction with existing pension schemes. Unless you had a generous employer's pension, which these days most people do not, it was difficult to see how you would ever be able to save enough money for a decent retirement. Added to that, in the old days, when people started working at 16 and retired at 65, they would have 40 years of employment in which to save for retirement. Nowadays, not only do many people not start work until the age of 21 at least, they almost always graduate from university with debts which take many years to pay off. Also, very few jobs these days are secure, many people may get divorced at some stage and, increasingly, employer's pensions are becoming a thing of the past, except for people working in the public sector who, by and large, still have comfortable salary-linked pensions to rely on in retirement.

For the self-employed, or those working in fragile businesses or industries liable to collapse with huge debts at any moment, the future is far from secure.

Many heavily advertised pension schemes have not performed well, or have been downright fraudulent, with the result that very many people have lost their faith in the pension industry to provide them with a proper pension. Pension funds are almost always invested in stocks and shares, which may perform well or ill and nobody knows what may happen in the future.

So – enter the huge rush to invest in property in recent years, as an alternative investment. As we have seen, it has been possible to put commercial property into a self-invested personal pension (SIPP) since 1989, but the majority of ordinary, individual investors have tended to steer clear of this sector.

The government announced its intention to allow people to put residential property into a SIPP from 6 April 2006, and then dramatically backtracked on this in December 2005.

So what does this last-minute reversal actually mean in practice?

It means that you can no longer wrap up property such as a second home or buy-to-let in your pension scheme, although you will still be able to put commercial property into a SIPP, as before.

In very simple terms, a SIPP is a 'wrapper' into which you can put pension assets. In the past, these have included equities, bonds, cash deposits and commercial property assets such as hotels, guest houses, nursing homes, ground rents and pubs and restaurants. This facility will continue to be possible from April 2006.

In normal circumstances, any profit made on your property is subject to one or other – or maybe all three – forms of taxation. Rental income is subject to income tax and all properties apart from your own home (at the time of writing at least) are subject to capital gains tax when you sell. In addition, all property, and all assets come to that, are liable for inheritance tax when you die, with the sole exception being assets which pass directly to your spouse or civil partner, so long as this is made clear in your will.

If you put your assets into a SIPP, by contrast, the assets become tax-exempt, although the eventual income or pension you receive is subject to income tax, as ever. It's just that while everything remains inside the SIPP, it is sheltered, in modern parlance, from the taxman.

All well and good. But by putting property – or any other asset – into a SIPP, you cannot ever take out the entire lump sum. You cannot, for instance, put an investment property into a SIPP, where you shelter it from income tax and capital gains tax, and then sell it, thereby pocketing a nice wodge of tax-free money. Why not? Because it is no longer yours. You have sold it, in effect, to the SIPP which now owns it.

A property-based SIPP acts in exactly the same way as any other pension fund, in that only a small proportion of the money invested may be taken out as a lump sum. The rest has to be kept in the fund, and you the pensioner take out an income which amounts to interest on the capital.

It is all highly complicated and, in some instances, it may not be a good idea to put money into a SIPP. Some people in any case would not be eligible for a SIPP, bearing in mind that the letters refer to self-invested personal pensions. If you receive a company pension, for instance, you may not be eligible as the pension is not then self-invested. Also, you have to have income or other funds to put into a SIPP in the first place.

Here, the labyrinthine rules and regulations are explained by SIPP experts.

Property investment expert Geoffrey Summers clarifies some of the important issues regarding SIPPs: 'If you put property into a pension fund, it is owned by the pension fund, rather than by you personally. The advantages are that if the property is sold, there is no capital gains tax payable by the pension fund, although the sale has to be properly conducted, and estate agents and stamp duty paid as usual.

'There may, however, be capital gains liability the other way round, such as when you dispose of your property to a SIPP.'

Supposing you have five shops, the SIPP can purchase all five, in a proper sales transaction. Obviously, the SIPP already has to have enough money in it to buy the properties, just as with an individual, and this can come from an existing pension fund or from contributions that you have made. It is clear that you cannot put property into a SIPP if there is already nothing in your pension fund. You don't just bung it in; there has to be a proper transaction once the SIPP is already set up.

The point about pension funds is that they operate independently of you, the beneficiary of the fund. This is because the fund is considered a separate entity from you, unlike when you have liquid assets in the bank.

If you have a bank account containing £100,000, this will typically yield interest of £4,000 a year on which you pay tax. You can also go at the capital as much as you like, eventually eroding it down to nothing.

If, however, you have £100,000 in your pension fund, you can draw down the interest or income after a certain age, but you cannot get your hands on the bulk of the capital. The incentive for keeping your money in the pension fund is that the money becomes free of tax. But the capital is unavailable to you for ever. You cannot get it out, whatever you try to do, once you have taken out the initial tax-free sum allowed, usually 25 per cent of the entire fund.

Exactly the same thing happens when you put property into a SIPP as with any other pension scheme. Another SIPP expert, James Hughes, of the City Trading Post, sheds some more light on the subject: 'A pension is basically a trust fund where you are the beneficiary. This is the case with all pensions, whether the funds are invested in equities or property. If you have £500,000 sitting in the bank, you can do what you like with it, but if it is in the pension fund you can never take it out even though you remain the only beneficiary.'

James Hughes takes issue with the popular conception that pension funds are a waste of money and all pension fund administrators are crooks and charlatans. 'The vast majority of pension funds have performed extremely well,' he says. 'The ones that backfired, which of course got all the publicity, were poorly managed. This is less likely to happen in future as not only do we now have a Minister for Pensions, but the problems of pension funds in the past have now been addressed by government. Government started looking at the prospect of putting property into pensions when it realized that there was no way of providing state pensions for enough people at current levels of taxation. People are living too long and they also want a more exciting retirement than used to be the case.

So, one might ask, why did the government change its mind on residential property and SIPPs at the last minute?

Some experts believe the Chancellor suddenly realized the system could be open to abuse, with already wealthy people wrapping up all their properties into pension funds, and benefiting from generous tax breaks. Maybe Gordon Brown bowed to pressure from some sections of the media.

Commenting on the U-turn, the *Guardian* – which had campaigned long and hard against allowing residential property into a SIPP – said that SIPPs would give £3 billion a year in tax breaks to already well-off property investors, and push up prices for first-time buyers who were trying to get a foot on the property ladder.

At any rate, you can still put residential property into your SIPP if you like, but it will no longer be protected from the taxman. In effect, this means you will wrap the property away from yourself without any financial advantages.

Other 'wrappers' such as bonds and ISAs and equity-based pensions also get protection from the taxman but you give up something in return, which is access to your capital. James Hughes believes that current tax treatment on pensions is 'brilliant' and the government is generous with tax relief. 'It's as if the government is saying to the individual: we are going to make pension provision your problem, but we will incentivize it for you. If they don't, and allow you to take your entire pension fund out, you can go to Las Vegas or on endless cruises and blow the whole lot. This means that large numbers of pensioners could soon be back on the parish and on benefits for ever. No government can stand that kind of drain.

'It is to avoid this kind of thing that both the tax incentives and the impossibility of getting the entire pension fund out to spend have been introduced.'

James Hughes continues: 'This is how it happened. The government said to itself: we want people to fund their pensions but they have gone off equities. Instead, they have been viewing properties as their "pensions". Let's make it better for them, but at the same time ensure that they will retain enough in their pension funds to see them out in comfort.

'If you buy property outright at £100,000 and it generates, say, 6 per cent rental income, you lose 22 per cent of that in tax; 40 per cent if you are a higher-rate tax payer. So, forgetting about other costs, you net, for instance, £4,680 per annum and after 10 years, this amounts to £46,800. If you sell after 10 years and have made a capital gain of £159,000, your net profit is £142,000.

'Now, if instead of this scenario, you put the £100,000 property into a SIPP, it is already worth £128,000 thanks to tax incentives. And the same 6 per cent rental yield amounts to the equivalent of £7,680 with no tax to pay. Over 10 years, this comes to £76,800 and the property is now worth £332,000. You can sell this property within the scheme without paying any tax at all, and have £308,000 to play with instead of £142,000.

'The big difference between the two figures is that you can take the £142,000 you have made on your property and spend it. The £308,000 you have gained instead from putting the property into a SIPP has to stay inside the SIPP.' Now, though, these figures apply only to commercial property, as before.

It is, in some ways, the difference between one bird in the hand and two in the bush.

'By putting assets into a pension scheme, you get twice as much as by just leaving funds in the bank, because of highly advantageous tax breaks. But the public have a bee in their bonnet about pensions, and that is why in recent years they have been putting money into property instead.'

The other factor is that for the ordinary unsophisticated investor, such as myself, pension funds, tax breaks and all such ramifications are hard to understand, whereas buying, selling and renting out property is easy to understand – and this is another reason why so many of us have been doing it. The other complication is that whenever you set up a pension fund, there are significant costs to be paid to the pension provider or fund manager and it is sometimes difficult to tell whether or not you ultimately benefit.

Of course, if I have £100,000 saved up for my retirement, I would rather have an annual income of £15,000 from it than one of £5,000 (if I can even get 5 per cent on that amount), but if I have had to pay a large sum to a financial adviser, would I be much better off? This is always something the ordinary investor, liable to be befuddled by smoke and mirrors, has to take on board. In general terms, the best advice is never to invest in anything you don't clearly understand, even if it seems extremely advantageous.

When you set up a SIPP, you are setting up a trust which is a legal entity in its own right. This entity can hold assets, be taxed, be sued. It owns the assets on behalf of the beneficiary and, as the beneficiary, you can draw income from the funds. A trust consists of assets owned by that trust.

Such trusts can also be advantageous when it comes to inheritance tax. Again, James Hughes explains: 'If properties or money are unwrapped, you are blasted by IHT and there is very little you can do about it. But if the assets are in a SIPP, they can pass to your descendants, who in turn become the beneficiaries of the pension fund. If you have a million pounds' worth of assets in a SIPP, your descendants can inherit it for their own retirement. This means that your children can have a nice juicy income on their own retirement, thanks to your SIPP taken out many years earlier. All this still applies, except that residential property no longer forms part of the scheme.

So – the next question is: how do you get the money or the property into a SIPP in the first place? 'You first have to have some idea of what you want to put into a SIPP. The SIPP has to pay stamp duty on the value of your property as you are in effect selling it, with the only difference that you don't go through estate agents. Otherwise, it is exactly the same transaction as when selling to a private individual. If there is a mortgage, this would have to be arranged in the same way as any other mortgage, with the rental income covering the repayments. There would be arrangement fees, valuation fees and all the other processes involved in setting up a mortgage.

'If you want to put property into a SIPP, it first has to generate rental income. You, or a tenant, can also be evicted by the SIPP for non-payment of rent! But the effect is that you pay stamp duty at a maximum of 4 per cent instead of inheritance tax at 40 per cent.

'This is how rich people have protected and tied up their assets for centuries.'

You not only need existing funds to start the thing off, but also to pay professional fees. Because SIPPs are complicated transactions it is essential, believes James Hughes, to go to an expert. 'It's the difference between going to a lawyer to draw up a legal contract and doing it yourself.'

Pay professionals to do it properly, he says. This is advice echoed by Robert Kiyosaki in his *Rich Dad, Poor Dad* books, and also by most rich people, who all pay professional financial advisers to sort out and maximize their assets. You just have to hope that your accountant or other adviser does not go down the same path as comedian Ken Dodd's accountant, who allowed Dodd to believe that money put in offshore accounts was totally tax-free and did not have to be declared to the HM Revenue and Customs.

The resulting court case made entertaining reading in the newspapers, but was less amusing for the comedian, who probably did genuinely believe he did not have to pay any tax on his considerable capital.

Dodd's case was maybe extreme, but it is all too easy for financially savvy people to delude the rest of us.

So far as setting up the SIPP is concerned, there will be a one-off fee to set the thing up and maybe a yearly charge as well. But the costs of setting up a property-based SIPP should be lower than for equities as there is much less activity connected with day-to-day running.

At the time of writing, you cannot just shove all your properties into a SIPP, as there is an upper limit of £1.5 million, and a yearly limit of £215,000.

Whoever dreams up these numbers, one wonders? Whoever is responsible, the same mindset has also instituted a whole host of regulations, just to make the matter even more complicated.

Here are just a few of the regulations concerning putting residential property into a SIPP:

■ The property must have been purchased on the open market and, if rented out, rented at a proper market rent.

■ No asset may be bought by the SIPP if the member has already owned it for more than three years.

■ No new investment may take place if the member has reached pensionable age in relation to the SIPP arrangement – normally age 65.

SIPPs will allow investment in commercial property by borrowing 50 per cent of the fund value. Once a property is invested in a SIPP, rental income will have to be reinvested in the fund and used to pay off any outstanding mortgage. Of course, as with any other pension fund, if you put rented properties in a SIPP, you will not be able to take advantage of the rental income until you reach retirement age – or the age decided on when you start to invest in this way. In any case, you would have to be aged over 50 to take out any funds for your own use as income.

You can only buy commercial properties for inclusion in a SIPP if you can afford the 50 per cent deposit. This means that if you have an existing SIPP containing £250,000, you can invest in a hotel or B&B home valued up to £375,000. Then the income will be yours free of tax. Any rise in the value of the property will also be tax-free. If the mortgage on the property is paid off by the time you retire, the rental income on investment properties can provide your pension. This is of course subject to income tax, but you could, if you wished, sell off the properties when you retire and take 25 per cent of the fund as a tax-free sum. If, on retirement, you have a SIPP of maximum value £1.5 million, this means you could take out £375,000 for your trip to Las Vegas or that round-the-world cruise – and still have £1.015 million in the bank. Not a bad retirement sum!

The things to watch out for, as with any investment in property, are a sudden downturn in property prices or rents, or upsurge in interest rates. It may also be the case that the pension fund administrators will want to let and manage your properties themselves, charging a 15 per cent management fee.

Once you have confirmation that you have enough money to start a SIPP, you will then have to fill in a form giving details of all old or existing schemes which you obtain from your pension provider, or a company handling SIPPs, and they will manage the transfer – for a fee, of course. Then, once the SIPP is up and running, you can either manage it yourself, or hand over the management to a financial adviser. The more you hand over the management, the more you pay.

The usual pension fund situation is that the fund is active and can be added to until you reach the age of 75, when it stops, and you have to buy an annuity. Also, usually when you die, your pension dies with you, however much it may have accumulated. But SIPP investors can keep the fund going beyond this age and also include their children and grandchildren in the pension, so they will inherit, although in time – when the Treasury gets round to it – this perk may disappear and be taxed along with other inherited income.

The two aspects which make property-based pensions attractive are (a) tax relief on your contributions and (b) tax-free investment growth, as all your rental income and capital gains will be tax-free. Supposing you earn £100,000 in a year, none of which you need to spend. If you put that entire sum into your SIPP you will not have to pay tax on it.

The generous tax-break position – if you see it as such – makes it possible for pension investors to gain much higher levels of return than ordinary buy-to-letters – for the same level of risk, according to Nick Braun, author of the book *Retire Rich with a Property Pension* (from www.taxcafe.co.uk).

Nick Braun believes that tax breaks will enable property pensioners to earn nearly double what a traditional property investor can make.

Geoffrey Summers, of SIPPs advisers Hartley-SAS, advises those who are interested in SIPPing into the future, to:

■ Start a SIPP now by making personal contributions, which must in general be based on income from an occupation or trade and not rental or investment income.

■ Maximize the value of your pension fund by making contributions at the highest level you can to benefit from tax relief. You can transfer money from an existing pension funds into a SIPP once it is set up, but this is not always in your best interests, so it is necessary to take professional advice (if possible, from more than one adviser).

■ Consider using your SIPP to start buying commercial property now. Interest rates or property prices may rise in the near future.

But – self-invested pensions are not for everybody. All advisers stress that they are an option, and dependent on your general financial circumstances. Also, you will definitely need to take advice if you are divorced or separated, or considering divorce, as former spouses and civil partners can now raid pension funds as well as other assets.

What is the answer now that SIPPs rules have been changed at the last minute? And where does that leave the investor who was hoping to channel residential investments into a pension fund?

It leaves investors who had already bought off-plan properties in anticipation of the new SIPPs arrangements in a mess. Such people were allowed to buy these properties on the understanding that they would not be habitable until or after 6 April

2006, when the change was going to take place. For these investors, the Chancellor has decided on a partial amnesty. They can still get the tax relief, provided they have bought the property through a properly set-up SIPP and if they sell the property before it becomes 'residential' (in other words, before it has been completed).

The drawback is that it forces investors to sell their properties quickly, and they may have to settle for a knock-down price. Also, any money they retain would be trapped in the SIPP for ever.

Readers who may have already invested money into a SIPP with a view to buying residential property will now have to choose another investment. They could buy shares, or put the money into unit or investment trusts. Another option is to invest in commercial property, such as factories and shops.

Alternatively, they could wait until the Government launches its REITS (Real Estate Investment Trusts), which is explained later in the chapter.

What you cannot do is get your money out of the pension scheme once it is in. According to the rules pertaining to pension funds, it has to stay there until you are over 50, and only then can you take out 25 per cent (as with any other pension scheme). However, you would still have to take an income from the rest of the pension. So you have no choice but to put the money in some other type of investment, or let it sit there, doing nothing.

A huge SIPPs industry was already well under way in preparation for the April 2006 deadline. This industry will now be disbanded, even after many investors have put money into the scheme in readiness. You may be wondering if these investors can now make claims for miss-selling, given that they have put money into a SIPP they now can't get out of, and that they can't buy residential property as they had been led to believe by the government.

The answer is probably no, as SIPPs and all selling methods concerned with them are not (at the time of writing) regulated by the Financial Services Authority. So whether the deal was set up by an estate agent, financial advisor of developer, there is nothing you can do if you have already put money into a SIPP.

You cannot sue the government over this issue either, as the U-turn was made four months before the new rules would have come into operation. It is wise to remember that you should never rely on the government to keep its word, as some financial writers pointed out at the time, particularly when it comes to money. Margaret Thatcher may have famously said, 'The lady's not for turning', but subsequent governments have had no such inhibitions.

The financial services industry has lost a lot of money promoting and selling the now non-existent residential property SIPPs, but whether or not the rest of us will shed many tears over this is debatable. One foreign property investment firm reported that it had lost nearly £400,000 from promoting SIPPs.

REITS (Real Estate Investment Trusts)

Although residential property can no longer be sheltered away from the taxman – unless a successive government reverses this – a new tax-efficient vehicle known as REITS, already well-established in America and Australia, could be the answer.

REITS, which is due to be available in 2007, work in much the same way as ordinary, non-property investments in that they are listed on the stock exchange and have a board of directors. The main difference is that they hold a collection of properties managed by a separate property firm. This means that individual control over the investment is lost, and that all your eggs are not in one basket.

Some REITS hold commercial property, some hold residential, and others hold a mix of the two. Property held in these funds is not liable for income tax or corporation tax, but does have to pay stamp duty and VAT. It is expected that the new REITs will concentrate on rental income from these properties, rather than capital gains.

Before REITS is introduced, investors disappointed by the loss of residential SIPPs should start investigating the possibilities. It is likely that REITS will be subject to a lot of government regulation (or interference, depending on how you look at it) in order to avoid abuses of the scheme.

Note: My own explanation of the U-turn on residential SIPPs is that the Treasury foresaw, just in time, that residential SIPPs could become hugely popular, resulting in lots of revenue suddenly becoming unavailable to them. This is likely to be the real reason for scrapping this anticipated tax break, rather than fears of abuses of the relaxation of previous rules.

When all is said and done, there is a lot to be said for behaving like a French peasant and keeping your money under the mattress, or failing that, in an easily accessible bank account. Though it is not 'sheltered' from the taxman, it is not subject to high fees from complicated investment schemes which can easily go horribly wrong.

My motto with property investment has always been: keep it simple!

Last word

As with any type of investment, there is no certain or guaranteed way of making money out of property. On the other hand, it has to be said that when you look at newspaper Rich Lists, at least half of the richest people in the world will have made their money out of real estate, one way or another.

And even those whose primary fortune does not come from property will almost certainly have invested a significant amount of their wealth in property. This tells you that there is a lot of money to be made from property. There always has been and there always will be.

So how can you maximize your chances of joining the property investment bonanza?

First of all, you not only have to have a definite 'feel' for property, but also be prepared to take on the responsibility of caring for bricks and mortar. One friend who invests in the stock market told me he would not want to have to be responsible for four or five ceilings falling down, ten tenants not paying rent and being in another country when the roof on one of his properties fell in.

Nobody wants these things to happen, but the difference between the successful and the unsuccessful property investor is that the successful ones know they can handle such events. If the whole thing simply terrifies you, then you may be advised to leave property investment alone.

You also have to be able to give it time. It takes more time and effort to invest successfully in property than in stocks and shares, and you have to be prepared to put in this effort. Any effort you expend in investing in the UK has to be doubled and tripled for successful investment overseas. And the more unknown or 'emerging' the market, the more effort you have to put in. Never rely on hype or marketing coming from those wanting to sell you a very expensive product. Do your own research, and then see whether your results match those of the developer.

I would say also that in order to make money from property, you really have to enjoy every aspect of the process. You have to actively enjoy viewing places, doing the number-crunching and also look forward to decorating, furnishing and marketing your properties. You have to get a buzz from it all – even when it goes wrong. You have to look forward to putting things right, rather than wringing your hands in despair.

Although I am a complete dumbo when it comes to numbers and figures, funnily enough this doesn't apply when I am working out figures when considering whether to buy, sell or rent property. Suddenly, my number-blindness leaves me, and everything becomes crystal clear.

The more research you put in, the more you are prepared to be hands-on, the less likely you are to make a very expensive mistake.

In my life, I have made very many mistakes over all kinds of things but looking back, I find I have made very few mistakes with property. This is because I have only bought after undertaking extensive research. And then, even after I have bought, I continue doing my research, to see if I have done the right thing, or could do better.

For instance, I bought a holiday flat on the south coast apparently on impulse. But talking to a friend about it years later, I realized I had actually put a great deal of research into the purchase. Before buying, I had investigated neighbouring towns and resorts, thought hard about the pros and cons of each and before buying, drew up a blueprint of my ideal purchase.

And then, after buying, I continued to investigate, to make sure I had done the right thing. And I still investigate, by viewing every new development, making forays into neighbouring areas to see if there is something better for me to buy, and making sure I keep thoroughly up to date with all small shifts in the market.

The result is that there are very few developments, very few properties, in West or East Sussex that I don't get to know about. And I keep expanding my area of expertise. I now know about investing in Devon, for instance, and I have also investigated Hampshire.

Wherever I bought, it would be the same story. At the time of writing, I would not feel happy about buying in Leeds, or Manchester, because they are too far away from where I live and it would be difficult for me to be there long enough to get an accurate feel for the places. But I can always investigate a neighbouring town or area to my own.

There are always very many things you can't control, so you have to keep on top of an ever-changing market as best you can.

For instance, my apartment is on the seafront. Now, I can control how I present the interior and it is up to me whether to sell or keep the place on. But even I cannot control what the sea does, or what damage the sea might do to my property. I have to accept that there are more hazards from being on water than from being inland, but know there is a special magic about being on water. Therefore, I have to sum up the pros and cons of this location, bearing in mind that all properties, all locations, have a fatal flaw. There is nothing that is perfect from every angle.

It also helps to have good taste, and to keep your taste honed and up to date by viewing the show homes of new developments, keeping an eye on all the magazines and looking at the current makeover shows on television. This enables you to be aware of how things might be changing, and know what's going on. One interior design friend says she works on a five-year timescale. When she designs a place, she can feel confident that it will look attractive and up to date for at least five years, after which it may well start to look dated. But she cannot plan an interior that will never date – that is impossible, she says.

The décor of properties abroad also dates. It is tempting to imagine that an Italian interior, or Spanish interior, is timeless, unlike a UK interior. But this is not true; nowadays, their ideas change as rapidly as anybody else's – and a Spanish villa with a tired, seventies look could be difficult to sell or rent.

You should also read the business pages of newspapers to keep up to date with interest rates, exchange rates, mortgage deals, bank account deals and investment opportunities. Some people are more interested in interior design, others more naturally turn to business and financial pages. But both aspects count equally, when investing in property.

Yes, it's all an effort but it should be a kind of effortless effort. It should come naturally, just as it comes naturally for sports obsessives to read and watch everything about their sport, even when the performance of certain individuals or teams makes them groan in despair.

Above all, investing in property should be an enjoyable activity. The more you enjoy it, the less likely you are to make terrible mistakes, as with anything else. The more you enjoy cookery, the more likely you are to cook wonderful meals; the more interested you are in fashion, the better you will look.

Property is exactly the same. You have to get a definite buzz out of the whole thing, and you can't mock it up. I like looking at even very nasty properties. They may not all please me, but I still find them interesting.

I wouldn't buy a nasty property, though! Or – at least, I wouldn't buy a property I found nasty. Other people, of course, may give the thumbs up to something I find unattractive.

But to be successful, you have to be confident about what you like and what you don't like – and why. There has to be some kind of chemistry between you and the property, as with people.

When the chemistry works, success will follow.

Appendix: Resources

Chapter 1: Determining the market

Auctions

Andrews and Robertson
Tel: 020 7703 2662
Allsop
Tel: 020 7494 3686
Clive Emson
Tel: 01622 630033

Savills
020 7824 9091
Ward & Partners
Tel: 01662 859999
Essential Information Group
Tel: 0800 298 4747
Web: www.eigroup.co.uk

Chapter 2: Using your own home

Information on property prices from

Net-houseprices.com
Mypropertyvalue.co.uk
Landregistry.com (England and Wales only)
Ros.gov.uk(Scotland)
Hometrack.co.uk

Rightmove.co.uk
Propertybroker.com
UpMyStreet.com
Neighbourhood.statistics.gov.uk
(Note: only the official government sites are free)

Leasehold advice

The Leasehold Advisory Group
www.leaseholdadvice.co.uk

Brighton, Hove and District Leaseholders' Association
Cornerstone Community Centre
Church Road
Hove BN3 3FL

Information line: 01273 705432
Web: www.leaseadvice.org
(This is a voluntary organization which holds drop-in clinics and
can also give telephone advice on leasehold problems)

Lease
The Leasehold Advisory Service
70 –74 City Road
London EC1Y 2BJ
Tel: 020 7490 9580
E-mail: info@lease-advice.org
(Government organization which gives advice on Leasehold
Valuation Tribunals and other leasehold matters)

Self-build

*SelfBuild and Design Mag*azine
Tel: 01283 742970
Web: www.plotbrowser.com

BuildIt Magazine
TrinityMirror Business
Tel: 020 7772 8300

Advice on self-build

Primelocation.com

Customs and Excise (advice on self-build VAT matters)
0845 0109000

Homebuilding and Renovating Show
Tel: 0870 010 9031
Web: www.homebuildingshow.co.uk

For film and TV locations

www.envenio.com
Tel: 020 7534 5757

Advice on inheritance tax

www.thisismoney.co.uk/inheritancetax

Islamic mortgages

Ahli United Bank
Property Finance
Tel: 0800 783 3323

HSBC – Home Finance
0800 587 7786

Islamic Bank of Britain
0845 606 0786

Lloyds TSB
0845 600 7786

Book

Hodgkinson, Liz (2004) *The Complete Guide to Renovating and Improving your Property*, Kogan Page, London

Chapter 3: Buy-to-let

Mortgages

Landlord Mortgages
Web: www.lml.co.uk

www.mortgageadvicebureau.com

Landlord Action

Evicting troublesome tenants quickly

Landlord Action, Ltd
Concorde House
Granville Place
London NW7 3SA
Tel: 0870 765 2005
Web: www.landlordaction.co.uk

Southern Private Landlords' Association
Tel: 01273 600847
Helpline: 01273 600747
Web: www.spla.co.uk

National Landlords' Association
78 Tachbrook Street
London SW1V 2NA
Tel: 020 7828 2445
Web: www.landlords.org.uk

National Federation of Residential Landlords
PO Box 11107
London SW15 6ZE
Tel: 0845 456 0357
E-mail: info@nfrl.org.uk

Inside Track Seminars Ltd
3rd Floor, Surrey House
34 Eden Street
Kingston Upon Thames KT1 1ER
Tel: 0208 541 2900
Web: www.insidetrack.co.uk

Instant Access Properties, Ltd
1 Grove Crescent
Kingston Upon Thames KT1 2DD
Tel: 020 8546 4277
Web: www.iaprops.com

City Trading Post Ltd
Godliman House
21 Godliman Street
London EC4V 5BD
Web: www.citytradingpost.co.uk
(investment properties in the UK and overseas)

Investment Property Portfolio Services
Tel: 020 8213 5222
Web: www.ipps-property.com

Buy-to-let.com
Independent Property Consultants
The Business Village
3–9 Broomhill Road
London SW18 4QJ
Tel: 08707 454601
E-mail: info@buy-to-let.com

Student properties

Bournston Student Homes
Tel: 0115 952 4960
Web: www.bournston.co.uk

Offplan investment

Urbanlogic
Fourth Floor
Fourways House
57 Hilton Street
Manchester M1 2EJ
Tel: 0161 236 5505
E-mail: guyd@urban-logic.co.uk

Book

Hodgkinson, Liz (2005) *The Complete Guide to Letting Property*, 5th
edn, Kogan Page, London

ARLA (Association of Residential Letting Agents)
Tel: 0845 345572
Web: www.arla.co.uk
(Useful information for landlords)

Chapter 4: Developing property

First-time buyers

Web: ukfirstimebuyer.com

New Homes Direct
Offplan and new homes from developers
Tel: 0870 432 0790
E-mail: developer-sales@new-homes-direct.com

Buying land

United Land Holdings plc
Tel: 01962 865000

Land Investment Association
Tel: 0845 1249857
E-mail: enquiries@landinvestmentassociation.com

Hayden James Land Acquisitions
Tel: 0870 8080 118
Web: www.haydenjames.co.uk

European Land Sales
Freepost NAT7984
98 Stadium Street
London SW10 OBR
Tel: 020 7242 4242
Web: www.europeanlandsales.com

Strategic land investment

Part Exchange Properties for Developers
Tel: 0870 420 4131
Web: movewithus.co.uk

Listed Heritage Magazine
Listed Property Owners' Club
Lower Dane
Hartlip
Kent ME9 7TB
Tel: 01795 844939
E-mail: info@lpoc.co.uk
Web: www.lpoc.co.uk

Ground rent and freehold investments

Information from:
Andrews and Robertson
Web: www.a-r.co.uk

Chapter 5: Holiday lets

Park and Holiday Homes
Monthly newsstand magazine
Information: www.magazine-group.co.uk

Marsdens Cottage Holidays (Devon only)
2 The Square
Braunton, North Devon EX33 2JB
Tel: 01271 813777
E-mail: holidays@marsdens.co.uk

VisitBritain guide to self-catering accommodation:
Tel: 020 8846 9000
Web: www.visitbritain.com

Park Homes
Tel: 0800 138 0053
Web: www.park-resorts.com/cmc

British Holiday and Home Park Association
PO Box 28249
Edinburgh EH9 2YZ
Web: www.ukparks.com

Chapter 6: Commercial property

Mortgages for Business
Tel: 0845 345 6788
Web: www.mortgagesforbusiness.co.uk
(mortgages for commercial and property development)

Also:
www.mortgages4commercial.co.uk
www.cpfconsultancy.co.uk
www.generalfinancecentre.co.uk
www.freshcommercial.co.uk

Assetz Ltd, 251 London Road, Stockport, Cheshire SK7 4PL
Tel: 0161 456 4000
WEB: www.assetz.co.uk
E-mail: enquiry@assetz.co.uk

The Guide to Commercial Property Investment 2005
Published by Property Investor News
Tel: 0208 906 7772

Chapter 7: Setting up a B&B

Bed and Breakfast News
Tel: 01565 65283
E-mail: mail@bandbnews.co.uk
Web: www.bandbnews.co.uk
(Monthly subscription magazine, also members-only website.
Contains ads for buying and selling B&Bs)

VisitBritain
0208 563 3000
Publishes *The Pink Booklet*: legislation advice on B&Bs

Finance:
Cumberland Building Society
Tel: 01228 403135

Walbrook Commercial Finance, Ltd
Tel: 0800 7312967

Supplies

Out of Eden
Tel: 01768 372 939
Web: outofeden.co.uk

Bed and breakfast insurance

JW Group
7 Market Street, Galashiels TD1 3AD
Tel: 01896 758 371

Chapter 8: Buying property abroad

Hodgkinson, Liz (2005) *The Complete Guide to Buying Property Abroad*, 4th edn, Kogan Page, London

General information on buying property abroad
Exhibitions

Homes Overseas Exhibitions (information line 020 7939 9852)
Web: www.international-homes.com

The Property Investor Show
Information: www.propertyinvestor.co.uk

Seminars about buying abroad

John Howell and Co.
The Old Glass Works
22 Endell Street
London XC2H 9AD
Tel: 020 7420 0400
Web: www.europelaw.com

www.fopdac.com
The official website of the Federation of Overseas Property
Developers has factsheets you can download for each country.

Information on mortgages and investments in France, Spain,
Southern Cyprus: Assetz Ltd, 251 London Road, Stockport,
Cheshire SK7 4PL
Tel: 0161 456 4000
Web: www.assetz.co.uk/investors
E-mail: investors@assetz.co.uk

Country Properties Overseas Department
41 High Street, Baldock, Herts SG7 6BG
Tel: 01462 895122
E-mail: overseas@country-properties.co.uk

Overseas Property Investments
Princess House
Princess Way
Swansea SAT 3LW
Tel: 0800 180 4544
E-mail: enquiries@opiuk.com
Web: www.opiuk.com

Auswest Property Group
Australian investments
Web: www.auswestpropertygroup.com
Dubai investments
Key2Dubai
Web: www.key2dubai.co.uk

World Property Centre
Web: www.worldpropertycentre.com
Cyprus investments
Web: www.cybarco.com

Portugal investments

Algarve Retreats
Tel: 0870 742 8100
Web: www.algarve-retreats.co.uk

Chapter 9: SIPPs

SIPPs advisers

SAS Hartley, Ltd
PO Box 1198
Bristol BS99 2QZ
Web: www.hartleysas.co.uk

Assetz:
Tel: 0161 456 4000
Web: www.assetz.co.uk

Region by region directory

Bulgaria

BULGARIAN DREAMS

Bulgarian Dreams is a UK firm based in the City of London that specialises in Bulgarian real estate. The market leader in its field, the company has been providing purchasers with the very best in Bulgarian properties for over 3 years.

Bulgaria was recently voted one of the most desirable new destinations for holidaymakers and is also perceived to be one of the premier investment countries in the world. As the levels of development and interest in Bulgarian property have increased, Bulgarian Dreams has capitalised on this and offers a simple yet highly professional introduction to the market.

Bulgarian Dreams was founded in 2002 by Robert Jenkin and Maria Georgieva and now employs over 35 people worldwide. At that time there were no companies able to help people purchase property in Bulgaria from abroad. Combining Maria's knowledge and contacts in the Bulgarian property market and Robert's skills in managing investment, Bulgarian Dreams was formed

In early 2004 the flagship Moorgate offices in London were opened and Bulgarian Dreams continued to expand, providing properties throughout through Bulgaria from the capital Sofia, to ski resorts like Bansko or the stretch of glorious Black Sea coastline.

The company was recently presented with a coveted Bentley International Property Award for 'Best Bulgarian Estate Agent 2005', the second consecutive year that the company has been awarded the accolade and is now expanding its office base into Miami, Dubai and Frankfurt.

Properties in Bulgaria offer incomparable value for money and the market is becoming increasingly sophisticated and stable. The general forecast is that property values in Bulgaria will continue to increase at a double-digit rate because of a rapidly developing mortgage lending market and increasing foreign direct investment in real estate.

The real estate market in Bulgaria is, after ten years of transition from communism to a functioning market economy, now starting to approach the conditions that already exist within more developed countries. As the country is now set for membership in the EU in 2007, the prospects for investors and owner occupiers alike just gets more appealing.

Potential purchasers and investors are increasingly turning to new markets to find the rental yields and capital growth that make financial sense. The market in the UK, along with the more traditional overseas property markets of Spain, France and Italy, have all seen large price increases and many purchasers are being priced out of the market.

Bulgarian Dreams is seeing capital growth of 15-20% with rental yields varying from 7-10% per annum. As the Bulgarian market stabilises, the environment for investment will continue to improve and as Channel 4's *A Place in the Sun* stated, Bulgaria offers "excellent value for money for foreign investors." Another huge advantage to the Bulgarian property market is that the country has very strong property rights. Compared to other popular European countries such as Cyprus and Croatia, Bulgaria has a much more stable and defined ownership system.

Having seen property prices increase rapidly in new EU member states, experts are predicting a similar growth for the 2007 entrants.

The upgrading of Bulgaria's tourism infrastructure is one of the highest priorities of the Ministry of Trade and Tourism and the Government itself, chiefly for its potential in generating hard currency revenues. Currently the main tourist areas are the ski resorts well known to Europeans and the Black Sea beach resorts long popular with East Europeans. In 2001 nearly 3 million tourists visited Bulgaria. This was up by 17% on the previous year and 2002 showed a further 10% rise on this figure.

Not only are the developments marketed by Bulgarian Dreams perfect for potential purchasers looking to benefit from a lifestyle away from home, but the Company also provides a full property management system. Bulgarian Dreams will, if the purchaser desires, furnish the homes with up to date interior appliances and fully manage rental agreements.

Two developments that highlight the quality of product available through Bulgarian Dreams are Windows to Paradise and The Orchard.

Windows To Paradise is a select development of studio, one and two bedroom apartments and penthouses situated just above the waterfront with 85% of the properties enjoying sea views. The scheme is located in the popular and emerging area of Balchik, just a short drive from the coastal town of Varna.

The exclusive scheme will benefit from the Gary Player golf course that is being created adjacent to Windows To Paradise and with a new marina also being incorporated, every apartment at the development will enjoy views over the sea, the golf course or the marina.

Bulgarian Dreams and world-renowned property development company, Manhattan Loft Corporation, have come together to launch Bulgaria's most exclusive and chic new development to date, The Orchard in Bansko.

The development is just a five minute walk from the primary ski lifts and offers a level of living above any other new build development in the country. Incorporated within the scheme will be 500 apartments, an ice rink, a luxury health spa, bar and restaurants providing a room service option.

There will be no better way to relax than in the 450 sq m lobby with its stunning glass atrium, generous lounge areas and roaring log fire. Residents will be able to enjoy the warmth and relaxation of the lobby while taking in the stunning views of the snow capped mountains and landscaped gardens.

For further information on any of the exclusive developments currently being marketed by Bulgarian Dreams, please contact, Tel: **+44 (0) 20 7614 1240** or visit **www.bulgariandreams.com**

Cyprus

Overseas Sun Homes is a UK based overseas property sales company that has links with property developers in many locations. Cyprus is one of the primary locations, with a wide range of property available for purchase on the west coast (in the areas of Paphos, Limassol and Polis), the east coast (Larnaca, Ammochosta and Famagusta) and Nicosia.

With its military links and legal and financial systems based on the British models, Cyprus is a logical location for the British buyer. Widespread use of English and driving on the left hand side of the road gives the country a feel of home. It's almost Britain in the sun! It's this sense of familiarity and comfort that has seen the country rise in popularity as a second home and retirement destination.

Overseas Sun Homes is able to give the prospective buyer a choice of over 50 quality developments on the south of the island, with the emphasis being on new homes. If you are looking for a property that can be moved into straight away, then there is a range of key-ready new properties and resale properties to choose from, with prices starting as low as £65,000.

Steve Bickerton, the proprietor of the company is pleased to be able provide his clients with a straightforward service that allows them to stay in control of how they go about buying their property.

"Some years ago when I first bought abroad, I found that there was a desire on the part of the agents with whom I was dealing, to be in control of the client from the first contact, right through to signing the contracts on the new home," said Steve.

"Whilst I appreciate the wish to stay in control from a business perspective, too much control can leave a client with the feeling that they are being pushed towards a purchase rather than being guided in their search for a new lifestyle. With that in mind, there's no pressure from us to get them to decide on a location, no pressure to get on a plane and certainly no pressure to buy."

"We like to think of ourselves as being able to provide the client with the information that they need to make an informed buying decision and, at the same time, to be with them when they need us. So that we don't fall into the trap of feeling that we have to 'get our money back' from subsidised inspection trips, as happens elsewhere, we ask the client to book a holiday in their chosen destination and then we'll meet up with them on their terms and show them around, when they want us to. Sometimes I'll make the trip myself, on other occasions it will be one of our local affiliates who will be on hand."

"We'll help with introductions to specialist mortgage advisors, currency brokers, banks and solicitors, all of whom are completely independent of us. Once the purchase has been made we'll stay in touch at least until the keys are handed over. How our relationship develops beyond that point is entirely up to the client – we'll be there whenever they want us to be."

Overseas Sun Homes has a comprehensive website at which you can look through its portfolio of properties. It can be found at **www.overseassunhomes.com** Alternatively they can be contacted on Freephone **0800 298 9243** or by email at **info@overseassunhomes.com** Whatever your choice of property in Cyprus, whether it's for investment, for holidays or for retirement, Overseas Sun Homes will be pleased to guide you.

J&JA property services

"a comprehensive service for today's overseas property investor"

J&JA property services offers two hot destinations, (and we're not talking just weather and beautiful beaches!) Two dazzling sun locations, both brimming with excellent investment opportunities, both ideal locations and both with their own unique attractions.

J&JA property services, a property services company based in Cyprus, offers a free property search facility and specialist advice on all aspects of the Southern Cyprus and Dubai property markets. Offering personalised practical solutions to our clients' property needs, we are unrivalled in our honest and down to earth approach to their expectations and requests. In addition to our unique composed approach in sourcing the right property for our clients, we are on hand 7 days a week, 52 weeks a year to offer impartial advice and information before, during and long after their purchase.

Our investment team have clear concise knowledge on the best investment opportunities Southern Cyprus and Dubai have to offer. Other matters in which we are able to assist our clients range from relocation issues, banking, car purchase, immigration matters, pension and tax matters, property management, in fact anything in relation to your investing and/or living in Southern Cyprus or Dubai.

New EU member, Southern Cyprus, is the third largest Mediterranean island and is strategically located at the crossroads of Europe, Asia and Africa. A legendary island basking in year round sunshine, Cyprus offers:

- Low crime rate
- High standard of living
- Excellent quality infrastructure
- Established stable market which offers a very high growth opportunity
- Year round tourism – ensuring excellent letting potential
- Strong re-sell market
- Attractive finance options
- Attractive tax incentives
- Banking and legal systems based on the English methods

Southern Cyprus is fast becoming the hottest sun investment location in Europe and the government's recently announced ambitious investment plans to capitalise on its strategic geographical location between the Middle East and Europe are making it even more appealing.

Dubai: the city of the future. The second largest of seven members of the United Arab Emirates, is a city that has risen from the sands at an astronomical rate to be labelled as the most exciting city in the world. Dubai's rulers have set about creating a city that very few modern cities can compare to. Development in Dubai is attracting world attention with residential, leisure and business facilities exceeding all expectations. The world's finest architects have been called upon to design buildings with amazing diversity and as a result Dubai is now home to some of the most impressive buildings the world over. Home to such incredible developments as the Palm Jumeirah, considered to be the eighth wonder of the world, Dubai has become one of the hottest investment spots of the world and just some of its offerings are:

- Year round sunshine
- One of the safest cities in the world
- Zero property and income tax
- Truly cosmopolitan community
- High standard of living
- Attractive payment terms
- Low cost of living
- Year round tourism – ensuring excellent letting potential
- Excellent capital growth potential
- Superb infrastructure (constantly being added to)

With property prices starting from £50,000 in Southern Cyprus and £80,000 in Dubai, now is the time to invest.

Both markets are witnessing strong capital growth, and both locations are year round markets attracting strong rental yields currently around 8%–10% per annum. In the more established market of Cyprus, a long time favourite with English buyers, house prices have trebled since 2000, and rose by 18% in 2004 alone. Cyprus will adopt the Euro currency in 2008, and in preparation for this already the cost of borrowing is falling which will further fuel an increase in property prices.

Dubai speaks for itself in that many newly released properties have a waiting list of potential buyers! Dubai is set to become one of the most exciting cities in the world incorporating such facilities as Dubailand, which, it is predicted, will dwarf Florida's Disneyworld and what will be one of the most exciting tourism, entertainment and leisure areas the world has ever seen. With world-class golf resorts, horse race venues including the Dubai Gold Cup, tax free shopping making Dubai a shopper's paradise plus a whole lot more, it is no wonder why property prices are on the increase.

Since our inception, we have consistently met the changing needs of our clients by being progressive, creative and innovative. Today, we continue to meet that challenge. J&JA's continued commitment to the needs, interests and expectations of our existing and future clients will assure we keep our goals, serving you better...

Julie Aristidou
Director
J&JA property services ltd
PO Box 52525
4065 Yermasoyia
Limassol, Cyprus

property services ltd

J&JA

Florida

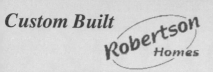

INVESTMENT IN FLORIDA
IS STILL A GOOD DEAL

Florida is most famous for Disney, Universal, numerous other attractions and of course the all year round climate. However, Florida along with California and Texas will see nearly half of the US population growth between now and 2030. With a depth of industry including of course leisure together with computer software, film and industry, the property market is tipped to continue a steady growth over the coming years and one has to remember with the influx of various nationalities, the market is a truly international market.

With this in mind, there are options to invest in the Florida market including the traditional short-term holiday home as well as long-term rentals, which is more akin to the normal buy to let market.

PARSON International, a high street estate agency based in the UK has a whole range of homes available from Condos and Hotel Condos to Town Homes and Detached Pool Homes. To provide an income with the least input in letting yourself, one of the up and coming areas for investment are hotel condos. These have already been very popular in areas like Miami and are now being developed in the International Drive area of Orlando. With prices starting in the low $200's and run by well known Hotel flags, these are excellent investments for the investor looking for no participation but with the ability to use oneself.

There are of course the long-term rentals including condominium conversions, usually no more than 10 years old, situated in premium locations, and providing an instant income and with projected annual appreciation. One particular development, Bermuda Dunes, located in the affluent area of Metro West, Orlando is on a golf course with an excellent specification, a good return and starting from the low $200's.

There are some superb detached pool home communities including Highgate Park on Davenport, 3 bedroom pool homes starting at $320,000, 4 bedroom detached homes at Chelsea's Landing starting at $349,000 further down the US27 and Moniticelli, Bridgeford Crossing with lakeside views, Calabay Parc at Tower Lakes, Villas Sorrento and Vizcay, also on US27 near the junction with I-4.

PARSON International, led by Managing Director, Kevin Parson an owner of homes in Florida himself, can offer advice as buyers agents on a whole different array of subjects including the buying process, bank accounts, management and letting of homes, visas, furniture packs, the right home to suit your budget and your objectives. As members of the National Association of Estate Agents, you can be sure of ethical, professional advice from an owner's perspective rather than a salesman's! Kevin Parson has been in the property business for almost 30 years, personally buying and selling his own portfolio as well as running his own business and multiple office area for a large corporate agency.

As well as selling homes in Florida, PARSON International also sells homes in the UK and mainland Spain. They have 2 offices in the UK together with offices in Orlando and the Costa Blanca, a truly international service.

For further information call Kevin Parson on **01379 650680**, **www.parson-international.com**

France

PIERCE & ELLIOTT
Real Estate

PIERCE & ELLIOTT REAL ESTATE is a highly professional developer and construction company that offers excellent service to clients interested in new built quality houses or holiday homes.

The Dutch established company with offices in Amsterdam and Carcassonne has a wide range of projects at hand in the regions of the Languedoc-Roussillon, Midi-Pyrénées and the Dordogne. The projects are distinct and vary in size, house type, price and al present various facilities. The types of projects that are offered for sale vary from individual villas to apartments, from holiday resorts to renovation projects. Also available are Domains of old farmhouses and "chateaux" that have either been constructed or are currently under construction. All types of clients with low and higher budgets will be proudly served. The projects are wide spread over the regions and can be found along the coast, in the mountains, in the midst of beautiful forests and some projects are even located inland in an astonishing hilly countryside within the vineyards. Most sites are dotted with stunning views over the Mediterranean or Pyrenees.

France is deservedly the most popular and preferred holiday destination in the world, and it is the sheer variety and timeless beauty of the country that make French holidays so appealing. Especially the Languedoc-Roussillon is magnificent as it is one of France's best keep secrets. It also offers the most diverse selection of weather as it is possible to ski and sunbathe on the same day in different places. Undiscovered, this gorgeous area has everything to entertain and inform the vacationer. Stretching in an arc west of the Rhone and along the Mediterranean to the Pyrenees, the countryside offers extensive contrasts in scenic beauty. The tranquil environment ever-changes from rugged river gorges, rolling hillsides, lush vineyards, fishing ports, to white sandy beaches, and lagoons. Its beautiful wide sandy coastline stretches for hundreds of kilometres towards the Spanish border with centuries-old beautiful villages which offer great value in elite and superb wine and cuisine, castles, churches, canals, Roman ruins, and walled cities providing intrigue. Combine that with the unspoilt ski possibilities in the Pyrenees and the amazing diversity of landscape, add a touch of some unique Spanish influenced cuisine, some great cities (Carcassonne) and you end up with a heady mix. Affordable pleasure and countless leisure possibilities are the keywords! Oops and…wine of course because the Languedoc Roussillon produces rich red wine in abundance and has the largest production of any area in Europe.

Since the start of their activities in France years ago, the regions, where the projects of Pierce & Elliott Real Estate are developed, have been appraised substantially.

Of course France, and especially the South, was already renowned for its climate, its history, its breathtaking scenery, its cuisine and its historical and cultural sights and is therefore well esteemed. However demographic changes, the increase in low cost air travel from numerous airports in the UK to smaller cities in France make many areas within easy reach for a weekend. The excellent accessibility by both car and TGV and the stressful life in the Northern European countries, together with the presentation of the Euro all have contributed in making these regions prevailing.

Other reasons that account for the eminence of these regions are the modest prices in terms of real estate, since one can still look for that hidden gem that is both affordable and a great investment for the future. The Côte d'Azur on the other hand is more expensive crowded and pretentious.

Last but no least the spending power of the North European clients has dramatically increased by the appraisal of their own houses in their home countries, accelerated by an overall low interest rate.

The past five years real estate in France has met a capital grow of substantial percentages. In the Languedoc-Roussillon and the Dordogne regions this was even over 10% per annum and thus much higher in comparison to other French regions.

Because Pierce & Elliott Real Estate, as a developer covers the whole purchase process meaning from actually buying the terrain to delivering the houses turnkey at finishing, they can offer attractive selling prices to clients, but also attractive investment proposals to investors.

At various stages investors can even be a partner with Pierce & Elliott Real Estate. At first, through the acquisition of land or a project and further at the level of the development and at the end on completion of the project, when the houses or projects have been finished. Investors have already successfully joined Pierce & Elliott Real Estate in various projects at various stages. All the investment projects that have been launched and finalised by Pierce & Elliott Real Estate so far, have had a return on investment above expectation.

Initial investors can be honoured with attractive remunerations. For those who want to buy a villa, holiday house or chalet Pierce & Elliott Real Estate offers a guaranteed annual income that is very much based upon the risk an investor likes to take.

Basically, there are two components regarding income out of investment in real estate:

1. Cash return from renting out;
2. Capital growth.

Pierce & Elliott Real Estate has investment schemes that meet these two components.

Firstly the client and Pierce & Elliott Real Estate sign a contract whereby is agreed to sell the house after five years.

The investor's income consists of an annual guaranteed income of 4% net. This means that all costs relating to the rental, such as maintenance, running costs, local taxes, etc. will be borne by Pierce & Elliott Real Estate. The investor receives verily 4% net. After five years the investor is free, thus not obliged, to sell the house and the capital gain is his. With an increase of 10% per annum, the return on the investment will be around 12.5% per annum. In this percentage the capital gain tax has already been excluded!

Secondly the contract allows the investor to have a guaranteed income of 6% net. In this case the capital growth after five years, after the property has been sold, will be split between the investor and Pierce & Elliott Real Estate. The overall return on investment in this scheme is around 10.5%. This is less speculative than the first possibility.

Thirdly and most secure option, is that the investor receives a net guarantee of 8%. After five years the property will be sold and the capital gain is a benefit for Pierce & Elliott Real Estate.

In the cited proposals the investor can make a choice from an insecure possibility (4%) to the most secure possibility (8%).

Of course if the investor desires to use bank loans to invest in properties, he can by means of leverage increase the return on his own part of the investment. Let's suppose that in all proposals, he will use a 50% loan at a rate of 5% (most mortgages are lower) the returns on own investments will be over 20%, over 16% and over 11%. These percentages will be higher in case the mortgage is a higher percentage of the investment.

To assure these schemes of investment Pierce & Elliott Real Estate has its own renting company, SARL Pierce & Elliott Loisirs that takes care of the rental, maintenance and key management. For investments in holiday resorts, Pierce & Elliott Real Estate has made arrangements with major international operating holiday rental companies that give mostly 4% or 5% (bank) guarantees on the rent.

In the above investment proposals, the investor has bought a complete house including furniture. However, one other good advantage of Pierce & Elliot Real Estate is that minor investment participations are possible meaning you can invest a small amount of money and still benefit from a fully proof guarantee. In that case the investor will be part of a SCI (Société Civil Immobilière). This is a sort of personal private company. The SCI, which contains several individuals, purchases a house and signs up a contract as stated above. In the SCI various investors with various amounts can be assembled. For instance four investors create a SCI and purchase together a house including furniture for €200,000. Their individual investment is €40,000, €50,000, €30,000 and €80,000. Pro rata to their investment, they are entitled to the same return on the investment, following the investment proposals, mentioned earlier.

Under all circumstances the investors/owners can make use of their own house, if they wish.

If this is desirable, the rent guarantees will be recalculated, although in off seasons the effects of this recalculation will be minimal. In this construction of investment the underlying security, namely the house, is even growing because of the capital growth.

As one can conclude Pierce & Elliott Real Estate offers a wide variety of potential investment vehicles with full securities, each with high returns of investment. It is important to know that that the proposals are flexible and can be adapted to the market situation during and/or at the end of the contractual period. It is also flexible in terms of self-use of the property.

Pierce & Elliott Real Estate also offers various projects with leaseback schemes.

The new changes in the pension legislation, allowing SIPPs (Self Invested Private Pensions) to invest *and* abroad *and* in the leisure market can be an extra incentive to boost the English interest to invest in French Property. For SIPPs the quoted investment schemes can be a very attractive alternative.

Other than the construction of houses, Pierce & Elliott Real Estate provides other services to clients relating to the property. These services include legal and tax counsel, insurance, mortgages, maintenance and key management. In addition Pierce & Elliott Real Estate offers bed & breakfast in the sumptuous Château Le Liet for its clients. For most of these services Pierce & Elliott Real Estate collaborates closely with well known and well established international professionals. Resale through our real estate agencies is another service.

Pierce & Elliott Real Estate has momentarily various projects under construction. Currently for sale are apartments in Canet-Plage (near Perpignan), individual houses in the Carcassonne area, chalets and apartments in the Pyrenees, holiday resorts in the departments Pyrenees-Orientales and Dordogne. For sale are also renovation projects in the Aude department and in Pennautier (at 7km from Carcassonne) where Pierce & Elliott's head office in France is situated.

You can see the projects at hand and the newest development on their website **www.pierce-elliott.nl**

For further information you can contact:
Mr. Martin Sint of Pierce & Elliott Real Estate in Amsterdam
The Netherlands
Tel: **0031 20 6205841**
Fax: **0031 20 6205867**
Email: **martin@pierce-elliott.nl**

St. Eutrope

- Département du Lot et Garonne
- 91 new holiday bungalows
- Habitable surfaces from 38 m² to 80 m²
- Minimum 1 bedroom
- Communal facilities
- 30 minutes from Bergerac
- Leaseback possibilities
- Prices from € 110,000 all in

Malibu

- Département des Pyrénées-Orientales
- 73 new apartments
- Habitable surfaces from 41 m² to 63 m²
- Minimum 1 bedroom
- Communal facilities
- Restaurant and bar
- Leaseback possibilities
- Prices from € 139,500 all in

Domaine Font Couvert

- Département de l'Aude
- 11 terraced renovated houses
- Habitable surfaces from 75 m² to 141 m²
- Minimum 2 bedrooms
- Communal facilities
- 25 minutes from Carcassonne
- Prices from € 169,500 all in

Coming up

In the department Ariège directly at the bedding of a large mountain lake at 30 minutes from the ski resorts and 1 hour drive from Carcassonne we will develop a holiday resort with 120 chalets. Prices approximately € 150,000 all in.

PIERCE & ELLIOTT
Real Estate

Greece

O'CONNOR PROPERTIES
THE CHANCE FOR A BETTER LIFE

O'Connor Properties, run by Chris and Mary O'Connor has been firmly established over the years with an international clientele.

Chris hails from Liverpool and Mary is an Athenian.

They were previously both language teachers and have always enjoyed and valued human contact.

We are considered to be one of the most experienced and well respected Estate Agents in Greece with a long list of testimonials from satisfied clients, which reflects the high quality of service we offer. Apart from making appearances on the Channel 4 programme in the U.K.

A Place In The Sun, we regularly assist with editorials and advertise in reputable property magazines and newspapers.

What type of properties can I expect to find with O'Connor Properties?

O'Connor Properties has a variety of properties available. From cottages, and Mani tower houses to beachside villas and plots of land for individually designed houses overlooking the sea – there is normally something to suit every taste and budget.

In addition, if you are working within a set budget, then O'Connor Properties will only show you properties that fit within your budget.

If you wish to have a house built, or renovated, O'Connor Properties can introduce you to English speaking architects/civil engineers/contractors, who can build or renovate your "dream" house at a very reasonable price. Their work is indeed exceptional, and combines all the modern facilities and commodities with the unique style of the Peloponnese architecture.

These architects/civil engineers/contractors are all recommended on the strength of recommendation of our clients who used their services and were highly satisfied.

What will O'Connor Properties do for me?

Chris and Mary O'Connor will be very happy to assist you all the way to your very own place in the sun.

Some of the things we'll do for you:
We offer advice on cheap flights and the best way to get here.
Upon request we book you into the kind of accommodation you would like.

We drive you round as many properties and villages as you wish, giving you information on the properties, as well as on the area (history of the area, cultural features etc).

Not only do we help you choose your "dream-property", assist you with all the legal matters and purchasing procedure, but we can also offer you advice on any other matter such as health and house insurance, transportation of your furniture (companies and legal advice), tax return forms, best shops, restaurants, and the "know how" of the area you wish to purchase a property.

I've chosen my house in Greece – now what happens?
You do nothing, your lawyer and our office will do it all.

We can introduce you to English speaking lawyers that can help you through the purchasing procedure, in fact you have to do nothing, they do it all.

This means that the property can be signed over to you in your absence and it is not necessary for you to be present.

Your lawyer will draw a deposit agreement between you and the vendor. He/she will arrange everything else, Greek Inland Revenue, Public Notary, Registry Office etc on your behalf.

Your lawyer will then have the deeds translated into your own language, and post them to you.

Recommendations
There are a great number of highly satisfied clients who will be more than willing to share with you their experience of buying, building or renovating with our company. Their e-mail addresses or telephone numbers are available upon request.

Press releases and T.V. coverage of O'Connor Properties
Homes Overseas July 2005 issue
The Daily Telegraph 17/07/04
The Times 6/6/03 and 2001
World of Property, a 3-page article in the
Homes Overseas April 2003 issue
International Living April 2003, the supplement of
The Evening Standard 3rd October 2001,
as well as many regional Newspapers such as:
The Journal June 16 2001, *The Evening Chronicle* June 19 2001
and others in Liverpool, Newcastle, Manchester, etc.

T.V. coverage:
"A Place In The Sun" Channel 4, September 2004
"The Richard And Judy Show" Channel 4, 2003
"A Place In The Sun" Channel 4, 2002

For more details please contact us:
Chris and Mary O'Connor
O'Connor Properties
Aristomenous and 18, Franzi St.
24100 Kalamata, Greece
W: www.oconnorproperties.gr
E: oconnor@oconnorproperties.gr
T: 0030 27210 96614 F: 0030 27210 96614
M: 0030 6977 524039

O´ CONNOR
PROPERTIES

Hungary

BUDAPEST – A VIBRANT CITY

Budapest is the beautiful, historic and architecturally scenic capital city of Hungary. Joining the EU in May 2004, is just one of the main reasons for buying in this vibrant and exciting city. With both new and classical apartments, there is a wide choice of properties, starting at low prices with the promise of good capital appreciation and average annual yields of 5 to 7%. Indeed, the last eighteen months has seen up to 30% appreciation and with demand still high, there is no indication of this abating. The majority of homes are studios, 1 or 2 bedroom apartments with rental demand high for all types and most areas. There are differing sizes and the largest is not necessarily the best for investment. Bare in mind when coming to resell, consider a parking space, as with most cities, it is at a premium.

The city is divided into districts, with the central districts of 5 and 6 boing the most popular around the business district and along Andrassy Avenue, the Champs Elyseé of Budapest. Districts 8 and 9 give good capital appreciation where during the communist years, little investment was made, whereas now, these areas are being brought up by The 'scruff of its neck' to become a desirable and improved area. Another excellent area is District 13 with its tree lined avenues and with probably one of the best capital appreciation areas. Because of the excellent transportation system, all areas are within 20 minutes of the main areas of the city. If you are looking for reasons to buy in Budapest then just look at the following:

1. Strong Rental Market
2. Low Property prices
3. Lowest Corporate Tax in Central Europe
4. 2 Million Strong City Population
5. Capital Appreciation 20-25% expected 2005
6. Well Developed Legal Framework
7. Budapest is comparatively Underpriced
8. Highest Foreign Direct Investment in E. Europe
9. Stable & Transparent Political Economy
10. Regeneration of this architecturally Beautiful City is underway
11. Five university campus

If you are looking for a sound buy to let investment in Eastern Europe, then look here. You can obtain further information from overseas property specialist Kevin Parson, FNAEA of
PARSON International on **01379 650680**

Mauritius

AIR MAURITIUS NON-STOP TO PARADISE

Air Mauritius flies five times each week non-stop from London Heathrow to the island of Mauritius and carries more travellers to this paradise holiday destination than any other airline. In fact, two out of three British visitors now choose the island's national airline.

From June 2006, the Air Mauritius services will increase to six flights each week and the airline plans to have daily services operational from 2007.

All Air Mauritius flights from London are overnight with a flight time of just under 12 hours. Flying overnight means travellers will be enjoying the white sand beaches and the warm, turquoise blue Indian Ocean just as quickly as possible.

On the London/Mauritius route, Air Mauritius operates modern Airbus A340 aircraft which has a three cabins...First, Business and Economy classes.

The company has recently purchased three additional A340 ER aircraft from Airbus and the first two will be delivered in late 2006 with the third coming into service the following year. The new aircraft will result in a complete cabin refurbishment across the existing A340 fleet and provide an exciting new service for passengers.

On board, travellers can also enjoy just a touch of the welcome and quality of service which makes Mauritius so special. Even the food on board will be an introduction to the tropical cuisine that awaits travellers on arrival.

In addition to the non-stop services, the airline also operates two flights each week from Heathrow via the Seychelles as part of a 'code share' agreement with Air Seychelles. So, travellers wanting to sample two Indian Ocean holiday retreats can take advantage of these additional flights.

In Mauritius, the airline also operates a fleet of helicopters for hotel transfers and sightseeing and Air Mauritius plans to totally revamp the fleet during the course of the next year. The plan is to purchase twin engined equipment which will significantly improve the number of flying hours that are allowed with the current fleet of single engined Bell Ranger helicopters. The new equipment will allow a lifting of some of the current restrictions and result in more flights over sea and built-up areas, plus night flying. This will add considerably to this very popular hotel transfer service and the many sightseeing trips that are now offered to visitors.

So, paradise is well served by Air Mauritius...
non stop flights to the Indian Ocean plus an
exciting service of trips for visitors when they arrive.

Trust Avis to plan your route to property prosperity

When planning a trip to research potential overseas properties, be sure you make the most of your time by arranging car hire in advance. Pre-booking with Avis guarantees you flexibility and freedom to explore from the minute you land. Our Avis representatives may also lead you to some hidden property treasures with their local knowledge!

When you book worldwide with Avis you can be assured of excellent, friendly service and wide choice of reliable vehicles. In Mauritius Avis offers the comfort and familiarity of a Nissan Micra, or the space and practicality of an MPV. Alternatively, make the most of the sun and stunning scenery in a Suzuki Jimny Soft Top.

Driving in Mauritius

Driving is the best way to explore the island and property hot spots. You are free to explore the island's more remote areas with extinct volcanoes, rugged mountains, dense forests and sugar cane plains. Or visit some of the local attractions including numerous top-class golf courses, the beautiful botanical gardens at Pamplemousses, or the Domaine les Pailles where you can see sugar refining and rum distilling.

To book you car whilst in Mauritius, call the local Avis reservation office on **+230 208 1624**.

If you are also visiting the other Indian Ocean Islands you can enjoy Avis car hire in:

- **Madagascar**
  – call the reservation office on: **+261 2022 61812**
- **Seychelles**
  – call the reservation office on: **+248 224511**
- **Reunion Islands**
  – call the reservation office on: **+262 262 421599**

Plan ahead and pre-book
Take advantage of Avis' early booking offers and discounts before you go, visit **www.avis.co.uk** or call Avis reservations on: **0870 60 60 100** (UK). Or contact your nearest Avis location.

Beau Rivage, Mauritius

Sweeping up from the middle of the sea, the magical island of Mauritius is often referred to as the 'Pearl of the Indian Ocean.' Inland its rich and varied landscape rises up in volcanic rocky peaks, cliffs and gorges, and waterfalls dot its lush green interior. Surrounded by beautiful, pristine beaches and dazzling blue sea with teeming underwater marine life, it's easy to see why Mauritius is such a sought after holiday destination.

Set beside a spectacular white sand beach at Belle Mare on the east coast of the island, the renowned 5* Beau Rivage is the flagship property of the Naiade Resorts Hotel Group (**www.naiade.com**). The typical thatched-roof villas and local architecture of this stunning hotel blend subtly into the surrounding environment creating a charming natural haven. All 174 spacious and elegant suites have impressive sea views from their private balcony or terrace.

Guests at Beau Rivage are immediately welcomed into an atmosphere of barefoot luxury, where every comfort is provided for.

Keen to reflect the rich and diverse culture which exists on Mauritius, the team at Beau Rivage has introduced aspects of Africa, India and China throughout the hotel. The island's historic past is celebrated during the week with insights into traditional food, customs, music and dance.

Guests are spoiled for choice when it comes to dining. The main restaurant, Rive Gauche, is subtly re-decorated each day to give an ever-changing atmosphere for evenings. For special occasions, the hotel's gourmet restaurant, Indouchine, has an enviable reputation for fine dining where meals are prepared and cooked according to each guest's tastes. Guests can also now dine casually with their feet in the sand at the Mediterranee, and seafood lovers can sample delicious fresh fish at Langoustine.

In keeping with its local ties, the hotel is the only one on the island to work closely with the Mauritius Art Academy who provides traditional and modern interpretations of the island's mixed heritage in music and dance, lighting and sound, under the velvet blue Mauritian sky. Night birds will love the late night jazz session at the Club Savanne on Thursdays, Fridays and Sundays.

The Spa Aphrodite aims to bring about a balance between body and mind by balancing inner energies. Using Oriental local beauty products and the Gatineau range from Paris, the professional team offers a truly indulgent choice of massage and beauty treatments.

Beau Rivage is as welcoming to families as it is to couples and honeymooners. All suites can easily accommodate two adults and two children, and the renovated kids club, mini-golf, and teenager's games rooms are very popular.

Ideal for weddings, Beau Rivage limits the number of nuptials to ensure they provide a completely personal service. Brides and grooms have tied the knot in the gardens in the gazebo by the lake, on the beach and even in the superb Maharajah Suite.

The perceptive team at Naiade Resorts know what to look for when creating a successful resort hotel. Beau Rivage is one of the most popular 5* properties in Mauritius. The Group also include the atmospheric feng-shui inspired 4* de luxe Legends, romantic 4* Les Pavillons, the ever popular 3* superior Merville Beach and the all-inclusive 3* Le Tropical. Naiade Resorts also own the tiny paradise island of Ile des Deux Cocos, which can be hired privately for weddings, honeymoons or Conference and Incentive groups. More recently the group acquired White Sands Resort & Spa in the Maldives, and Desroches Island Resort in the Seychelles to add to its discerning Indian Ocean portfolio.

Seychelles • Mauritius • Maldives

We have a passion for excellence and our intention is to simply be the best

5th Floor Chaucer House • 13-14 Cork Street • Mayfair • London WIS 3 NS • United Kingdom
Tel : 44 20 7 499 67 77 • Fax : 44 20 7 495 78 77
Email : marketing@naiaderesorts.co.uk • www.naiaderesorts.com

Scotland

Thinking of moving north of the border?

ESPC
SOLICITORS PROPERTY CENTRE

For the widest choice of homes in east central Scotland, visit **www.espc.com**

SELLING PROPERTY IN SCOTLAND

When selling in Scotland, the procedure is somewhat different to that in England, because, in Scotland, in the majority of cases your solicitor will also act as estate agent. The solicitor will therefore both sell the property and deal with the issues of transfer of title. Even if you, however, decide to use a separate estate agent, it is wise to alert your solicitor to the fact that you wish to sell your home, before putting it on the market. This is because the process is usually much faster in Scotland than it is south of the border. Your solicitor will need to make sure your title deeds are in order, check the amount remaining on any existing mortgage you may have, and generally prepare to be ready to deal with offers when received. .

In Scotland, 'offers over' is the most widely used basis for arriving at a selling price, in which the seller hopes to achieve a final price in excess of the quoted figure (upset price). Depending on the desirability of the property, the selling price tends to be between five and 15 per cent over the asking price, although in a very buoyant market, the price premium can be 30 per cent or more.Interested parties may, through their solicitor, submit a 'note of interest' in buying your property. Although not absolutely legally binding it is accepted practice that once a note of interest has been registered you will not accept any offer without giving the others who have noted interest the opportunity to make a bid for the property. Once you receive a few notes of interest, the next step is to set a 'closing date' for offers. Nobody knows what the other offers may be, and while it is most common for sellers to accept the highest offer, it is not always the case.

There is also the 'fixed price' option, where the seller indicates that he will accept the first offer for an exact figure. In any case it is practice in Scotland for offers to be submitted by a solicitor acting on behalf of the purchaser.

Once the seller has accepted an offer verbally, bear in mind that it is not legally binding. Traditionally purchasers get a survey and valuation of the property before submitting an offer but in certain areas the practice has grown of offers being submitted "subject to survey" If the offer has been made "subject to survey" any verbal acceptance will usually indicate that this condition must be withdrawn.

The prospective purchaser will be expected to have the survey carried out as soon as practicable and on the basis that the survey and valuation are satisfactory withdraw the condition that the offer is subject to survey. The seller's solicitor provides the buyer's solicitor with a written qualified acceptance. This is the beginning of the 'missives' – the exchange of formal letters between both parties' solicitors, stipulating price, date of entry, items included in the sale, and a number of additional legal conditions. After the missives have been concluded, there is a binding contract for the seller and the buyer and neither party may pull out without penalty.

The seller's solicitor will then exhibit the titles to the purchaser's solicitor to allow them to identify the nature of any title conditions, will deal with the discharge of any loan security over the property, will obtain necessary searches in the Land Register and from the local authority and generally deal with the detail of ensuring the sale transaction goes smoothly and is achieved by the contractual completion date.

by Lorna Wharton, corporate communication manager ESPC (UK) Ltd
For further information, please contact:
Lorna Wharton/Simon Fairclough
t 0131 624 8888   m 07917 014 090   lorna.wharton@espc.com

Spain

THERE'S STILL SOMETHING SPECIAL ON THE COSTAS

Spain is a country rich in history and culture, and the area in and around the Costa Blanca, Calida and Almeria is no exception. With the cities and towns of Alicante, Murcia, Orihuela, Torrevieja, Cartagena, Elche and La Manga all close by, there is a wealth of museums, galleries, parks and gardens to explore.

Spain too, is the home of Fiestas and almost all year round you will find celebrations of some historical or religious event, accompanied by colourful processions, impressive firework displays and, of course, plenty of eating and drinking.

Buying a new home, especially abroad, is a very important decision, so whether you are looking for a holiday home, investment or permanent residence, it is imperative that you receive sound advice and help from the outset.

When you purchase an overseas home through PARSON International, you can be assured of our expert knowledge, not only in the field of home buying, but also the way of life and legal procedure. With their network of local partners located in the heart of the areas we promote, we can assist and advise before and after you buy, in particular the Costas along the coast of Spain.

Our local partner on the Costa Blanca, as well as having a complete choice of homes along the Costa Blanca, Calida and Almeria, is licensed in Spanish law and will give you the professional advice needed to smooth your path through the complex legalities associated with buying a home in Spain. Our partner will also advise on mortgages, finance, health services, schools, buying a car and property maintenance.

With Spain only around 2 hours flying time away, the area is ideal for the weekend away, holiday or indeed permanent living. With the prospect of capital gains tax being reduced from 35% to 15%, there us a further added incentive to buy here.

As we are an independent, unbiased company, not tied to any one developer or construction company, PARSON International have a large selection of new and re-sale homes to offer including bungalows, villas, apartments, fincas both on the coast and inland.

If you are considering buying a dream home in Spain, make PARSON International your first call on 01379 650680. Alternatively visit our website **www.parson-international.com** for further information and you can also see us advertised on Real Estate TV Sky Channel 250. We also exhibit at major shows throughout the country where our friendly, knowledgeable and experienced team can assist and tell you everything you want to know.

PARSON International
Victoria Road
Diss, Norfolk
01379 650680
www.parson-international.com

Sales of homes in
Spain, Florida, Cyprus, Bulgaria and Hungary

Switzerland

Why SWITZERLAND?

Switzerland's about punctuality, mountains, cheese and watches!

Is it that why Phil Collins, Tina Turner, Roger Moore, Alain Delon, Michael Schumacher, Jackie Stewart, Brian Ecclestone and many others, live in Switzerland? Some say: "No, it is for tax reason only."

A closer survey shows a more complex image. WETAG CONSULTING, the leading real estate agency in Ticino, the southern part of Switzerland, sells every year property worth dozens of millions of Euros to foreigners – up to 75% of its total sales volume. "I always ask our clients why they decided to move here," says Ueli Schnorf, one of the owners of WETAG. "They regularly point out 5 or 6 important factors which gives Switzerland a hard-to-copy edge over other destinations." These are:

1. Diversity and beauty of nature
Indeed, since the mid 1800's Switzerland is ranking uninterrupted amongst the *world's top ten holiday destinations*. It is rare to find within a two or three hours' distance (Switzerland measures roughly 300 x 200 km) Europe's highest mountains with glaciers, and subtropical lakes with palmtrees and bougainvilleas.

2. Security, and general standards of living
Switzerland shows a *low criminal rate. Victimisation risk is amongst the industrialized nation's lowest*. Polls list Zurich, Geneva, Berne at the top of *"World's quality of life"* – *surveys*. No *other population is considering itself happier* than the Swiss[1,2].

Interesting to add here: For more than 100 years now 10-20% of Switzerland's population are foreigners, a quota at least double as high as in any other European nation. Nearly everybody is speaking more than one language; the country's official languages are four (German, French, Italian, Rumantsch)!

3. Health infrastructure
Switzerland's compulsory health system is amongst the world's most expensive, but also the *world's most sophisticated*. Who is carried in emergency to the next hospital can be sure, he is in excellent hands.

4. Political and economical infrastructure
A well founded democracy with several large parties and extensive rights for each citizen make quick changes nearly impossible, thus giving a *high degree of continuity for the individuals* and a feel of stability.

Public service has a long tradition and is working well. Schools, communication services, transport, post, police and justice are efficient and transparent; the famous banking system is maintaining a wide number of branches for locals' needs.

5. Tax law

On a worldwide scale Swiss taxes are ranging in the better midfield but are still *Europe's most attractive*. Most Cantons abolished inheritance and donation tax.

Furthermore there is this Swiss tax specialty attracting wealthy foreigners: Several Swiss Cantons offer to foreigners taking first residence and declaring not to work (but living from their wealth) a attractive fixed yearly flat tax.

* * * * * * * * * *

Welcome to Switzerland? Yes of course, but:

Laws foresee certain restrictions for foreigners wanting to live or to buy property in Switzerland:

Who Intends to stay just for holiday purpose is restricted in buying not more than one property, with a maximum surface of 200sq.m. of net living area, and grounds not exceeding 1000sq.m.

Who wants to take first residence may buy property without restriction, as Swiss citizens can. But he will be subject of approval of residency first. Residence will be granted for working reason (the employer will apply for the permit, confirming the working contract). Independents or persons not intending to work will have to give proof of their financial possibility to maintain themselves.

Since foreigners living in Switzerland are more than a million, the well-known stars - some of them with flat-tax-agreements – are only the much-bespoken peak of an iceberg. It is the above-mentioned bundle of factors that makes the attraction of Switzerland; we may summarize them as "quality of life."

Ueli F. Schnorf, phD., economic historian.

Owner of WETAG CONSULTING Immobiliare, exclusive affiliate of Christie's Great Estates, founding member of EREN (European Real Estate Network), member of RELO.

---

[1]ranking as number 1, 2, 5 for 2003 and 2004 alike, amongst 215 cities worldwide (Mercer Human Resource Consulting's yearly "Quality of Life Report").
[2]"World database of Happiness", R. Veenhoven, State of Nations, Erasmus Univ. Rotterdam.

Turkey

Secrets of
Property Investment

Right Time – Right Place – Right People – Right Action

Searching for a dream home in the sun, a holiday sanctuary and an investment security for your future? – Look no further, Turkey has it all! The crossroads between Europe and Asia, Turkey is a living testimony to its people, culture and a tradition dating back to the dawn of time.

From the Mediterranean to the Bosphorous, the Dardanelles to Noah's Mount Ararat, fabulous coastlines, breathtaking scenery and some of the world's finest beaches are waiting for you to discover. Add a financial index making your pound go much further, a stable government, copper bottomed international ownership laws and you begin to see why so many say:

> **"Turkey is the property Hot Spot that once was Spain."**

With Turkey moving ever closer to full **EEC** membership property prices continue to increase at a rate. The message is clear…The time to move is now.

> **"When others see the boat – you've already missed it"**

Two UK directors took the leap of faith to build villas in Dalyan. Their success spawned a friendship with the Oruc Brothers, Cumali, Ahmet and Ramazan. Marketing man Colin Bentley joined the group and Oruc International was born.

Success is built on a deep rooted knowledge of Anglo-Turkish requirements, years of hands on experience and a commitment to quality and service, Oruc have developed into a One Stop Turkish Property Shop able to answer all your questions and meet your property requirements.

International Property Success Often Comes Down to:

Right Time – Right Place – Right People – Right Action

The Media listing Turkey in the world's top three property hot spots universally agree that the time to invest in Turkish property is now!

It's time to live your dream!… It's your move!
CALL: **0845 166 47 57**   VISIT: **www.orucinternational.com**

Location,
Location, Location

From action-packed beach resorts like Bodrum and Marmaris to the tranquil unspoilt paradise of exquisite coastal villages like Dalyan and millionaire marina towns like Gocek... *Turkey has it all!*

Don't compromise your dream. Take advantage of inspection tours, visit several locations. Listen to advice from respected experts like ORUC, talk to other property owners, weigh the information, complete your research and due diligence then MAKE a decision. Buying your dream home in the sun should be one of life's most exhilarating and rewarding experiences. To make that leap of faith you must MAKE a decision and take ACTION.

New Build or Resale
The structural integrity of Turkish new builds is secured by stringent new government regulations. Great bargains and good quality can also be found in the Re-Sale market. Again thorough research and informed advice will help you make the right decision. Full service companies like Oruc offer structural surveys, advice and costs on alterations, additions and improvements. New or Re-Sale, there is plenty of options and the choice is yours.

Buying *'Off Plan'* is popular with UK customers. Better still can be building your very own bespoke Villa. ORUC International's reputation was built delivering luxury bespoke villas to order. They are there for you today from concept through design, architect planning and construction with our experts on hand to help and support you every step of the way.

One Oruc Villa owners described her experience of designing, fitting and furnishing her dream home in the sun as *"Possibly the world's ultimate retail therapy."* It should be fun, it should be exhilarating and it should be a shrewd financial investment.

Whatever your Requirement:

Bespoke Luxury Villas	**Luxury Apartments.**
Re-sale Properties	**Off Plan Properties**
Property Rental	**Inspection Tour**
Property Maintenance	**Property Management**

Oruc International... One Stop Property Shop for everything Turkish
CALL: **0845 166 47 57**   VISIT: **www.orucinternational.com**

The Darling Buds of
TURKEY!

"The tragedy of life is not that it ends so soon, but that we wait so long to begin it." Anonymous

The Darling Buds of May! Remember those days of not so long ago, when life was good, summers were long, the sun always shone and people were lovely like Catherine Zeta Jones and David Jason in the TV show. When all the pink bits on the map belonged to Queen and country, Britannia Ruled the Waves, UK bands rocked the world and Bobby Moore's England won the World Cup. The Mini was King, full employment universal, put down £25 and buy a house. Yes Great Britain was… *Great!*

Our land has witnessed huge change since McMillan through Thatcher into Blair's Britain. Life is not as relaxed as it was. Places to go, people to see, things to do. Pressure, rigour, reports, risk assessment, performance monitoring, targets, health and safety, deadlines, paperwork, re-training, Initiatives, initiatives, initiatives Pressure more pressure… S-T-R-E-S-S

Did you ever here of anyone lying on their deathbed say:
"I wish I had spent more time in the office?"

Rigour, pressure and stress appear essential elements to modern living, the price we pay for progress and sophistication. So why are so many choosing to escape to a home abroad? Maybe they are saying pressure and stress is a reason to seek refuge in the sun, living in another land with different values and cultures that offer the old values that we once prized so highly.

Whatever the motivation *Several Million UK* residents own property abroad! Whether they are searching for a sanctuary, a place in the sun, a Shangri-La for retirement or merely a good investment, millions have made the decision to live their dream and invest in a second home abroad.

"The future belongs to those who believe in the beauty of their dreams." Eleanor Roosevelt

It's time to live your dream…   Build your second home in Turkey
For everything Turkish Call Now   Oruc, your One Stop Property Shop

Oruc International… One Stop Property Shop for everything Turkish
CALL: **0845 166 47 57**   VISIT: **www.orucinternational.com**

Peace & Tranquility

"Rest is not idleness, and to lie sometimes on the grass on a summer daylistening to the murmur of water, or watching the clouds float across the sky,is hardly a waste of time." Sir J. Lubbock

So what is the big attraction of Turkey? As a starter the strong British pound gives UK buyers a big advantage in the overseas property stakes. Turkish properties currently offer outstanding value and a sound investment. As they move ever closer to EEC membership and their economic index closes on the pound and euro; capital growth can be significant.

Indeed many Oruc Villas have shown 30% per annum capital growth in the past three years. That is a 90% capital growth in just 36 months. Add to this an average rental income of say £8000 per year and the investment moves to a level that positions Turkey as one of the world's top locations for property investment.

Now add Mediterranean weather, crystal clear waters, stunning coastlines, magnificent cuisine, wonderfully hospitable and respectful people and a rich culture that dates back to the dawn of time and you see why so many Brits are choosing to buy a second home in Turkey.

Why the Jason – Jones, Darling Buds of May introduction?
Go to Turkey, meet the people share their culture and relax. You'll soon rediscover the lifestyle, values and traditional qualities we once prized so highly in our land when it was the Great Britain we loved…Turkey today – Perfect just Perfect!

"Happiness is not having what you want, but wanting what you have.'
Rabbi H. Schachtel, The Real Enjoyment of Living

It's time to live your dream!… It's your move!

Oruc International… One Stop Property Shop for everything Turkish
CALL: **0845 166 47 57**   VISIT: **www.orucinternational.com**

The Magic Numbers

Holidays, international travel and property development abroad is big business.

Why Turkey?

FACT 15,000,000 UK tourists in 2005

FACT Tourists numbers doubled to 30 million by 2010 (*Source* Turkish Govt)

FACT 25% UK tourist increase predicted for Turkey 2006

FACT Top 3 holiday destinations for British tourists

FACT Top 3 countries to invest in a holiday home (Ch4 Survey)

FACT As much as 500% growth in property prices in past 10 years

FACT Turkish property outperformed UK stock market over last 10 years

FACT Turkeys Ministry of Culture and Tourism predict huge growth 10 year growth

FACT Turkish Prime Minister promised – Tourism top of his agenda

FACT Dalaman tourist centre designated priority development region completion 2007

FACT £300,000,000 allocated to protecting the cultural heritage

FACT Turkey's property boom has been likened to Spain in the 90's

FACT The Turkish Government has the Two stage plan for tourist investment

FACT Stage 1: 2004-2006 near completion.

FACT Stage 2: 2007-2010 huge benefits to investors who start now

PLUS **Great People, Lifestyle, Climate, Scenery, Coastlines, Cuisine, Culture, Tradition**

It's time to live your dream!... It's your move!

Oruc International... One Stop Property Shop for everything Turkish
CALL: **0845 166 47 57**   VISIT: **www.orucinternational.com**

Investing in Turkey

Turkey is the bridge between Europe and Asia so with its fast growing economy and rapidly developing infrastructure, Turkey offers many opportunities for property investors.

In 2004 more than 17 million people visited Turkey and this figure is expected to double in the next few years. Future projects are planned such as more leisure facilities, including golf courses, health resorts and sports stadiums that support international events. The first Formula One race on Turkish soil was held in Istanbul earlier this year.

The country's economy has been successfully stabilised through a number of tough reforms following a series of crises in the early 1990s. Their GDP has grown by an average annual rate of 8.4% over the past two years; inflation has been brought under control from 30% in 2002 to 8% in 2005 and unemployment at 10% is under the E.U. average. These figures have helped boost investor confidence with only $1 billion in 2003 and to more than $14 billion in 2005. Prospects for the economy are looking good, especially as the Government are committed to maintaining tight fiscal control, while continuing economic reforms and accelerating their privatisation programme.

Furthermore, as Turkey begins the process of aligning itself for EU accession, property prices across the country are set to rise in line with properties in similarly attractive areas of Europe. The combination of foreign and domestic demand for holiday homes is fuelling an unprecedented building boom along the entire west coast of Turkey. Legislative changes, which relaxed restrictions on where foreign nationals could purchase property, have also encouraged more buyers. As a result of this property prices are rising rapidly, particularly in areas popular with tourists or the rising Turkish middle class. For example, property values in the Aegean resort of Cesme have risen by up to 50% in two years thanks to demand from Turkish buyers in nearby Izmir. So now is the right time to purchase an investment property or a second home in Turkey.

Property prices and the cost of living are still much lower than other Mediterranean neighbours and Spain so if you invest now you can expect to see a substantial increase in your investment. Buying in Turkey is like buying in Spain fifteen years ago because properties are affordable, good value for money and the rental return is good. In the last five years Turkey has seen a considerable increase in the sale of properties to foreign nationals. Cumberland Properties and Management in Bodrum, one of the leading Estate Agents in the area reports an increase of 50% in property sales over the past year.

Serious crime and crime against property and the individual are very low in Turkey meaning that investors and their assets are safe and secure.

The Aegean and Mediterranean coastline of Turkey stretches for over 1000 miles, dotted with the small ports and resorts that are proving increasingly popular with tourists and homebuyers. The property market in coastal areas is dominated by newly built villas and apartment blocks. Eric Kaya of Cumberland Properties and management advises buying off plan as a good investment because the property price will normally increase before the property has been fully paid for.

Bodrum, one of the property hotspots, is one of the prettiest resorts along the Aegean coast with its beautiful harbour, whitewashed houses, narrow winding streets, glorious beaches and incredible castle. Like the whole of this coastline, there is an amazing variety of fishing villages and up-market towns. Anything is possible on the coast nowadays from dining on the best seafood sitting on candlelit jetties in the sea to windsurfing and paragliding or taking a private cruise on a wooden yacht (gulet) to eating al fresco with the local fishermen. There are five star hotels and excellent shopping such as, to name but a few, Emporio Armani and Cacharel as well as local boutiques. Alternatively, just outside the seaside resorts are villages where you can still see and take part in Turkish traditions

The demand for accommodation in popular resorts is high, especially between the months of May and September. This makes it easy to rent out quality holiday properties for a good rental return. Indeed rental properties can provide yields of 5-10% per annum in the bigger resorts such as Fethiye, Bodrum, and Didim although the returns are somewhat limited by the length of the holiday season and the market is still small in overall terms.

Buying property in Turkey is similar to but simpler than buying in the UK. However, there is a requirement to obtain permission from the military for the purchase of a property prior to completion because non-nationals are only permitted to buy within a designated town area. This can be simply dealt with by appointing a conveyancing solicitor in Turkey who makes the application automatically while handling the sale transaction.

Investing in Turkish property will reward you with considerable capital gains and potential income from renting out during the holiday season. Couple this with stunning climate and the arrival of Turkey as a chic and fashionable tourist destination and you can see why professional investors are now putting Turkey at the top of their list for investment. And best of all, it is no further than the popular Mediterranean destinations, being just three and a half hours by air from the UK.

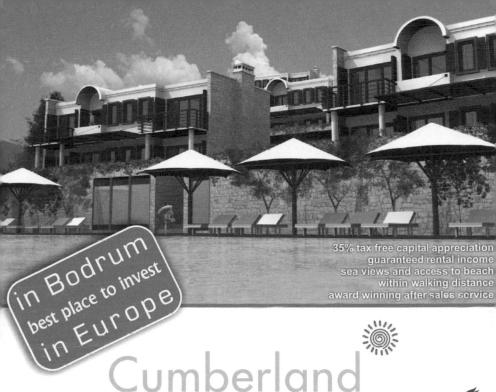

Index

Index of advertisers

Also available from Kogan Page in *The Complete Guide to...* series:

The Complete Guide to Buying Property Abroad
fourth edition, Liz Hodgkinson

The Complete Guide to Buying and Renting Your First Home
third edition, Niki Chesworth

The Complete Guide to Buying and Selling Property
second edition, Sarah O'Grady

The Complete Guide to Buying Property in Florida
Charles Davey

The Complete Guide to Buying Property in France
third edition, Charles Davey

The Complete Guide to Buying Property in Italy
Barbara McMahon

The Complete Guide to Buying Property in Spain
Charles Davey

The Complete Guide to Letting Property
second edition, Liz Hodgkinson

The Complete Guide to Renovating and Improving Your Property
Liz Hodgkinson

The above titles are available from all good bookshops. To obtain further information, please contact the publisher at the address below:

Kogan Page
120 Pentonville Road
London N1 9JN
Tel: 020 7278 0433
Fax: 020 7837 6348
www.kogan-page.co.uk